PRESIDIO
PRESS

BALLANTINE BOOKS
NEW YORK

BLOOD MAKES
THE GRASS
GROW GREEN

**A Year in the Desert
with Team America**

JOHNNY RICO

A PRESIDIO PRESS TRADE PAPERBACK ORIGINAL

COPYRIGHT © 2007 BY JOHNNY RICO

PUBLISHED IN THE UNITED STATES BY PRESIDIO PRESS,
AN IMPRINT OF THE RANDOM HOUSE PUBLISHING GROUP,
A DIVISION OF RANDOM HOUSE, INC., NEW YORK.

PRESIDIO PRESS AND COLOPHON ARE
TRADEMARKS OF RANDOM HOUSE, INC.

ISBN 978-0-89141-897-9

LIBRARY OF CONGRESS CATALOGING-IN-PUBLICATION DATA

Rico, Johnny.
  Blood makes the grass grow green :
  a year in the desert with team America /
Johnny Rico. —1st ed.
      p. cm.
  ISBN-13: 978-0-89141-897-9 (alk. paper)
  ISBN-10: 0-89141-897-0 (alk. paper)
  1. Afghan War, 2001—Personal narratives, American.
  2. Rico, Johnny.   I. Title.
  DS371.413.R53 2007
  958.104'7—dc22
  [B]   2006048452

PRINTED IN THE UNITED STATES OF AMERICA

WWW.PRESIDIOPRESS.COM

9 8 7 6 5 4 3 2 1

BOOK DESIGN BY BARBARA M. BACHMAN

DEDICATED TO SERGEANT "PETEY" BILLY, WHO,
IN EXCHANGE FOR THIS DEDICATION, GAVE ME
RITZ CRACKERS WHEN I WAS HUNGRY

FIREBASE COUGAR, 21 FEBRUARY 2005

Join the Army, see the world,
meet interesting people—and kill them.

--pacifist badge, 1978

"Let somebody else get killed."

"But suppose everybody on our side felt that way."

"Then I'd certainly be a damned fool to feel any other way.
Wouldn't I?"

--Catch-22

Anyway, I'm sort of glad they've got the atomic bomb invented. If
there's ever another war, I'm going to sit right the hell on top of it.
I'll volunteer for it, I swear to God I will.

--The Catcher in the Rye

ACKNOWLEDGMENTS

I'd like to acknowledge myself for all my hard work on this project.

Myself and no one else.

Well, maybe, I'd also like to acknowledge "Antonio Burns" for his mentorship and friendship—may we always never have Canada.

But that's it.

Just myself and Antonio Burns.

. . . and my agent Lorin Rees for enduring my ever-changing mind. But that's it—for real this time. No one else. Just myself, Antonio Burns, and Lorin Rees. Not a single other person.

Except maybe Mike Lucier for trying to tell me it wasn't possible to start and end a book with masturbation which made me attempt it. And Professor Tony Robinson for his four-year stint of patience while I slowly finished that master's thesis. And Eric Samuelson and Sean Miller for their friendship.

But, for real this time, that's it.

These are the only people I want to acknowledge: Myself, Antonio Burns, Lorin Rees, Mike Lucier, Tony Robinson, Eric Samuelson, and Sean Miller. If you're not on this list, then too bad, because these are the only people I'm acknowledging. Except Wade, Allen, and Nate. And that is it, the list is closed, thank you very much.

Oh yes, and Anna for neck kisses. Love ya, babe. And my parents. Can't forget the folks. So these are the only individuals that I wish to acknowledge within my debut book: Myself, Antonio Burns, Lorin Rees, Mike Lucier, Tony Robinson, Eric Samuelson, Sean Miller, Wade, Allen, Nate, Anna, and my folks.

And not a single other goddamn soul . . .

———

. . . okay, after a moment of further consideration I've decided to acknowledge everyone I've known throughout my entire life after the year 2000, but no one I've known prior to 2000. So if I've known you at some point, within the last seven years, fine, you're acknowledged. Prior to that, well, tough luck, as they say.

Except for that English professor I had in 1999 who gave me a "D" on my creative writing project.

Yeah, I want to acknowledge him, too . . .

But, seriously, that's it.

CONTENTS

The first thing I want you to know is that I was ordered to write this book.

The sergeant major, right after he told us at Cusher's funeral that nobody owed us anything and took back the medals he gave us, told us—all of us—that it's our duty to tell our Army story. That there was a lot of negative publicity circulating out there about the Army and that each one of us has an Army story, and it was our responsibility to have it be told.

I'm not sure this is the story the sergeant major had in mind, but he didn't specify. He just told us to tell our story.

So that's the first thing I want to tell you: that I'm under orders.

I write because I want to be a good soldier.

I want to follow orders.

The second thing I probably need to explain is that I'm in Afghanistan.

I'm in Afghanistan in a small three-room concrete operations building that sits in the corner of Cougar Base, a tiny one-hundred-man firebase located near nothing. A representative modern-day Alamo complete with clay brick walls that's somewhere in the desert wasteland, accessible only by helicopter or very brave drivers willing to traverse territory thick with Taliban rascals.

At this very moment, I'm half-ass masturbating. Limp-handed, not really focusing. I need to get serious or just zip up right now. I decide to commit and intensely focus on my third-grade teacher. I empty into my hat. I just read in *Jane,* a women's magazine, which I'm surprised to find at an infantry base in Afghanistan, that if you look at pornography every day you're considered an addict. I realize, without equivocation, that at this point, after a year in the desert, I'm fully addicted to pornography. I've masturbated my way through the war. Three, four, five times a day—whatever it took to get the job done.

That's the level of commitment and dedication and sacrifice I'm talking about here.

I step outside the command building and smoke a cigarette, one ear toward the door for lingering radio traffic that I'm supposed to monitor. It's okay for me to smoke a cigarette now because I've quit my habit. It's okay to occasionally smoke if it's not a habit.

I'm stalling, I decide as I go and take a piss by the clay perimeter brick wall to our base that was built by a Taliban commander. I tell everyone that a Taliban commander built our outer perimeter wall, and they think, "Well, that's weird." But it's not weird when you consider that he did a good job and he charged us only thirty thousand in U.S. funds. It's not like we knew he was a Taliban commander—that is, until he was done. Well, almost done. There was no point in arresting the guy before he finished the wall.

It's time to quit stalling. I head back into the operations building and unplug the six-million-dollar incoming radar system, which, strangely, uses an ordinary wall socket despite all its casings and panels and such and which also happens to use the only wall plug that has a matching socket to allow me to plug in my laptop to finish the book. The six-million-dollar radar system shows that we've been attacked by enemy rockets eighty-three times tonight. The truth is we've only been attacked once, but that was earlier in the evening, and I've almost forgotten about it now—if I'm being completely honest.

I could've unplugged the coffeemaker. I chose the six-million-dollar incoming radar system because to do so means something. That's the level of commitment, dedication, and sacrifice that I'm talking about here.

The last thing I have to tell you is that there are places where I've monkeyed with the story.

The old axiom is that truth is stranger than fiction. Most readers will never guess the parts where I did this, thinking that I exaggerated some of the more absurd surreal moments. Let it be our secret that these are the parts that I haven't touched.

There are many reasons for why I made certain changes.

The first is that for me to tell a story, it becomes necessary to condense time lines and rearrange scenes so that you don't have the reality of weeks of nothingness except baking in the warm Afghan sun filling page after page. Necessarily, time lines and sequences of events have been rearranged and characters blended and others dropped altogether. There were over one hundred individuals at each of the three main firebases I write about, and I don't have the luxury or the inclination to include everyone.

And sometimes, it's just hard to say exactly what happened all the time. Firefights are a good example of this. When someone is shooting at you, and you are shooting back at someone—just two typical human beings trying to kill one another—objective perception goes out the door. What seemed an entire morning firing bullets was sometimes only forty minutes. Thinking backward, even immediately after the event to the orders of movement and the sequences of events, often produces vastly different stories from all involved, each story held and believed with a dedicated passion to objectivity and a claim to a clear and concise memory. Yet, no two accounts agree.

And things also have a way of growing in memory. Two bad guys become six. Rifles become machine guns. And so it goes.

I think the responsibility of writers is to convey the feelings that exist in the moment, the moment of that sharp and immediate pang of sour smiles when your heart suddenly starts pumping ice through your veins and breathing becomes difficult and visual perception takes on the appearance of the cinematographer on *Cops,* with unsteady frames and jostling scenes, running through a backyard chasing perpetrators. When reality suddenly slips a notch or two into insanity and the world is alive with flying bullets and the idea of death becomes very real and immediate.

This story is a lot like that.

I stare at a blank screen and start to write and then quickly delete the sentences I just wrote. It's difficult to write the first sentence. The first sentence leads you down a path that you're forced to commit to. I decide I'll hold off on the first sentence. I don't know where this story will lead me, and I don't want to commit to some path I'm not yet sure of. I'll write the first sentence last. One of those cute little habits writers have. Finish, and then go back and add the first sentence. Some sort of life-and-death rebirth circle-of-life type of crap.

Here we go.

**BLOOD MAKES
THE GRASS
GROW GREEN**

Chapter 1

NIGHT PATROL:

Dancing with Cornflakes
in Afghanistan

I was somewhere in the desert *at the edge of civilization when the psychosis begin to take hold.*

My heart beats securely and steadily, buried deep somewhere in this gear I wear. It's buried by bulletproof plates and flack vests and tactical vests and ammunition and global positioning system handheld devices and maps and red star cluster flares and grenades and canteens and cigarettes and gum and Jolly Ranchers, but my heart is in there somewhere. I can feel it thumping securely somewhere deep inside. I feel encased, entombed in a catalog of military waste. My hands, sheathed in thin trigger-ready gloves, feel like distant attachments, moving inexplicably without my knowledge as they crinkle and fist and smooth themselves in nervous fidgety tics. Something's cutting into my hip. Some buried harness or piece of equipment isn't fitting well. Something is always sitting wrong. You reorganize, readjust, refit, and go back out, and something's always cutting you, biting you.

My green night vision goggles with their scratched exterior lens make me think that the scratch is out there beyond my Humvee all-terrain vehicle flying through the open desert. I'm always wondering what's beside that building or on the side of the mountain, and I have to always remind myself seconds later that it's only my scratch. My little lens scratch. I can't get foreground and background to come into focus simultaneously. I keep rotating my focus lever until I get tired and just leave everything blurry. It's like playing with rabbit ears on an old decrepit television; you can't get good reception no matter how much you mess with it. My night vision goggles keep slipping. I need a new mount. Mounts are hard to come by. Some guys had been waiting for mounts before we left for this deployment. The mounts had supposedly been "on order" for the last six months. I should've just gone online and bought a new mount myself from a private company, and then I'd have had mine in six weeks like everyone else. It was the principle of the thing, though. I didn't want to buy any more of my own gear. I've already spent thousands outfitting myself for the war, and I refuse to spend one dollar more.

So I sit here instead, one eye shut and one eye open, behind a green lens that's increasingly slipping, cutting the vision in my one good eye in half. I focus on the weird light patterns that you get when you close your eyes after staring into a lightbulb and watch them float around this black vacuum like fluorescent ghosts that drift quietly in a luminescent world. The form of the residual light is what I can only describe as cornflakes. Relaxed, slowly drifting cornflakes. In my mind's eye I am zooming in to join them, dancing with them and floating.

Just dancing with the cornflakes in Afghanistan.

I feel relaxed. Is this meditation? Just sitting here floating and dancing with the phantoms of residual light that remind me of cornflakes?

The radio crackles next to my ear. I am suddenly brought back to the mission. To reality. We're in the Humvee. I can't understand what he said. He said something that sounded like ". . . on the hill; over?" Was that a question? Is he asking me a question or giving me a command? Should I call him back? No, I won't, I decide. He'll call back if it's important.

We pull to a stop, and I look sideways out my window. I see two red lights of some vehicles way off in the distance on a mountain across the valley. They're moving. My vision shifts. And then I notice they aren't distant vehicles. They're the taillights of the other Humvee. The one only five feet from my own. I shake my head. I have to get straight in the head. Stupid night vision—there's no depth perception, no peripheral vision, no detailed texture that allows for easily identifiable scale or size comparison.

My vehicle moves forward as I struggle lamely against the piles of ammunition on my right side between me and the legs of our gunner, who's popped up through the roof manning the .50-caliber machine gun mounted on top. To my left is the metal door. My legs—damn, my long fucking legs are awkwardly bent and pressed intensely into the metal frame of the seat in front of me. I am surrounded by metal. I hate metal. It's so cold and unforgiving and sterile and harsh.

I wish I could surrounded myself with sock monkeys. Soft sock monkeys. My grandma used to make me sock monkeys, monkeys made out of used socks. They were not only soft but strangely comforting and safe, despite rather grotesque grimaces perpetually framed on their faces. Those monkey faces were the type of faces I imagine child molesters get when they spy their prey: big wide eyes and extreme exaggerated creepy pedophile smiles. Maybe I don't want to be surrounded by sock monkeys, but perhaps a towel, a nice soft towel or a bathrobe, the kind I used as a blanket when I'd curl up on the heating vent with the family cat when I was just a little boy. Me and the cat underneath a towel. That'd be nice.

I rip off my helmet and breathe deeply, sucking air and choking on it as if I'd just emerged from a pool and a long swim underwater. Am I the only one who gets claustrophobic just wearing my gear? I want to rip it all off and run around the Humvee naked, flapping my arms and immersing myself in the cold air of early winter while yelping like a bird. Yes, the bird yelping would be a nice touch. I'd surely get discharged for that. Psychological discharge. Why the psychological discharge? "Well, sir, he was yelping like a bird and running around naked while on a mission." Anything to get me out. I can't afford to stay in. They're saying I'm going to be stop-lossed.

"Stop loss" means you can't get out of the Army. That means the Army lets you go when they want to let you go. Just hearing the words makes me sick to my stomach. Sudden sickness as an electrical charge rips through my intestines and I feel my bowels loosen and lose their solid form. My stomach acid churns on itself. My head pounds. My breathing rises. I have so much to do, so many plans, so many timetables and life schedules to meet.

My old professor is leaving, moving to Philadelphia. I have to start doing research with him, make up for all the time I lost in the Army being inactive in academia. He's my ticket to graduate school and my doctorate.

My best friend, Sean, is teaching at Metro State as a part-time professor, and I want to do that too. But time, my time, is slipping. The more years that separate me from academia, the harder it will be to get hired.

Sean and Eric and Elizabeth's dad and I are all supposed to climb Kilimanjaro in Kenya in the spring of 2006. They're all carefully planning and manipulating to get time off.

My sister has secured a job for me in Antarctica for the fall of 2005, and if that doesn't work my ex-employer keeps talking about holding my old job for me. But how many years can I expect to hear this offer, which comes every year with a little less frequency?

And I'll miss out on all of it, sitting at some lonely Army base two years after the date I was supposed to get out of the Army, finding that all my plans have passed me by because the Army had to keep me past my normal enlistment term to go to Iraq.

I'm going to miss out on my life.

I feel sad about my supposedly intentionally noble decision to join the Army and serve and protect my country after September 11 and to take a three-year break from my career. It seems to be turning into a disastrous move. I hate to feel this way—that serving my country will have been the worst mistake of my life—but if I get kept an additional two years beyond when I was supposed to have been let go, it will have become exactly that. I don't want to regret serving America. But with all the hard work I put into creating a career, crafting my little niche in the world, and obtaining an education, I can't afford to take a five-year detour. The only lesson to be learned is to not make the mistake and give them a few years because they'll take from you as many as they want. This is my advice to the youth of America: Don't serve. You'll regret it if you have anything else you want to do with your life. And that three-year contract you're going to sign? Read the fine print; they can keep you as long as they want.

We pull to a stop. We're on a cold windy ridge studded with ragged poles, with flags and pennants waving off of them. My intuitively deductive mind figures out that it's some type of Haji marking system.

"What's this?" Cox asks.

"Some type of Haji marking system," I cleverly remark. I sit down Indian style on a smooth face of rock and stare off into the darkness for some seriously intense observation. Below the ridge is nothing but darkness. I might as well be staring out into the voids of space beyond the galaxies where there are no stars. I get the sudden feeling that I'm sitting on the edge of an abyss that leads to a free fall of never-ending darkness.

No. Wait.

Scratch that abyss comment. I see some wheat fields down there, or something.

Never mind.

Everybody's quiet. There is some brief scatter of conversation, which is quickly muted. It's too cold to be talkative, and besides, it's no fun talking in hushed whispers.

I scan my sector, but my thoughts keep drifting. I wonder exactly how big Amanda's breasts are. They seemed so perky and sizable, yet the last time I went to feel them under the pretense of innocent cuddling, I quickly realized she had on a Wonderbra.

I think about the movies I want to play during my shift as radio guard tomorrow. I think it's time for a rotation of the classics. *Gone With the Wind, Casablanca,* maybe *The Maltese Falcon.*

I bet Amanda has big nipples. Big pink nipples. I haven't seen them, of course, but I've felt them sliding in and out of my fingertips. I'm not paying attention. I have to pay attention, scan my sector, soldier-the-fuck-onward. I have to shake this extraneous thought, get back to the mission at hand. I have to pay attention, stay sharp, stay frosty. I wonder if Amanda likes having her nipples sucked?

This is how it's done. We move to invisible over watch positions in the middle of the night for patrols. No one is aware of our presence in small concentric circles outside our firebase. Most of Afghanistan is in chaos, under the control of thugs and warlords. But for a two-kilometer radius around Firebase Dizzy, we are in control. And we control this two-kilometer radius with a vivacious indifference and mediocrity.

That's the level of commitment and dedication and sacrifice I'm talking about.

Later, back at base, the soldiers drop from the Humvees and jump off roofs and dismount as orange-cherry tips of cigarettes break the blank lightless vacuum of the night. We're at a tiny Special Forces compound separated from our parent Cougar (Charlie) company chain of command, providing security so the Special Forces can do missions without having to worry about their base. It's a choice position that we're all happy to have, because simply by working in a Special Forces base, we get three hot meals a day, and soda, and Internet and phone access to contact our loved ones back home, even though we're somewhere in central Afghanistan about a day's drive from any other U.S. forces deep behind enemy lines in Taliban country.

In the adobe operations building with its secret hallways and back rooms, my gear falls off in random clumps and piles around the floor. The operations building is a complete mess, with empty Kool-Aid mix cans and candy wrappers littering the floor. Mulbeck, my nighttime counterpart in the perpetual task of radio guard, and two other soldiers are inside in T-shirts and socks, laughing at the movie *Old School* playing on the television.

I enter the walk-in supply closet and offer a secret meal of milk and tuna to Brian, the kitten I adopted when we first arrived. Underweight and pitiful, he had been close to death. But I nursed him back to health and put a little meat on his slender kitten frame. Specialist Walker, our medic, used a laser to remove a growth from his eye, and he is now a happy plucky kitten, who perpetually pours forth affection toward those of us who saved him. I pull him from the rain tarp I'd buried him in and laugh at his confused sleepy-eyed bewilderment and feed him as I gently stroke his little head. When I finger the black patch of fur over his eye, he droops his head and purrs.

Hiding Brian in my shirt, I go outside and climb onto the roof of the operations building, where I keep an extra cot. The rooftop is a tangled mess of wire and electrical cords running in every direction, the result of years of quick fixes by whoever happened to have the slightest bit of electrical know-how. Every day our power goes out for an hour or two, and each quick fix only compounds the problem of split wires and jerry-rigged transformers. Various antennas for radio systems point up at odd angles, unstable, rigged with duct tape, leaning too far one way or another.

I do a perfunctory search of my cot and the immediate rooftop for the tarantula-sized leaping and biting sand spiders, and then snuggle deep into my sleeping bag. The cool desert air engulfs my body and causes light goose bumps to rise up underneath the desert camouflage uniform that I've been wearing for over a week. When you only own three sets of clothes, you stop caring about changing them.

I rest my hands behind my head and stare up at the stars as I turn on my iPod to listen to the Beatles as I pet Brian. You can *actually* see the stars. Not just the stars, but the milky dust of the cosmos, a hazy twilight mist floating in a vacuum that somehow seems to accentuate the smallness of everything under it. A blitzkrieg of brilliant points of light breaking the blackness of empty space with fierce determination. With the power grids and neon and fluorescent noises turned off, the stars are so bright you can taste them.

I suddenly sit up, filled with a sense of anxiety that rises from my stomach to my neck. This is what premonitions would feel like if I believed in them. That awkward feeling something is wrong with the world, that you forgot to turn off the oven before you left home.

And then the horizon explodes.

Momentary microsecond daylight and speckles of Fourth-of-July sparklers rip the night apart.

The hairs on the back of my neck flicker upward to a position of attention. Seconds later, there's a booming rolling echo, which topples a minipyramid of empty cigarette boxes that had been in position for days on a picnic table in the courtyard in front of the operations building below me.

I stand up and run off the edge of the roof. In midair I grapple in the

darkness for the ladder and half catch it as I fall to the earth. The Beatles sing their famous silly little walrus song from the iPod in my pocket.

On television, inside the operations building, Will Ferrell runs
naked down the street, yelling to empty streets that he is going streak-
ing. The four soldiers laugh, mesmerized by the magic image. We're
impervious to the sound of explosions and assume they belong to our
own mortar section, firing outgoing rounds of illumination to help our
own patrols see the side of some hillside far outside the base. Or something. Explosions are always going off in Afghanistan. You start to dis-
regard them after a while.

Mulbeck waits for the scene to be over, for the money shot of Will
Ferrell backing his ass into the faces of his wife's friends as he climbs
into a vehicle. Only after that scene does he finish his sentence into the
walkie-talkie: "Um, tower three, what do you see from your position
again? Say again. Over."

Tower three crackles through the cheap Kmart walkie-talkies that
are our primary form of communication in Afghanistan and are closely
listened to by the Taliban. I had only read how the United States monitored Taliban communications. It wasn't supposed to be like this: them
monitoring us. Even the local Afghan Army soldiers had more advanced and better-working walkie-talkies—a point of great contention
for all concerned. "Um, yeah, we got some serious fire out here by Taliban Bridge to our west. About 2400 mils." And then, a beat later, "Holy
shit, we've got RPG fire, machine-gun fire, the fucking works! It's a
fucking Schwarzenegger movie out here!"

Ten minutes later, our quick reaction force is heading out of the
gate in four up-armored Humvees along with the Special Forces group
whose base we're assigned to secure. I spend the next thirty minutes in
my flip-flops walking in and out of the operations tent, tracking their
movements over the radio.

And then reality snaps.

Our soldiers are ambushed en route to Taliban Bridge.

It was a trap to lure them outside our well-defended base.

I listen to the chaotic crackle of them being ambushed en route and
the subsequent firefight, and move back to the picnic table to smoke a

cigarette. I've actually quit, but I always make an exception when some-one has the possibility of dying. Garbled yells of soldiers in the midst of strenuous conflict come in through the night air. The radio is choppy, with everybody transmitting over everybody else. A Humvee has been blown up, and at least one soldier has shrapnel wounds, and all our fel-low soldiers are out there in the desert in the thick of it surrounded by flying bullets and explosions and death at any second as they fight their way back to base.

And back at Firebase Dizzy in the operations tent, they sit in mute silence transfixed watching the movie *Old School,* laughing at Will Fer-rell's wild antics, immune or indifferent to their fellow soldiers fighting for their lives less than a kilometer away outside the base's walls.

And in the medical aid station, which I run to with ragged breath to warn the medics of possible incoming casualties, they are calmly perus-ing gang bang porno where petite blond white girls are nailed by big black cock. They wave me away. Yeah, yeah, we'll be ready.

And in the chow hall two soldiers are having a midnight snack talk-ing about who is going to get the most pussy on leave.

Does nobody care? Our boys are fighting for their lives, and nobody is anxious?

See how they fly like Lucy in the Sky, see how they run . . . .

I climb the ramparts to our base's rear wall and watch the fireworks display. It's pretty.

I am the eggman . . .
I am the eggman . . .
I am the walrus, coo coo cachoo . . .

An hour later, our soldiers come back weary and exhausted. They stum-ble to bed as the leaders stay to meet a few more Special Forces soldiers in the gravel motor pool in the center of the base. Intense hushed con-versations break the night as I spy on them from the roof of the opera-tions building, where I'm purportedly attempting to go back to sleep.

I'm brought back to childhood when I would stay up listening late into the night on private conversations, my mom and dad arguing while I had one ear to the heating duct, which channeled and amplified their angry yells back to me.

I can't fall asleep.

There is too much tension in my chest. It feels like an oily grease coating my shivering guts. I'm afraid. For most soldiers who've had service in Afghanistan or Iraq, this is nothing. Not even worth mentioning. I didn't even go out on with the quick reaction force, and I'm afraid. I'm afraid for them. I'm vicariously afraid. I'm afraid because less than a mile from me there were explosions and people who want to kill me.

Just last week I had my first baptism by enemy fire. I hid behind a haystack and felt exhilarated. Now I'm afraid for myself last week when I wasn't afraid.

My mind is flooded with regrets. I wish that, in gratefulness for being alive, I would think only of the moments and textures that have made me happy in life. There are so many.

Making love to Angela with her gripping my hand tightly and then moving my face to see hers in the dark beneath her new white flowered sheets, which smelled like strong laundry detergent, as she whispered that she loved me. Lit candles cast a soft glow over the room and its warm red cherry oak furniture.

A light coating of dog hair on the carpet at Grandma's house, sitting on the floor watching the television and happy just knowing that Grandma was nearby in the kitchen baking.

Sitting with my best friend, Sean, on the peak of a Mayan pyramid in Guatemala, trading memories and aspirations for future histories not yet realized while looking down at the thick jungle canopy beneath us, which was coming to life slowly with the waking of the jungle's nocturnal shift as an oncoming storm fermented on the horizon.

There are so many things to be grateful for. So many things to be proud of. Yet, my mind is filled with a deluge of variations of myself from the past that I've fought hard to forget, to ignore. I'm embarrassed at the person I've been. I want to divorce myself from my past, point fingers and scream that the other person is an impostor, a fake. Have him arrested and given to the proper authorities for immediate execution!

That last year of graduate school. I would walk the few blocks, which always seemed to be in autumn, to the Blockbuster on the corner. Cigarettes and wine and seclusion and Blockbuster videos. That's all I did for an entire year. I laughed when they looked up my record and told me I had rented two hundred movies. I thought it was funny. But now I'm disgusted. Two hundred fucking movies. What a waste of life. And that's to say nothing about the endless hours spent playing video games. I should've been working out, or gotten out of the house, gone hiking, called Eric and played Frisbee in the park. Gone for runs. Done something with my life instead of wasting it as my eyes burned up the replay of bad celluloid.

Women. Jesus Christ, women. All the women I had been too embarrassed to ask out. Eric and me going to Vegas and me being too shy and inhibited to talk to a single woman. Same with Sean in Mexico. Them secure already with girlfriends, just watching me to see if I'd ever make a move on someone, if I'd ever get some courage and approach a woman. The obvious excuses that I came up with and their kind but ultimately misguided statements meant to comfort me in my shyness. Lame attempts to validate my own petty excuses. Jesus, what wasted early twenties. Why did it take me so long to not be shy?

I remember being at a bar, some local dive, leaning drunk against the bar with the room spinning, holding on for dear life. The woman behind the bar moved in slow motion, her long flowing chestnut hair swinging behind her as she turned with her flashing telegraphed smiles. I wanted to ask her out, but I couldn't speak. I kept trying to make small talk, but it kept coming out as "I'll take one more beer." I was depressed as hell about something. She kept giving me pitying looks as she set one drink down after the other. I grabbed a paper coaster, thinking I'd leave her a cute message that she'd find after I left. I wrote that I thought she was cute but that I wasn't always a sad drunk; normally I was funny. I left my phone number. Pathetic. I kept positioning it, angling it off the gutter of the counter, but that damn male bartender kept coming by my area with his rapid cleaning, clearing away the clutter and almost tossing it. I kept grabbing it from his hands and repositioning it so that she'd see it. When I went to leave, I looked back to see my coaster soaked in ripples of static beer, the ink soggy and un-readable. She never saw it, thank God. But just knowing I did that, just knowing I was that pathetic, makes me cringe.

I was nineteen, I think. I asked a girl out at Costco, where I used to work. She agreed and I went home and excitedly cleaned out my car and spent an hour fussing over my hair, which probably looked silly anyway. I bought flowers. Who buys flowers? Not on first dates, not anymore. That's too eager, too needy. I can't believe I bought flowers. I showed up in the parking lot. I waited forever. Went through a Nine Inch Nails CD twice. Finally asked somebody when she was coming out, and they told me she had gone home hours ago. It was one of her friends I asked, one of her friends who worked late at night closing the store up. She started laughing. She couldn't help it. She tried not to, but she couldn't help it. It had been a joke, you see. Don't you see? It was only a joke. She was never going to go out with you. It was a joke.

I remember sitting down the street in my car staking out Kirsten's house. Sitting there listening to the Smiths over and over. They were singing about a girlfriend in a coma. I laugh thinking about the melo-drama. I cried quietly as I saw her bring home a guy from the club, a guy I knew she didn't know. They entered the house holding hands, pausing on the front porch just long enough for me to see them kiss. A few minutes later, I watched as all the lights went off. And there I was down the street under the big oak tree, just quietly crying away the predawn hours. Was I ever this pathetic? Was this really me?

There is a flood of names and voices and faces. Girls I called too much, too soon; I was too excited, too eager. I remembered their slow but steady and sure rush to get off the phone with some polite excuse. And I was always too damn polite, playing into their lie so as not to make them feel uncomfortable even during their dismissal of me. I want to erase everything prior to age twenty-two, just obliterate it, have it never have existed.

So many mistakes.

And that's all I can think about. My mistakes. All I can think about are my mistakes, my quiet shameful secrets, my embarrassments, my lies, because I'm suddenly afraid of dying. And I'm ashamed at the parts of my life that I've already wasted.

How did I get here, again?

How the hell did I end up in the Army?

I think back to my friends and family and my childhood.

I think back to my life before the Army and try to remember exactly why it was that I was so eager to join up.

Chapter 2

THE END OF THE WORLD

Our neighborhood in Davenport was a wonderful place of long, warm Iowa summer evenings that seemed to stretch into forever. Catching lightning bugs in glass jelly jars, living in the sort of imaginary worlds that only seven-year-olds can see, we found the old dilapidated boarded-up houses in our neighborhood enchanting. They were mysterious fortresses to be breached, explored for abandoned loot. We would be on our swing set pretending the ground was lava, not to be touched, when one of the drug dealers who lived behind us would suddenly run through our yard, cutting underneath the monkey bars. Our only response as the police chased after him was to squeal with horror that they were touching the fiery lava.

In this happy childhood I learned that America would die in a horribly cataclysmic death.

My father told me that America was going to end.

We were moving through the junkyard looking for a radiator pump or a fan belt, whatever it was we needed to keep our family car mobile. I was perched on a stack of tires listening as he towered above me, looming back and forth, bigger than life, inspecting the engine of an ancient Honda with his penlight for salvageable parts as the final vestiges of daylight seeped away. I adjusted my thick brown plastic-framed glasses and stuck my hands in my secondhand winter coat as I quietly listened to him above the light hoarse whisper of the wind.

"Nobody makes a quality product anymore. Everything's been outsourced to the bottom dollar. Nobody takes pride in their work anymore. Now it's just about how much money you can make as quick as you can. It's disgusting," he said through pursed lips as he scanned the junkyard for value.

"Everything's owned by the Japanese now. They're going to own this country soon enough. This used to be a respectable country, Stephen. This used to be a respectable country," he said more to himself than to me as he stood there surveying the junkyard, hands on his hips. "Of course, that doesn't matter; the country's not going to last much longer. America's dying, Stephen. She's dying, and I can't stand to see her die."

We drove back in our small Honda with the rusted paint as night and a gentle snow fell on the city. I was buried deep in layers of warmth, in sweaters and T-shirts and jackets and gloves, but my father was only in his T-shirt and a vest that had the stenciled name of the heating and air-conditioning company he worked for. I always marveled at his ability to handle the cold. It wasn't just that he handled it well; it was that he seemed to belong in it. His full mustache twitched on top of his curling lip and underneath his thick brown-framed glasses that matched mine. His eyes darted intensely back and forth across the road in front of us.

"The problem is, Stephen, that people don't care anymore," he dryly intoned as the snow fell and the tires made a lulling comforting rhythm against the wet asphalt. "If you can't buy it at a Kmart Blue Light Special, they don't want it. People don't care about democracy, and that's why democracy doesn't work anymore. You want religion? You want God? Try checking aisle three; we're running a special this week on God. He's half off for one week only, and you can take off an additional seventy-five cents if you have a coupon."

It was my father who first taught me about America.

My father was an aging hippie who never abandoned his youthful ideals or his political ideology. He only grew more bitter and angry over time as his beliefs festered and congealed in what he perceived to be a sea of moral despotism and greed. He told me that market special interests had coopted the legitimate authority of government. He talked about the law and how it was purposefully used to marginalize particular demographics within society for various nefarious purposes. He talked of democracy and capitalism and the responsibility of citizens. And, of course, as a young child I understood little of what he said.

Sometimes at night he'd let me watch old war movies, hopeful he'd instill a healthy fear of violence in me while I was still young. Some of my fondest memories are of him sitting on the couch in the dark living room, which smelled slightly of cat urine, long after my mother and sister had gone to bed. We shared a package of Oreos as I sprawled out on the floor watching *Platoon* or *Full Metal Jacket*. He winced and sighed in disgust at the violence, but I secretly grew titillated and excited as soldiers ran around with guns and shot people and then later, back in America, cried in horror over their experiences.

I too wanted to cry in horror someday over painful experiences.

And then, when I was twenty-one years old, although I hardly spoke to my father anymore, I broke his heart. I got rid of our family name.

Chapter 3

JOHNNY RICO NEEDS TEN DOLLARS

pulled up to the bank drive-through window.

I looked like complete shit.

I was a twenty-one-year-old piece of shit.

I was shit incarnate.

My very molecules were composed of nothing but shit.

My face was smeared with soot and grease from my job changing tires, and my hair was at a bad stage during my attempt to grow it out after my failed decision to go bald as some type of fashion statement. Tall and skinny and awkward, I sighed restlessly in my seat as I squinted into the long bank window that ran the length of the drive-through positions. The cute attractive girl was giggling as she read the documents that revealed my embarrassment. She looked up briefly and smiled. But she wasn't smiling with me; she was smiling at me. She called a friend over, and then another. And then it was the three of them laughing hysterically, each raising her head in turn to stare out at me.

Changing your name in a society so dependent on identification is a messy process. It's not just the obvious things you have to adjust, such as ordering a new Social Security card and a new driver's license; it's the situations like this you must prepare for. Like when your grandmother writes you a ten-dollar check for your birthday under your old name of Stephen Hites, not quite understanding that you're something different now and you're so broke that you feel pathetic because you're eagerly anticipating ten dollars.

This ten dollars is going to make your day.

This ten dollars is going to let you eat.

So you drive up to the bank, you write out the deposit slip for cash, and, because your account has been switched over to your new name, and the check still has your old name on it, you send through one of the ten photographed copies of the court order for name change that you keep in your glove box for just such occasions.

And then, if you're me, the girl inside, barely able to control her laughter, speaks into the intercom and says, "You changed your name to Johnny Rico? You don't look like a Johnny Rico. What makes you think you're Johnny Rico?"

And then the buzzer clicks off with a squelch.

They're all inside laughing at you.

But now you have to say something.

One look inside told me everything I needed to know. They didn't think I was cool. They didn't find me attractive. They thought I was a dork. I was a tall skinny dork trying desperately to be cool through the pathetic adoption of the name Johnny Rico—a name, if there ever was one, that comically and absurdly pretended to be suave, to be cool, to be handsome, to be everything I was not.

A response was expected.

I looked behind me, hoping to see another car, something to force this embarrassing episode to quickly collapse in on itself, but there wasn't one. I was the only person at the bank. I sighed and leaned forward to depress my end of the speaker.

What was I to tell them?

Was I to tell them, speaking back and forth over the drive-through speaker system while sitting in the bank parking lot, about how the changing of my name was an ideological move? That it had nothing to do with wanting to break my father's heart, that it had nothing to do with trying to be cool? Was I to start a line of questioning about why it is that in a society where we choose everything about ourselves from our careers to our homes, where we pick and choose from a hodge-podge of ideas and identifiers, the things we want to be identified by, it seemed absurd to me that we don't also choose the very thing that perhaps identifies ourselves the most? Our very names?

Or was I to start discussing, in the available fifteen seconds, the ideological philosophies of the 1950s Robert Heinlein book from which I stole my name? Was I to tell them that the protagonist in the book, my character, the *real* Johnny Rico, realizes that choosing one's country, one's political identification, needs to be a carefully deliberated choice that is taken with a symbolic act of military service and that I was, in fact, intoxicated by the idea of someone, even a fictional character, exercising that level of concern and care about notions of citizenship in a world when citizenship is so loosely realized by the randomization and location of geographic birth and the nationality of one's parents? Should I have told them that my name change was actually a political statement? That this was my metaphorical "crazy in the head" way of stating that I wanted to be an American? That this was me choosing my country and being "reborn" and that this act of individuality was so typically American in its indulgence of individual freedom that I had thought it an appropriate gesture? That I was offended by all the Americans who adamantly believe in America only because this is where they were born and who, unlike immigrants to this country, never actually had to choose this country over other countries and raise a hand and affirm belief in our shared ideals?

Was I to tell them that I was completely crazy and that even though I was only twenty-one years old and was only supposed to be concerned with getting laid and drunk that these ideas kept me up at night?

Inside, one of the girls whispered to the others, and they all broke out in renewed laughter at me. All last vestiges of any type of customer/business relationship had been destroyed, and we were now in junior high school. I depressed the button that allowed me to speak and meekly said, "I just liked the name." I leaned back and shrank into my seat, trying to hide.

I heard the hiss of the vacuum tube sending my ten dollars as she

Chapter 4

ANGRY ARABS

During college I was in an apartment with my pseudogirlfriend of the moment, Ashley, and five of six angry Arabs who lived there. I say pseudogirlfriend because my relationship with Ashley mostly consisted of watching her do cocaine while I got drunk. There was supposed to be some type of angry love triangle in the room: myself, Ashley, and her spurned lover whom she had left to be with me. I'd met Ashley during our seminar on indigenous politics. We had skipped out on the lecture regarding the political mobilization of the marginalized voice of Central America's indigenous Indians and made out in a toilet stall in the women's bathroom and continued our courtship at the annual Columbus Day protest.*

But under the sharp haze of a cocaine high, neither Ashley nor her ex-boyfriend much cared about our lost and unregulated relationship structure. Ashley's handsome, suave, *GQ* ex-boyfriend was from a rich Turkish family. He was a visiting student at our university, majoring—of course—in political science.

Political science seemed the bastion and stronghold for anti-American sentiment on campus. It wasn't just anti-American sentiment; it was anti everything. Anticapitalism, anticorporation, anti the entire fucking system. And I'm not knocking it; I was a card-holding member

---

* She was my blond, blue-eyed, trophy something or other. I was her . . . To this day I'm not quite sure what I was.

and to some degree still am, although I temper my criticisms with a real-world understanding that not even the corporations of the world nor the Defense Department can be all evil all the time.

There we were, me intoxicated and them high, talking about how much we hated everything in the world. Cutting over one another, all excited and worked up into a political fervor, frothing at the mouth when we weren't inhaling or swallowing our next round of poison.

I distinctly remember that the conversation was about the United States' involvement in the perpetuation of globalization, which, of course, had to be evil. Whether we were right or wrong didn't matter; the point was that we were all agreeing quite eagerly and making ourselves angrier in the process. We, unfortunately, knew just enough to put some element of truth in our comments but lacked the discipline or care to be accurate.

"Fucking hate Americans," Ashley stated, ever the English major, as she folded her arms underneath her small but pointy and perky breasts. "They think they can consume anything and everything they want in the world, and they don't give a fuck if some third-world schmuck has to pay the price so that we can buy things cheaper."

"The American military is what props up capitalism. That's all it is—a price support system for America's corporations," said one angry Arab friend of Ashley's as he settled down deep in the couch cushion and passed on a joint that was circling. "Central America was militarily taken over in the last fifty years to ensure cheap production and natural resource markets for the corporations. They're all in bed together. It's a mass conspiracy."

"Do you know that you Americans spend three hundred billion dollars a year on your military?" stated another with annoyingly pretentious reading glasses.

"The Bush administration," Ashley's ex-boyfriend went on as he took another line from a plastic plate, "the Bush administration refused to sign the international treaty on land mines! LAND MINES! Who can be against land mines! What they want is more children to lose arms and legs. They don't care. It doesn't happen here so you don't care about it?"

Another one of Ashley's angry Arab friends stated in quiet sad contemplation, "Do you realize how much education that buys? Three hundred billion dollars? How much food that buys the hungry? But why educate an entire generation and decrease your crime rate and your resulting social spending for an entire generation if you can buy more bombs and planes to kill more people, right? Am I right or what?" We declined to discuss the relative merits of his own country of origin, Saudi Arabia.

I was agreeing fervently, so it must have been the fault of the alcohol when I said, "Yeah, I'm thinking of joining up, actually. The military—the Army; you know? Be all you can be?"

A long uncomfortable silence permeated the room.

And then, after a moment, they all stumbled over one another to support me in my endeavor. "Sure, sure, yeah, the Army needs good men," said one.

"That'd be pretty fun—get to travel; see the world," said another.

The angry Arabs were all very supportive.

Chapter 5

THE FIRST THOUGHT

Years later I eased back in my black swivel chair and practiced a few "snap pivots" from desk to file cabinet. I flicked the lights on and off a few hundred times. I banged my head on my desk a couple of dozen times in mock simulation of rage. I threw coffee stirrers across the room at the garbage can. I sunk only three out of a package of one hundred. I practiced sucking in my cheeks and holding them for thirty-second intervals.

This is how I spent my days prior to the Army. Not really in rehabilitating my probation clients and improving their lives or in protecting the community, but in managing the numbers, in presenting my statistics. I was good at helping clients who were "approximately" finished with the requirements of their probation order get off of probation so I could have more free time. On my laptop I'd make charts and graphs for my supervisor that purported whatever it was I could purport to make my caseload look positive. Sure, all my cases looked superficially as if they were headed toward the crapper, but what you, supervisor, have failed to notice is the long-term indicators, and if you notice my chart here, this is a normal visible decline that exists in all client cycles, and actually these indicators highlighted in red project a bright statistical report at the end of the quarter with many early terminations for good behavior and few instances of recidivism.

Everything was relative.

I was also good at finding reasons to send clients to jail. So good that periodically my supervisor would inform me that there was no more room in the jail and I couldn't send another one for a while. After hearing this, I'd slink back disappointed to my cubicle and slump angrily into my seat, realizing I would have to deal with my clients.

I worked very hard at the appearance of keeping busy. I started an in-house GED program. I started workshops for clients to help them with résumés and the interview process. I started after-school study groups, and then once the programs were started I'd pawn the work off to other officers also anxious to appear busy and ambitious and sit back in my cubicle throwing coffee stirrers in the trash can.

In the evenings I'd attend graduate school, putting the finishing touches on my second master's degree. And, for lack of anything better to do, I volunteered with my college professors who were caught up in fits of social altruism to do research for low-income housing coalitions that I, in reality, cared little about. I volunteered with Sudanese refugees, helping them acclimate to American life.

Whatever it took to make the time go by.

Worst of all, I was seeing three therapists concurrently.

I had become addicted to the soft gentle quiet that exists only between the ticks and tocks of the clock in therapists' offices.

I attended drug rehab classes with my clients in my free time to facilitate their own attendance, and I kept going long after they failed and went to jail, sucked in by the raw expression of emotions by people who had nothing left to offer the world.

Hear that?

That's the sound of violent desperation crying.

It was addictive.

All I needed now was to start a fight club.

I wondered where I had gone wrong.

Every magazine I read teased me about the difference between what I should have been and what I was. I flipped through an article on the CIA's new "around the world" detention flights and thought about the life of the pilot who flew covert flights into Algeria at two o'clock in the morning. I bet he had some stories. And a quiet pride at bars that he couldn't even discuss his job. I flipped through an *Outside* magazine and saw a story of career mountain climbers who took tourists to the summit of Everest. That was a hell of a job, too. That wasn't a probation officer type of job, of which there were thousands upon thousands across the country. I should've been a researcher with primates in central Africa, or a Special Forces commando. Something that would make people the slightest bit interested when I told them about my occupation, instead of just letting their eyes glaze over when I told them I was a correctional officer.

I bounced a ball against the wall of my cubicle and thought about my options. I suppose the next step was to start the Ph.D. But was more school really the answer? The last time I noticed any discernible improvements in my own intelligence was two undergraduate degrees ago. I was on the cusp of an important year: choose one way and you get to keep your integrity; choose the other and you slide slowly into middle-aged middle-class suburban oblivion. A few more years and I'd be married with a child on the way and shopping for minivans. And wouldn't that be terrible.

I stared down at an Army recruitment ad in my magazine and started contemplating.

Chapter 6

THE AQUA SWEDISH BLENDER INCIDENT

"**Do you see that?**" I asked. Terry looked over my shoulder at my trophy. "It's Swedish," I proudly responded to a question never asked. I'd seen it on a shelf from three aisles down. It was an aqua blender. It was Swedish. It completed me.

I was in Bed Bath & Beyond with Terry, a bartender whom I'd met online at match.com. Terry enjoyed spending time with friends and family, having fun, listening to music, taking long walks on the beach, and listening to the rain. I barely remembered her name. All that mattered was that she was uncontrollably attracted to me.

I held the box in my hands and imagined its placement in my retro aqua appliance–furnished kitchen. *This is it,* I thought. *If nothing else, I'll never have to worry about my kitchen again. No matter what else happens, my kitchen is always going to be good. That's one corner of my life I don't have to worry about anymore.*

And then as I stood in line to make this purchase, happily pulling out my Fonzie the Bear Providian MasterCard with the fifteen-thousand-dollar spending limit, flexible purchasing options, no annual fee, low APR, and free airline miles for every one hundred dollars purchased, I froze.

Two weeks later I rid myself of all my material possessions. I posted signs around my low-income apartment complex that advertised free things in Apartment 302. It was a blowout clearance sale. Everything had to go! I moved furniture into the hallway, taping signs that asked those passing by to adopt a couch or an entertainment center. Small index cards offered the name of the couch or the entertainment center and its birth date, and suggested that maybe the reader could provide this piece of furniture a good home.

I moved everything I couldn't get rid of to the middle of the Denver University college campus in clandestine night operations.

Soon my apartment was empty. I was living in a one-bedroom, one-bath, empty apartment save for the sleeping bag in the corner and the card table on which I kept life's essentials: stereo, DVD player, laptop, printer, and PlayStation.

Realizing I had nothing left to live for in my apartment, I moved a few blocks away to the Westin in downtown Denver. I thoroughly enjoyed life at the Westin, which offered me a bar in the lobby, valet service to go to work, and a newspaper outside my room each morning. But at two hundred dollars a night, I had to end my stay. Besides, it was somewhat absurd having a hotel room two blocks from my apartment, which I was still paying rent on and to which I returned every day to water my plants.

Chapter 7

┌─────────────────────────┐
│   **SEPTEMBER 11, 2001**   │
└─────────────────────────┘

September 11, 2001.

I was at the towering concrete courthouse, which looked exceedingly out of place rising from the interstate in this otherwise mundane rural suburban county, which had been left behind by the economic success enjoyed by the rest of the Denver metro area in the late 1990s.

I was in the juvenile division at the windows, looking out at the planes at the distant county airport all bunched up in the air, stuck in some strange holding pattern, each landing one after the other.

Everywhere across the country, the communication of what transpired was instantaneous. No one was showing up for court, and I sat in the empty bleachers with my work group, the district attorney, the public defender, and various attorneys in quiet patience, waiting for the courthouse to make a determination regarding the day's docket. The district attorney, a pugnacious balding Hispanic man, was spitting venom onto the names on the docket of people who were absent, making promises we knew he couldn't manufacture to put them all in jail for missing their court hearings regardless of what was happening in New York City and Washington, D.C.

I made frequent trips out to the hall to call Eric, who gave me a play-by-play of what was going on as he sat transfixed by his television back at home.

Want the awful horrific truth? One of those secret truths that we all harbor but few share? Like how we might feel upset at having to front airfare to fly home for a funeral? That type of truth?

To be perfectly honest, it was an exciting morning for me. I didn't feel horror or sadness; rather, I reveled in the excitement. Sure it was horrible, what with all the dead people and all, but I couldn't help but smile at the energy surrounding it all.

I would never have guessed then that two years later I would eventually return to the scene of the crime and serve alongside the U.S. Special Forces near the same area where the Taliban was born, and where Mullah Omar, the Taliban leader, met secretly with Osama bin Laden in the days prior to September 11.

I popped into my supervisor's office at the edge of "shantytown," which my cubicle section was known as. The office was the informal break area for the entire juvenile probation team, composed largely of women (all of whom, I should note, I wanted to sleep with), which congregated there to swap gossip. They were deep in political conversation. Normally they discussed the sleeping cohabitation habits of our coworkers or the quality of someone's pineapple upside-down cake.

But today there was news on the tip of everyone's tongue, producing a palatable energy to be consumed and discussed and regurgitated.

We were at war.

The front page of the *Rocky Mountain News* displayed a color photo showing a greenish image through night vision goggles of Army Rangers jumping into Afghanistan.

The invasion began.

At the time, nobody knew what this meant. The Soviets had spent the better part of the 1980s in Afghanistan getting their asses handed to them and losing thousands of soldiers. This could be an all-out war for America lasting for years. And that was the thing—no one knew.

And everybody in the office was trying to share in this nexus of history, as if discussing it and bringing up relatives and ex-boyfriends who used to be in the military in some vague capacity could somehow in this moment make them closer or more connected and part of this unique 'moment in history when the entire crux of foreign policy shifted from the dying residue of Communist containment to an endless war against terrorism. At that precise moment, those young men jumping into Afghanistan, those Rangers, were the tip of the spear for an entire nation of anxious observers.

Then, with quick reflexes, I caught the barest pause in the conversation and, with great bravado and male machismo, said, "If this thing goes any further, I'm signing up!"

The conversation silenced.

Their faces slowly turned to polite indulgent smiles. I'm the little retarded boy in the room who says he wants to be president, and the adults can only offer empty supportive gestures of encouragement.

I'm sure that a few I couldn't see exchanged raised eyebrows and smiling eyes and laughs. Tall, skinny, lanky, nonaggressive, quiet Rico suddenly throwing himself into company with the Army Rangers and trying to be tough.

"Well, that's a sure way to win the war," said Officer Costas, her words absolutely dripping with sarcasm, breaking the awkward silence in that way that invites raucous laughing.

I immediately realized my stupidity and backed out of the office, embarrassed. I returned to my cubicle in shantytown, feeling ashamed and silly.

I slumped in my chair. If I was going to enlist, why didn't I just quietly do it and surprise everyone with actions instead of words? This was what I despised about tough posturing of the type I would later find so abundant in the Army. Usually it was hollow.

Suddenly I was that guy who bragged about how many fights he'd won, how many chicks he had screwed, how big his dick was. I couldn't let myself be one of those guys. Machismo was the epitome of hollow posturing, an open declaration to the world of fears and inadequacies that was revealed in what you bragged about. Real men didn't need to brag or act tough about jack shit. By my own logical reasoning then, this meant that I wasn't a man.

So I grabbed my car keys and went down to the recruiting station and signed up for the U.S. Army.

Chapter 8

SATAN AND HIS LEAGUE OF ARMY RECRUITERS

Recruiters *are* **the devil.**

Let's not mince words.

They're not the devil so much as they're no-good lying untrustworthy bastards.

I'm many things: hypocritical, selfish, deluded at times; but one thing I'm not is a sellout. I can't look people in the face and lie to them and be fine with it.

Wait.

That's not true. That's actually a lie.

Sometimes I'm quite good at lying. But I could never lie to somebody who was about to sacrifice three years of their life.

Not the way these guys can.

If there's a special tier in Dante's Hell, it's reserved for recruiters.

Upon entering an Army recruiting office you're assaulted by oily superficial country-boy hospitality, "Hey, buddy! How's it going! Thinking of joining the Army, are ya?" Smiles are plastered and superficial, and it's easy to read the recruiter's real thoughts underneath the thin veneer of friendship: "You little fucking punk, I hate your guts and I'm going to try and screw you over."

The first thing they tell you about is the money. I could get a twelve-thousand cash bonus for signing up for just three years! I wasn't too impressed with the twelve grand (which over three years and after taxes came out to be just a few grand a year, barely covering the rather drastic deduction in income I was going to take), but I was interested in their sixty-five-thousand-dollar student loan repayment program. Sixty-five thousand dollars would pay back a lot of international trips that I had racked up on student loans.

What they don't tell you is that actually receiving these benefits once you're in the Army becomes a task of infinite difficulty. They don't tell you about the chain of command that will be completely indifferent to helping you obtain your promised benefits, and they don't tell you about the packets of paperwork that will be repeatedly lost, that you'll submit over and over and over again before you see that first dime.

There was never any opportunity for consideration. Every incentive, every cash bonus, every school loan repayment program was going to disappear immediately if you waited to think it over. The next time you walked in, they would offer you nothing. It was important to jump on board Team America as soon as possible.

The recruiters made no distinction among the prospects. No variety in their methods. To them, everyone was eighteen years old, right out of high school, and as dumb as a brick.

"Hey, buddy, ya thinking of joining the Army?"

"Actually, yeah, I've been thinking about it."

"Do you have a high-school diploma?"

"Actually, I have a master's degree in qualitative and quantitative research methodology for criminology, and I'm almost done with my master's degree in political science with a dual emphasis on political psychology and foreign policy relations."

"Great! Great! Can I tell you about some of the job training that you can get in the Army? How'd you like to be a welder, maybe? That way when you get out of the Army you'll have some valuable skills you can fall back on."

No matter what you asked, you never received a straight answer. In the Army, you could be anything you wanted to be! You want to be a Special Forces commando and get all the best schools like scuba school and HALO parachute school? No, there's no test, it's no problem; just sign this paper and *that's what you'll become!*

———

After a week of visiting various recruiters, I signed up.

When I was asked what I wanted to do, my response was simple, "Infantry."

I saw no reason to get a job in the military that I could perform in the outside world at a higher pay scale. In fact, the only job in the military that really couldn't be done in the outside world was that of the frontline combat soldier. No, if I joined the Army I'd be doing the one thing you couldn't do in the outside world: I wanted to be an infantry combat killer.

The recruiter assumed I would be going into the officer corps and told me how to get in touch with their ROTC officer. I stopped him. I would be going in as an enlisted grunt. A private. If I was going to do the Army, I wanted the deluxe gold all-inclusive package. My life was suddenly veering into absurd territory; why not fly straight on until morning and see where I ended up? It was more that I loved seeing just how far absurd situations could be taken. Sometimes this required my temporary cooperation.

I write this section with particular hatred at both myself and the nameless bureaucrat at the in-processing station who lied to me. We were signing page 96 of contract series Delta when the nameless bureaucrat who was temporarily assigned to me read in his lightning-fast voice as if he were doing an auction, "Andyouarecommittingforatermofthree-yearsbuttobeextendedtoeightyearsattheneedsoftheArmy."

"Whoah! Hold on a second," I stated, grabbing the page back from the nameless bureaucrat and scanning it for the keywords I was looking for. The nameless bureaucrat sighed. I had been stalling, wanting to review the contract carefully. They weren't going to sneak anything past me! Hell, I was educated! I wasn't some dumb kid!

"What's this eight-year thing? I'm only signing up for three." The military had this clause whereby, if necessary, they could call you back up for service for a period not to exceed eight years in the event of extreme emergency. Super-extreme emergency. Like nuclear war, World

War III, everybody-in-the-regular-Army-is-dead type of emergency. At least, that's how it was sold to me.

"I don't know," I waffled.

And it was really the hand on the shoulder that disturbs me most, in retrospect, because that's when this nameless bureaucrat turned in close to me and said, "I'm not trying to pull one over on you here. I'm not trying to do that, really. I want you to know everything that you're going to be responsible for. And I'm telling you, right now, at this moment, this is not something you have to worry about. This has never . . ." My eyes were watching his lips move in slow motion, slowly enunciating each word. ". . . in the history of the entire Army . . ." Lies. ". . . ever been used."

The thing was, I felt bad for not trusting the guy when he really hadn't been anything but polite with me. And if he was willing to touch me on the shoulder, then hell, he must be on the up-and-up, right?

"This is like nuclear war, World War III, everybody-in-the-regular-Army-is-dead type of emergency, okay? They have never used this in the history of the United States, and I doubt they ever will. But everybody has to sign it. It's just some outdated thing that's still in here because, for whatever reason, nobody's ever bothered to take it out."

I sighed, smiled apologetically, and signed my name.

I walked out of the large looming courthouse-looking building in downtown Denver that served as the central processing station for all the military in the Western states, feeling depressed instead of happy or excited.

Had I really just signed up for the Army at twenty-six years of age?

Had I really just signed up for the infantry as an enlisted man? The infantry? The infantry was full of tough men who liked to fight and were aggressive! I wasn't aggressive! I wasn't aggressive at all! In fact, I hated tough male posturing almost more than anything else in the world. What the hell was I thinking? Why hadn't I signed up for a more appropriate job that stimulated my brain, like intelligence or computers?! I could learn how to operate computers.

Had I really thought through this decision?

A sudden panic washed over me, and I was barely able to control myself, to stop myself from rushing back into the building, knocking over the guards at the door, racing up the flights of steps, charging into the room where I had signed the papers, grabbing them forcefully from the sergeant who might still have them in his hands while he laughed with the other recruiters over the latest sucker he had just enlisted, and diving dramatically out the third-story window, papers in hand.

Instead, I just sighed, staring wistfully up at the third-floor window, which I knew there would be no diving through, and put my hands in my pockets. Though it was still early, this was quickly turning into another cold, windy, bitter fall day in Denver.

Chapter 9

EATING DORITOS IN THE MIDDLE EAST

quit my job and decided to go travel before I had to show up for basic training in Fort Benning, Georgia. I figured I might as well head to the Middle East and do some advance location scouting before the Army eventually sent me there to kill somebody.

My goal was to hide under the guise of a traveling Canadian until I felt safe, and then reveal my true superhero identity as an American and engage the local populace in dialogue, in debate. I wanted to see firsthand if they hated us. Unlike most Americans, I didn't mind if they hated us. Hell, I kind of even hated us.

I traveled to Morocco and Lebanon, and by the time I arrived in Egypt, I was mentally exhausted and wanted nothing more than to hide from the world.

And now they were trying to get in again.

I kept looking up from the book I was reading, noticing an almost peripheral phantom movement from the corner of my eye. Then, convincing myself that in my self-imposed isolation I was semidelusional, I'd look back down at my book.

And there it was again.

The slight subtle jiggle followed by a long pause.

These bastards were applying a methodology now.

The Dorito fell from my mouth to the crumbs in my lap. My eyes darted to the door. I jumped off the bed and got on all fours as I crawled to the door. I already had a desk and dresser pushed up against the door. Maybe it was time to add the room's single chair?

I quietly listened to the telltale distancing of rapidly retreating footsteps on the stained soiled orange carpet outside my hotel room.

I looked around my disheveled Cairo hotel room, which stank of toilet cleaner and hurt the eyes with its scratched pastel furniture set. I had been in my room for three days subsisting on Doritos and Coca-Cola from a vendor across the street. For three nights I had dreamed of strange and peculiar shadowy Arab figures hiding in the accentuated shadows from the small pale lamp next to the bed, searching my room as they traded quiet laughs. It wasn't until this same afternoon, when two hotel employees casually unlocked the door and walked in on me while I was sprawled out on the bed jerking off to mental imaginative musings of my friend Amanda, that I'd realized they weren't dreams at all.

They had actually been in my room during the night while I lay there, probably lost in sleep and casually massaging my groin.

I became a novelty of sorts. The angry masturbating American in room 321. I'd go downstairs for my Doritos and Coca-Cola, and the young hotel employees would make the jacking-off motion real quick and subtle-like with their fists and then blend it in with whatever other movement they were making. I could only smile through clenched teeth: "Yes, yes, I jerked off. You caught me jerking off. Very good for you. Very funny. Very amusing."

Furthermore, I was the guy who had gotten into a yelling match with every single one of the college students working at the hotel in the so-called office center, which was really not much more than an overheating, humming, late-1980s desktop computer that cried and moaned with every double mouse click.

I was sending an e-mail home late at night when the desk clerk, with little else to do but man an empty desk, approached me. Light friendly conversation ensued, genuine on his part and awkward, as always, on my part. I explained to him that I was American, something he could tell before I told him, and asked what he thought about Americans. I told him that in our country we had been told that the Middle East countries hated us because of our support of Israel and our military base in Saudia Arabia. At first he gave me the safe answer, saying, "No, we love Americans. Many Americans come to Cairo. Tourism is very important in Cairo."

Tourism *was* very important in Cairo. It was interesting how hard the Egyptian government's tourism bureau tried to funnel you into prepackaged group tours and nice safe respectable hotels the moment you set foot on the ground at the airport. Even with my two-o'clock-in-the-morning landing I struggled against the swarming false friendly smiles that offered me comfortable quarters and guided tours in English. I exited the airport by myself, anxious to flag down a taxi and make it on my own, and distinctly remember them at their airport kiosk looking out after me forlornly. As if they had been, at that moment, both aware and afraid of the more unpolished country I might discover.

"Listen," I told the young Egyptian, swiveling around in my chair and abandoning my e-mail home for the moment. "I don't want any of that 'love America' crap. I don't want the Egypt that caters to tourists. I want real Egypt. Be honest. I'm not your typical American. I'm not going to get offended no matter what you say. I just want the truth."

And then he gave it to me.

He told me how America had manufactured the September 11 attacks and framed Osama bin Laden as an excuse to start a holy war against the Muslims of the world. A war that had been started, as a matter of fact, since I had brought it up, by America's unflinching support of Israel.

I responded with one of those laughs that pretended to be casual and only slightly amused but was obviously already agitated, owing to a raised blood pressure and a slightly elevated tone in my voice, which tended to get more high-pitched the more incredulous I felt. "That's absurd! It's common knowledge, common knowledge that Osama bin Laden has hated the United States for years. You're arbitrarily creating facts to fit this false reality."

The young Egyptian responded with stressed laughter of his own that I was ignorant and, like most Americans, completely unaware of the reality of foreign politics. At this point he was joined by two more of his fellow coworkers.

And then it quickly devolved until we were yelling. Finally, frustrated and realizing that all rational debate had gone out the door with the appearance of his friends, who succeeded in reducing our discussion down to a Rico gang bang as they all laughed around me, winning the debate only by reason of their overwhelming numbers and the force of their laughter, I closed out my e-mail and went up to my room. I hoped that the Army would send me to Egypt someday so that I could kill them.

I had spent the week touring Cairo. I kept to the slums, venturing into the slightly prosperous areas only for meals; I would eat at Chile's, T.G.I. Friday's, or Pizza Hut before returning to the polluted over-crowded decay that made up most of Cairo. Whenever I traveled, my picky eating forced a necessary and immediate and consistent attitude adjustment whereby I'd suddenly profess to love corporate America as I argued through bites of Big Mac that I loved McDonald's. Afterward, when I had returned safely to the States, I'd criticize the same corporations endlessly, suggesting some obscene relationship between the rise in McDonald's franchises and the decline of civilization.

I ignored the historical artifacts I had already seen in television shows and instead spoke to shopkeepers and store managers, and tried to let the impoverished ambience soak through to my very core until I suffered a slight nervous breakdown when a taxi driver refused to take me anywhere but the pyramids of Giza.

I finally relented and went to see the stupid pyramids, where my taxi driver took a single, disinterested, slightly out-of-focus photograph of me rolling my eyes, with the rising wall of one of the pyramids in the background.

And it was after my trip to the pyramids that I decided to finish my days in Cairo masturbating and watching Egyptian cartoons on the staticky television set while the hotel employees, still amused by my anger earlier in the week, tried to get into my room past the hotel furniture moved up against the door.

Chapter 10

WHEN JOHNNY COMES MARCHING HOME AGAIN

My mother stood in the doorway crying, with my stepfather's arm around her, as I hefted my slight book bag containing two pairs of white athletic socks, two pairs of plain nondescript underwear, black pen and paper, reading book, and plain white T-shirt. I told my mom that it was simply an "advised" packing list—a recommendation, really—but my mom, bless her heart, wanted me to start my tour of service in the Army off right, so she had gone to both Kmart and Wal-Mart to make sure Johnny went off to Uncle Sam with perfectly matching socks and underwear. I had tried to convince her to buy boxer shorts, the only kind I wore. But in my bag I had two pairs of tighty whiteys.

The recruiter was outside in his black government-issue car to take me to the hotel. We rode in silence. I remember some complicated pass system at the hotel that you had to stay at before flying to basic training. You got a ticket and showed it for your free dinner and signed in at the desk by such and such a time and then found your name on the bus manifest to head downtown—and so on and so on.

In my room a small, skinny, pimply nineteen-year-old kid was reading Dungeons and Dragons books. He immediately latched onto me as some type of indulgent authority figure who would placate all his fears about his impending service as an airman in the Air Force who was to paint airplanes in Germany. Would he die? What if they couldn't identify his body? Would he have to kill somebody? What would the front lines of war be like? As he held back tears and I patted him soothingly on the back, I wondered whether or not he'd sleep soundly enough to let me get in one last night of good solid masturbation.

I ate dinner at the table reserved for incoming recruits. I felt woefully out of place, surrounded by six or seven nineteen-year-old kids who were all talking about how they were going to be SEALs and Rangers and Special Forces soldiers. They were awkward, skinny kids who traded stories about getting caught with beer and outfoxing the detention officers at their high schools.

I hit the bar despite an invitation to a gang bang on one of the incoming female Navy recruits on the third floor. I desperately wanted my last night in the free world to have some feeling of significance. It was a hotel bar near the interstate, and it had a crowd of regulars whom I quickly became friendly with. Soon we were all laughing and drinking and making toasts to my upcoming venture. At some point we were joined by another regular, one everyone apparently didn't like. David was a Vietnam veteran, the obnoxious drunken type of veteran who made you regret all your sympathy for Vietnam vets. He was supposedly some Special Forces crack commando who had done this and that and was quickly driving everybody away with his crude behavior and jokes and mannerisms and pathetic need to dominate every conversation.

He asked me about my own business at the hotel, and I lied. I told him I was on vacation, too embarrassed to tell him that I was joining the Army.

As the night wore on and it was just me with my Vietnam vet friend hanging on me with his brandy breath in my face in blasts of laughter, one arm around my shoulder, ordering us both another round of shots, I considered going up to my room. But the idea of hanging out in my room with that scared kid spilling his fears about the military didn't seem that inviting.

So I did the only logical thing I could think of. I hid in a bathroom stall near the lobby and tried to sleep.

The next morning I was in line for the bus manifest. A voice called out my name from the back of the line, "Rico! Hey, Rico!" Embarrassed that somebody I knew would see me in line to join the bus for the losers heading into the Army, I looked around quickly, hoping against chance that there was somebody else named Rico in line.

"Hey, Johnny Fucking Rico!" the voice called out.

He meant me.

I turned to see one of my recent probation clients extending his hand to shake mine. A good kid, whom I liked considerably, he had been let off probation early because he hadn't been a threat to much of anyone besides himself. But still, I was now on the same career path as my former clients. I just remember wanting to cry.

The bus dropped us off at the in-processing station where I had signed the contract, and it was then that they found an error. I had arrived without my college loan paperwork, which I had been told I was supposed to submit at a later date. Stating that if I went into the Army today I'd have to go in without getting my loan repayment, I called my recruiter for a ride back home and opted to try again the following week.

And this is what we call silly. A surprise return home after dramatic good-byes had already been said to Mother. Calling my friends back up to say that, actually, well, actually I still had one more week before I had to go into the Army, so even though we'd already had our emotional good-bye party and our final drinks and hugs, if they wanted to do something this weekend I was available.

And most of all, having to do it—all of it—all over again.

Chapter 11

WELCOME TO FORT BENNING:

A Covenant Controlled Community

Perhaps no ride is more dreaded by young soldiers than the first bus to basic training. You're picked up at the Atlanta airport by civilians and herded outside to the parking garage in the early hours of the night. You sit by a curbside awaiting the bus, smoking final cigarettes and posturing to all these other young men who decided to join an organization whose sole task is killing and destroying. I smoked in silence as I watched the younger boys jockeying for position with one another, swapping stories about how much pussy they got before they left for the Army and what type of cars they drove back home.

The ride from the Atlanta airport to Fort Benning, home for all infantry trainees, is about two hours by bus and is a quiet, lonely two hours of watching shadows flit by the window. You are too anxious to sleep. Eventually you arrive and expect to be met by screaming drill sergeants that embody the reality of that enigmatic figure we've all seen in thousands of wasted hours of television and movies. But the first stop is reception, not basic training.

At reception you're taken to a bare room and told to empty out all your contraband into a clemency box. Foolishly, most do, emptying their magazines and pornography and cans of chew into the box, not realizing that there's virtually no supervision at reception and that they could've held on to their addictions for another couple of weeks. In the late hours of the evening you're led by a real Army soldier (who in reality is some loser who hasn't even gone to basic training yet and just delayed his entry into the Army by claiming a fictitious injury and thus stays perpetually at the reception battalion) deep into four-story metal buildings that house incoming trainees.

I imagine it's a lot like the feeling one gets on entering prison for the first time. Young boys hang loosely, swinging on metal railings from floors far above as you enter the interior courtyard, hooting and hollering and blowing kisses and yelling out things like "Fresh meat!" which is usually followed by raucous laughter. You're given a urine-stained pillow, a green canteen, and a metal cot with a moldy mattress, where you try to catch an hour of sleep before wake-up.

You wake up at 4:30 in the morning and join the tail end of a line of seven hundred other trainees spending two hours in silence, immobile, slowly snaking back and forth across a cement courtyard until you get to the mess hall. Once in, you are packed tight as a drill sergeant yells at you to get "Nuts to butt, nuts to butt, men!"

You eat in five minutes, shoveling food down your throat, looking down and not talking. You retire to your bays where you clean until lunch, wait two in line, eat lunch, and then do the same until dinner. Between meals they call periodic formations in the parking lot to make sure nobody's run off. Strange medical ailments and mysterious diseases suddenly occur that weren't there only days earlier when the trainees received their final medical clearance at the in-processing centers in their home state. Soldiers are dropped from the rolls as they return home, relieved not to have fully committed to their mistake.

In the barracks the trainees are as tight as wires, largely left unsupervised save for the occasional "walk-in" by a huge sergeant rumored to have killed fifty-six Somalis during the *Black Hawk Down* incident. Fights occur frequently in the latrines. You're perpetually harassed and hassled to see if you'll bite back. If you don't, the harassment becomes exponential. I, mild-mannered and purportedly more mature than most of the others simply because of my age, still managed to get into three fistfights during this two-week period. Suicide cases were already developing around the building on different floors; one kid threw himself off the top floor to the cement courtyard below. You heard crazy ridiculous rumors of things like rape, which you prayed were crazy ridiculous rumors.

During work details I'd talk to another older college guy as we compared barracks assignments. His barracks seemed pretty calm and easygoing. The soldiers I was with were caught up in the melodrama of reenacting a low-rent *Lord of the Flies* production with themselves as the starring characters.

Trainees were engaging in Code Reds on one another in the middle of the night, beating one another with bars of soap put into slack socks for ridiculous infractions such as refusing to share candy, mostly because they had seen *A Few Good Men* too many times and thought that Code Reds were supposed to happen in the Army. Every night I'd hear the light dancing of a congregation of toes on the linoleum floor suddenly speed up into a frenetic rush, followed by a loud smack and then some poor soldier crying out in pain, baying the way I imagined an old coon dog would.

Cliques and leaders developed within the barracks room as they jockeyed for positions of political authority and power. The leaders' only real task was to guide us to formations, guide us to and from the chow hall, and ensure that the bathroom was kept clean. Dramatic episodes in which leaders and their enforcers screamed at us over such seemingly inconsequential infractions as our inability to clean the bathroom were frequent. Disposed-of leaders screamed at those who had disposed of them and then got into fights with the newly appointed leaders. Grown men cried and screamed.

I sat there day after day, staring at the bottom of the top bunk and wondering what the fuck I had gotten myself into while all about me the barracks seemed to perpetually erupt in chaos as recruits fought, cried, and screamed. Maybe I was too hasty with my decision to enlist; I couldn't imagine that the officer candidate school trainees conducted themselves in the same way.

And then it happens. One day your section leader of the moment runs up and tells you to pack your bags. You're going downrange. You're going to basic training. And the drill sergeants pick you up outside and march you to your new barracks, and there's much screaming and yelling and gnashing of teeth.

Chapter 12

DOWNRANGE TO BASIC TRAINING

t's hard to maintain the dignity and composure you normally feel from having traveled the world when you're screaming that you're a killer while saliva hangs off your lip and you're doing jumping jack number 507, which means that at this point your arms aren't so much raising up and down in a unified arc as flopping around aimlessly.

It's hard to maintain the dignity and composure you normally feel from having been a working professional while you've got a shaved head and are wearing a stained dirty white sweat suit doing push-ups outside the chow hall in front of two hundred other people while screaming at the top of your lungs, "I AM THE QUEEN OF BATTLE, DRILL SERGEANT! I AM MY COUNTRY'S STRENGTH IN WAR, DRILL SERGEANT!"

It's hard to maintain the dignity and composure you normally feel from being a college graduate when you're in the subremedial grenade-throwing class and are rolling back and forth in the leaves, screaming at the top of your lungs, "I'M A GRENADIER, SERGEANT! WATCH ME BLOOOW!" This while a sergeant, who if not in the Army would probably be working the night shift at the local Texaco, tells you to "Keep 'er rollin', college boy."

But then, it would be hard to maintain the dignity and composure of age and experience throughout any part of the Army. Suddenly, my old skills were useless. There was no need for someone who could extrapolate data sets from research models or wax philosophically on the consequences of hemispheric defense policies. Surrounded by nineteen-year-old kids and treated as one, I soon found myself mentally regressing. During training cycles in basic training, I'd sneak away into the woods to smoke a contraband cigarette with two other trainees who in the civilian world had been living at a juvenile detention facility before entering the Army. The fact that it had been guys like myself who had put them there no longer mattered. My entire previous life no longer mattered. I was now reduced to that high-school mentality in which you sneak off campus for a smoke, or hide dirty magazines from your parents.

Halfway through basic training, I got the reputation as the chronic shower masturbator. Which, ironically, would have been accurate except that nobody had a valid reason for believing so. Late at night I sneaked away to the showers to eat a Snickers bar, when, unknown to me, someone saw me from behind and silently woke up the rest of the platoon to bust in on me whacking my Johnson. By the time he had gathered them, however, I had completed my Snickers and was leaving. I exited the bathroom as my platoon entered. They laughed and called me a shower masturbator. I retorted with my mouth full of my last bite of chocolate, "Ahm not a shuwer masburbabor." But, not wanting to get into trouble for eating a Snickers and having to pay the usual three-hundred-dollar fine for eating contraband—for I knew that one of our platoon snitches would surely tell our drill sergeants in the morning if I admitted to it—I simply nodded and informed them I had indeed been masturbating in the shower.

There were only a few mild hiccups during our basic training rotation cycle: the occasional AWOL soldier, the occasional late-night fight in the bathroom that landed someone in the doctor's office with serious injuries. A soldier who tried to kill himself, and we were then required to keep a twenty-four-hour guard on him. And when the soldiers on suicide guard fell asleep on shift, the guard duty doubled to four guards up at all times. And then when one of *them* fell asleep it doubled again, and so on and so on until our entire platoon was hovering around this poor bastard, just staring at him as he lay on his single bunk, which had been moved to the middle of the room. Every time he started to fall asleep, he'd be waked up. He took it well until after about four days of not sleeping, when he went crazy and tried to kill himself again. Only after some guys in our own platoon devised a plan to kill him was he removed and taken somewhere else, and we were allowed to sleep again.

My drill sergeants, who were all working on their online degrees in criminal justice from E. Army University (lots of Army guys want to be cops), learned that I had a master's degree in criminology and had been a probation officer. My offer to help a single drill sergeant with a single paper soon turned into my doing every assignment and paper and taking every test for a group of drill sergeants. In exchange they offered me whatever I wanted. No longer was I available for "scuffing up." At night, while other soldiers were buffing the floors up above in the barracks to a high shine, I was downstairs in the drill sergeants' office laughing with the lot of them, eating take-out pizza and guzzling soda.

We finished our training with a strenuous twenty-five-mile road march, which ended in an infantry indoctrination ceremony at the top of a hill, where we baptized our warrior spirit by drinking Kool-Aid from a large bowl. This was supposed to represent some kind of Viking tradition. Torches burned around us, making us look very much as if we belonged on a set of *Survivor*.

I was supposed to feel pride, but I only felt silly.

Chapter 13

AIRBORNE AIRBORNE ALL THE WAY; AIRBORNE AIRBORNE EVERY DAY

After basic training came Airborne school. I coasted easily for the three weeks and was in "Jump Week" when the Friday before graduation I went out to the clubs with a good friend, Berger, whom I had met in basic training and who had been talking to a cute girl flirting with us in the corner. Berger whispered in my ear that she seemed the sort to be filled with all types of insidious venereal diseases and suggested we leave and hit the next bar.

In the parking lot, Berger showed me her purse. Her Hello Kitty purse.

"What do you think we should do with it?" he asked as he flipped through credit cards and ID cards.

"What the fuck did you do?"

"I took her purse."

"I can see that—why?"

"I don't know." Berger seemed suddenly concerned.

I grabbed the purse from him and said, "Berger, you can't keep her purse."

"I'm not going to give it back to her!" he yelled defensively in a drunken slur.

"No, I suppose you can't," I stated. I walked up to a trash can and put the purse inside. "There; at least nobody else will find it now."

And that's when I felt the arm on my shoulder.

—

For a weekend I rotted in jail in Columbus, Georgia, outside of Fort Benning. Wasn't the first soldier, won't be the last. But once again, the contrast between my old life and my new one was upsetting. I used to put people in jail. Now I was in jail.

Finally, on Sunday evening, I was released for a phone call. I called the Airborne barracks for a friend named Greg, who I knew didn't go out that much and would most likely be in his bed. I had the CQ desk send a runner up to his room to tell him that a nasty death had occurred in the family. Grandma had died. It was very sad. I was even able to manufacture tears to the sergeant who answered the phone. Thankfully, Greg was willing to take a taxi out to us late Sunday night and bail me out of jail. I left Berger in our shared cell to rot but promised I'd be back.

After finishing my exit processing I took a taxi with Greg back to the barracks to grab my credit card so I could get cash to bail out Berger.

When Berger was released, we raced back to Airborne school for our graduation as the morning sun appeared over the horizon. Our company was forming up outside on the gravel in the early morning twilight. We ran inside, changed into our uniforms, jumped into the rear of the formation just as Sergeant Airborne called the formation to attention.

Sergeant Airborne walked back and forth on his small cement podium. "It appears that we have a couple of impostors in our midst. It appears that we have some who should not be here. Who's our lucky winner, Sergeant Rodriguez?"

Sergeant Rodriguez let out a big game-show holler and then shouted, "Private Berger and Specialist Rico come on down!"

We reported front and center. Sergeant Rodriguez smiled at us and whispered "Nice try" in our ears as he walked by and turned to face the training company. "These two hotshots stole a purse last night. They are thieves. But worse than that—they are purse thieves. They steal from women."

I looked out on our training class of two-hundred-plus soldiers whom I had worked with for the past three weeks and saw four hundred plus eyes filled with disgust. Laughter started from somewhere in the rear and then rippled forward, gaining momentum. Soon the entire company was laughing as we were forced to do push-ups and flutter kicks and dirty dogs.

I was dropped from Airborne school and put on official "shitbag" status. For the next four months I was in limbo, awaiting the outcome of my court case. I shifted between the four training companies like an unwanted virus. Regardless of my protests of innocence, in each training company I went to I was given the worst treatment possible. This was to be typical behavior of the Army mentality—a broad disinterest in details or in nuanced defenses such as "I didn't do it; it was my friend." All that mattered was that I had been arrested for it, and that was everything.

Eventually, as the months passed, the Army increasingly forgot to inform incoming classes about us, and we took on a mystique as the weird guys in perpetual holdover status. Never training with the new classes, but always there. I started working at the Airborne school doing behind-the-scenes demonstrations and helping the NCO staff set up the training apparatus for instruction. When the dummy falls from the three-hundred-foot tower and his chute doesn't open and he hits the ground? Yeah, that was me dragging him off the field in the distance.

When our court case came up, I negotiated with the DA as if I were still a probation officer cutting a deal for a client. I had both of our cases reduced, and we were awarded a year's unsupervised probation with eventual omission of the charge from our records if we stayed out of trouble. To have gone to trial would've meant an additional six months in Airborne holdover hell. Free of my burden and with my good name mostly cleared, I was then switched to RIP status, which meant that I was to await the start of the class cycle (RIP, of course, being the acronym for Ranger Indoctrination Program).

Recognizing that I had made a big mistake, I wanted to quit the Ranger program as soon as possible. I couldn't help but laugh at myself. I was twenty-six years old and had made the same mistake as all the little eighteen-year-olds do who thought they were going to be Special Forces and Navy SEALs. I had thought I was something I wasn't.

Which, of course, is the whole reason why some people become Rangers and people like me don't. Sometimes I imagine that if I had wanted Special Forces badly enough I could have made it. But then I feel that saying "Yeah, I could've; I just didn't want to" would discredit the sacrifices and honor of those who did make it. I didn't, and quite possibly there's no chance I could've made it at all. But I tend to believe that anyone can accomplish anything they want as long as they apply themselves. I didn't and wasn't willing to.

On my first day, they picked us up at Airborne school and made us run to the 75th Ranger Training Regiment compound with our green duffel bags on our backs. This may not appear to be that difficult, but these were packs that weighed eighty or ninety pounds. And none of us were in that good shape following the leniency that is the Airborne physical fitness program—at least in comparison with the infantry physical training we had been doing in basic training. We were dropped off in a blacktopped area that looked like a basketball court. But there were no hoops. Instead, walls that towered twenty feet in the air listed the names of all the Rangers who had died in various conflicts.

We did various exercises on the black asphalt for a couple of hours, all of us panting and unable to support our own weight any longer with even one more push-up. The Ranger instructors would offer us water from a passing water hose as sweat poured like a leaky faucet off our noses and chins, which were always at an awkward position in the middle of an exercise. Then we were taken for a five-mile run, which ended in an obstacle course on a hillside. So then we ran some more, up and down the hill, up and down, over and under barbed wire and poles and through the mud. When we finally got to the top, wheezing and gasping for air, our hearts pounding, we ran through it again. And then again.

Fuck this, I'm too old for this shit, I thought as I lay under the tree getting an IV from a medic.

So I joined a long and not so illustrious list of quitters. After enduring a speech that informed me I would never amount to anything if I quit this program, I held up my hand and promptly quit. Never amounting to anything would be fine with me.

Within the secret Ranger compound, in the rear, behind several layers of razor wire, was a building that looked like a condemned apartment complex. Considered perpetual and lifelong worthless "shitbags," there we were left to our own devices. We'd do PT early in the morning with a sergeant who cared very little for his job, and then we'd be released for the day. An evening formation was called to make sure we were all still present and accounted for.

The weeks passed with ease. It was a wonderful time to be in the Army. We would be drunk by noon and spend the afternoons playing Risk and other board games on the top floor of our building, which we ruled like kings with impunity. And then one day we were called into formation.

Forty of us who thought that orders would never come down and that we'd spend the rest of our years in the Army in the "worldwide open deployment" program at the 75th Training Detachment were called out to go to Korea.

I wasn't going.

I would go to Hawaii.

I packed my bags, bought a plane ticket home, and called for a taxi. I was getting the hell out of Fort Benning.

Chapter 14

ALOHA HAWAII

I rose up from the ground and raced across the baseball diamond before collapsing in the dirt, holding out my small tree branch in front of me and screaming, "BANG! BANG!"

"You didn't get me!" yelled the soldier who was lying prone in the grass behind the dugout.

"Yes, I did!" I screamed back. "You're dead!"

"No, I'm not!"

As soon as I arrived at my unit, I began my infantry training. We'd go to the park and hold sticks in our hands, the weapons being too much of a hassle to draw out of the arms room, and practice our battle drills as we sprinted low over the grass and then collapsed onto the ground and held our sticks out in front of our faces and yelled.

Our barracks and unit headquarters were located along the perimeter of a building that helped frame a large empty parade and physical training field complete with climbing ropes. The entire quadrant represented the 3rd Brigade Broncos. Each of the four buildings, which took up a city block on each side of the quadrant, represented one of the brigade's contributing battalions. The long rectangular barracks battalion buildings were broken up into four even sections, each representing a company. And in each company area, the platoons were divided by the floors and hallways of the building. The buildings were exceedingly old and decrepit. Some still supposedly contained bullet holes from the

Japanese attack on Pearl Harbor during World War II, although I could never find them. And interspersed on the sides of the buildings were palm trees. And all basked in the warm and mild tropical Hawaiian sun.

I was the newest member of 3rd Platoon, Charlie Company, 5th Battalion, 2nd Infantry of the 3rd Brigade combat team of the 25th Infantry Division.

It would be the start of another series of disappointments.

The 3rd Platoon, normally manned with thirty-two soldiers, had recently lost half its ranks to an epidemic of methamphetamine addiction that had circled like a raging outbreak of cholera. The 5th Battalion, 2nd Infantry hadn't been deployed since Korea—and for apparently good reason. The 5th Battalion was largely considered to be the bastard child of the 3rd combat brigade. The 3rd itself was considered to be the unfortunate brigade within the 25th Infantry Division. And the 25th Infantry Division? Well, it had the unofficial title of being the Army's least prestigious division, not having been deployed since Vietnam. There was a rumor, frequently recalled, that the secretary of defense had said he "wouldn't trust the 25th to guard food depots."

Here we would practice the most modern cutting-edge warfare available. Such as trench fighting, which had come in handy when we jumped in at the tail end of World War I.

Some lieutenants, however, didn't take training seriously. At times they attempted to infuse a sense of innovation in their tactics. This was always frowned on. Our platoon leader, Lieutenant Michael, attempted to outflank the cardboard cutouts of the enemy which were on a hilltop.

"We can't outflank them, sir?"

"No, you can't outflank them, Lieutenant. They're cardboard. They can't move," said the major, who was acting as the game master.

"But in real life, I'd outflank them," Lieutenant Michael replied.

"This isn't real life, Lieutenant. Now, just assault the mountain head-on and take your casualties."

I enjoyed being a casualty because I got to lie down in the sun and soak up the rays like a cat lolling in the afternoon light. My regression in maturity to the level of a nineteen-year-old fully complete, I tried to die as often as possible. All the dead soldiers would lie on the ground in grand lifeless gestures of dramatic death with arms and legs sprayed wildly.

"What's going on over there?" one would ask as he popped up his head slightly, trying to get a view of what was up ahead.

"I think we just won!" another who was facing the proper direction would exclaim. "No, no, take that back, take that back. We just lost some more guys." And then, as an afterthought, "Boy, I wish I had died over there. It looks really sunny over there."

Another would quickly turn his body around, pretending to have died facing the other way, and respond, "Oh yeah, damn, it does look sunny over there. Fuck, we should've gotten killed over there."

It was very important for all of us to go through this training so we wouldn't make the same mistakes on the battlefield. Like throwing grenades into a house that was filled with our own soldiers. Every time we had our after-action review, we'd learn about some mistake that would throw Lieutenant Colonel Marcus into a raging froth.

"Okay, where—I said where—is the farmer? Didn't you see the farmer? Your contact was the farmer? You were told to be on the look-out for a farmer? Anyone? Anyone? A farmer?" the lieutenant colonel would ask, hands on his hips, his equipment all clean and his uniform pressed as he stood in a puddle surveying his weary men encrusted with mud and filth.

Some staff sergeant would consult his men in hushed whispers and then meekly move forward. "Um, sir, we uh, we uh think we killed him about an hour ago."

During nontraining garrison cycles we exercised two to three hours a day. We ran around post singing cadences about killing people and pulling the dead bodies of our fellow soldiers out of helicopters and how we all wanted to be Airborne Rangers.

Our lieutenant and platoon leader, Lieutenant Michael, was a graduate of West Point and of the Ranger leadership school. Consequently, he thought he was better than everyone else. To my dismay, his intelligence and competence at everything he tried only supported his own general theory of himself. I too could only conclude that in all actuality he probably was better than the rest of us. He spent his days in the Army e-mailing friends and reading magazines and then occasionally giving us pep talks about how he expected us to follow him into the yawning maw of death. Then he'd retire for the day to grab an early lunch at Quiznos.

Our tiny wrinkled platoon sergeant sometimes showed up at work and sometimes didn't. And when he did, he chain-smoked Marlboro red cigarettes, quickly pawned his work onto everybody else, and then searched match.com desperately for women.

As a college graduate with typing skills, I was quickly assigned the position of RTO, or radio telephone operator, which in the old World War II movies was the guy who carried around the radio and always got shot in the head. In garrison he was the personal assistant, secretary, and receptionist for the lieutenant and platoon sergeant.

Most of our time was spent with mind-numbingly dull tasks like checking inventory lists for missing equipment.

Something would go missing, I'd report it in a deficiencies list, and nothing would be done about it. A month later, somebody would freak out about the missing night vision goggles, and I'd be sent all over base to track them down or create another deficiencies list. It was very important for the Army to have lots of lists of all the equipment that didn't exist.

As I finished my first year, that's pretty much all I thought the Army's purpose was: the creation of unending streams of paperwork.

Paperwork was created for everything. For every bullet fired, for every pen ordered, for every comment made about a soldier, a series of reports had to be filled out exactly right. A misplaced period sent the entire document back to the beginning of a long chain of incompetent hands. Prayer helped as you sent paperwork up to the company, which sent it to one of the S shops (which handled everything in the Army), which then sent the paperwork to the battalion, which sent it to the brigade, which sent it to the division. Usually, at the division level somebody would kick the document back down for a misspelled word, and it would take another few weeks for the document to climb back down the ladder to arrive back at the platoon level. This, of course, is assuming that the document didn't get lost along the way, which it almost always did.

Chapter 15

IN COLD BLOOD AND CALM PULSE

It was an early morning battalion-sized run. The rain fell and the air was dark and constipated with moisture. A sergeant to the side of the formation called out, "One killer! Two killer! Three killer, four!" And beside him the running battalion of infantry soldiers repeated it in a deep chorus of tenors between haggard deep breaths, their bodies keeping the steady pulse and rhythm of the run in check with left foot, right foot, left foot, right, as their sneakers splashed in the puddles in the street.

Our run culminated in a park near the barracks, where we stood at the silent position of parade rest, our arms folded behind our backs, our only movement the gentle up-and-down restlessness of our heels, squishing in soaked sneakers. A platform had been set up, and Lieutenant Colonel Marcus appeared on the podium as "Eye of the Tiger," the theme song from one of the *Rocky* films, blared from a set of loudspeakers.

"Men," Lieutenant Colonel Marcus informed us from his position high above, "on September 11, 2001, our country came under attack. Terrorists ripped at the very heart of our country." He looked up and paused for us to solemnly digest his words. "Now it's our turn for payback." But no one was really that moved. In fact, it seemed downright silly. It was now the fall of 2003. September 11 had happened two years ago, and Afghanistan had already been "taken care of." Everybody was focused on Iraq. Afghanistan was so last season's war. There was a whole new country to occupy this year. Six months out from September 11, memorials and speeches still seemed poignant and necessary. Two years later, such speeches were received with tired sighs and sarcastic eye rolls.

"We are going to war. I've received orders for the 5th Battalion, 2nd Infantry Bobcats. We are going to be part of Task Force Bronco and deploy with 3rd Brigade this spring for a year in Afghanistan," he said.

And as we stood there in the rain listening to the beat of a bygone 1980s band's single, and the recycled propaganda of our battalion commander, who was telling us we were going to be serving in a war zone for a year, I tried to sort out important questions in my life, like whether or not *Lawrence of Arabia* should be a four-star rating in my top-films-of-all-time list when I considered its obvious strong production values, or if, despite its worldwide acclaim, I should go with my own gut and award it only three stars. I didn't know, and this question baffled me and would take much further consideration.

Lieutenant Colonel Marcus ended by saying, "Go forth, in cold blood and calm pulse."

Later in the day I was printing strawberry and tulip cover sheets for all our weapon database books. I was trying to infuse our platoon with some aesthetic sensitivity, but I was being fought tooth and nail by our new platoon sergeant, Sergeant First Class Derrens, who'd arrived after our last platoon sergeant went AWOL with seventeen years in service, three years away from retirement. Sergeant Derrens, while laughing at my tulip cover sheets, requested that I search out more death-oriented graphics. I lied, stating that none were available in the small folder of graphics on the antiquated computer. We compromised and went with a series of foxes, which were feral hunters but also cute and cuddly. It was the only act of rebellion I could manage to inject a playful contrary sensibility into the atmosphere of aggression.

I pasted the last of the pictures onto our machine-gun folder and headed outside to have a smoke in front of the CQ desk. The CQ desk sergeant was laughing, and the private who worked with him was doing elevated push-ups with his legs off the top of the desk. The CQ sergeant poured water on his head and laughed and threw reading magazines at him as the private screamed out the number of his push-ups. I worked my way over to the side of the building, where my good friends Ryan and Diego were talking.

Ryan Daniels was a handsome, aging, sarcastic, frat boy. Diego was a cynic and jaded humorist, who delivered deadpan ironic lines and had an eye for the decline of civilization.

"Guess we're going to Afghanistan, fellows," I stated. I always used words like "fellows." I purposefully used them. It was a part of my token rebellion.

"Well, actually, Rico, Afghanistan is such an old term. That was this morning. Now it's affectionately known as "The Ghan." You see, before you can instill any melodrama into a place, you have to have your own post-hand short script, your own language that develops about a place," Diego said as he took a long drag from his Marlboro.

"Just think of all the awful memories we'll have! Ten years from now when we're all homeless drunks we can be scarred by the memories of the Ghan! And then we can start telling people who don't care about what we're saying, 'Back when I was in the Ghan . . .' It'll be wonderful!" Ryan said as his voice collapsed into laughter.

"What's going on in Afghanistan? I thought it was all over with," I said.

"Haven't you heard? Ryan and I went over to the computers after lunch. The Taliban are planning this big spring offensive, which coincides—quite nicely, if I may add—with our arrival in country," Diego stated like a game-show host selling a prize. His face took on a smarmy smirk.

A big Taliban offensive?

This was good news, indeed!

All of us in the infantry, myself included, were most fearful of not seeing any combat at all. It was the worst shame that an infantryman could endure, a grudging reluctant admission that he had never actually performed the job that he had trained for.

I drove home to my apartment, hoping desperately that the Taliban had the strength of their convictions to follow through with the offensive. I offered a quiet prayer to God, whom I really didn't believe in, to protect the Taliban and keep them in good health so that they could attack us and we could later kill them.

Chapter 16

THE FINAL WEEKEND

The entire company of one hundred men stood at parade rest on the basketball court in the warm afternoon sun. We yelled "Cougar!" (Charlie Cougars!) as we were called to attention and then stared lamely at our bald-headed Captain Zimmerman, who was giving us another uninspired speech.

Captain Zimmerman specialized in giving uninspiring speeches.

"Men!" he pleaded. "Don't do anything stupid. It's bad to do stupid things! Doing stupid things is bad!" From our captain's repeated overt simplification of everything he tried to convey to us, I gathered that his opinion of us wasn't very high. "We can't afford anybody to do stupid things because we're going to war. And we need all of you for the war. We can't afford to lose anybody. War is something that takes teamwork. War is something that's a group effort. It's a community of all of us, and we're going to war and we need you all. You all need each other. Together we will kill Taliban. Many brothers, many backgrounds, killing Taliban together."

I couldn't help but smile at his transfusion of war with the gentler sensibilities of community and brotherhood. Captain Zimmerman was a man who saw the glory and potential of mankind revealed in the civility of cooperation. If we cooperated, we could go and wage war together and kill people in countries where we had never been.

"Let me tell you a little story," he continued. We all stared blinking in the sun, one hundred and twenty people thinking random thoughts about their final weekend of freedom. About how they were going to finish an argument with their girlfriend, or advance to the next level in some video game they were working on. I was trying to decide whether I wanted to go to Subway or Quiznos after work and was having a serious interior dialogue and debate with myself as I carefully weighed the various sandwiches available at each location against one another. "My little story is about four soldiers that went out to North Shore a few weekends ago. Perhaps some of you heard of this. Four soldiers went out. Only two came back." He paused for dramatic effect.

"Why did four soldiers go out and only two come back?" he repeated. "It's because they didn't think. They didn't use . . . common . . . sense." He paused heavily, accentuating the words "common sense." Captain Zimmerman also saw the glory and potential of mankind revealed in the application of thinking and common sense. If we applied thought and common sense, we could go and wage war together and kill people in countries where we had never been.

"They went out drinking, a little night on the town. And that's fine. And it's good that they went out in a fire team. It's good to be with buddies. Always have your battle buddy. Battle buddy is good! That part of what they did was good! But then, after they went drinking, they decided to go for a late-night swim, and that's where they didn't use any common sense." He seemed to be finished, completing a pace with an abrupt turn. And then there was silence.

And then: "Battle buddy good! No common sense bad!" Little giggles erupted from undefined points within the formation. "Drugs, men. Drugs. Don't do them. Drugs are no good. If you want to get high, go on a trail run with me up Koli Koli Pass; that'll get you high. A real high. A natural high. No drug high can beat a natural high." More giggles and laughter, this time joined by my own smirk.

"Sex with married women—don't do it. Sex with underage women—don't do it." "Sex with underage women" was added after some platoon was discovered gangbanging a major's sixteen-year-old daughter. "Sex with men—don't do it."

And, finally, after some more nonsense, we were released.

I got a hotel downtown on the Waikiki strip. A seedy place smacking of desperate vacations by a financially strapped clientele. It had the air of a Midwest casino that eagerly wants to be seen as Atlantic City or Vegas but can't get the smell of Missouri out of the air, and you realize that it's not the same and should just give up trying.

I spent the evening with Ryan and Diego and almost missed out on the entire deployment by choking on a bone buried inside a piece of pork that made me throw up at the table, much to the chagrin of our fellow diners. Instead of partying long into the night, we all preferred to retire to our separate rooms to be alone with our thoughts.

Final evenings before deployments seem forced. You're forcing everything. You're trying to force relaxation. You're trying to force important thoughts that contemplate the adventure you're about to embark on. But you can't force it. The contemplation comes to you later in little spurts as you've finished climbing a mountain and, winded, you lean against a Humvee. That's when it comes to you. And then only in broken bits and pieces.

I looked out from my window and just enjoyed watching the street below. I was dating this pretty little thing of a nurse named Kaitlin, and I invited her over. I didn't want to go out and party. I just wanted to stay in and watch movies and bring a bottle of wine back up to the room. Enjoy the comfy bed and the fluffy pillows and the smell of commercialism and vacationing and sunscreen in the air. And while I waited for her arrival, I realized that for the first time since being told months earlier that I was going, I felt slightly anxious. It wasn't a fear of dying or of getting harmed—the war seemed over for the most part, and statistics were on my side—it was more a fear of the unknown. Not knowing what living conditions would be like, not knowing if I'd hate every second of it.

I felt small and insignificant as I thought back to all the soldiers who had come before me. All the soldiers who had been to Afghanistan. All the quiet fears of thousands of soldiers before me. And with Iraq. All the thousands of small private mental theaters of anxiety and unanswered prayers and unfulfilled desires that must've gone out, been sent out to the Universe in the middle of the night to be swallowed and not responded to. And then my mind just kept going further back. I started imagining the horror of all the soldiers in Vietnam. A real war. A horrible war in which many people died.

And I drifted back not only to the American soldiers in the two World Wars, in the Revolutionary War and the Civil War, but to soldiers all across the globe throughout the course of civilization and history. My mind boggled with the sheer immensity of the image. All the people who died in the name of some cause, at the behest of the desires of their kings or leaders, to be sacrificed in power plays, or simply killed over land many times over by a great many people all claiming to own it, all while the land remained apathetically indifferent to their sacrifice.

My own slight anxieties felt unworthy in the light of such enormous events. I was a tiny bubble floating in a hurricane of problems and anguish and real soldiering gripes. Just a tiny bubble of self-pity.

Mostly, though, I was excited. This was what I had joined the Army to do. This was my once-in-a-lifetime chance to be a part of history. This was my gift to my older self, who would someday have the memories and the experiences that I hadn't yet gotten to play with or own.

Kaitlin came over, and she was very sweet to me, catering to my whims, allowing me to order her around like a servant. We both thought it was funny. We kissed and played and hugged and talked about how I'd be going for an entire year without sex, and we both laughed, and I feigned cries of agony and told her not to remind me.

And on Monday, I left.

ARRIVING IN COUNTRY:
AN E-MAIL TO MOM

Dear Mom:

So it's some godforsaken early hour in the morning, and I'm at an air base in Turkey with eyes propped open by coffee and nicotine, and I'm eating stale French fries I bought from the Turkish guy selling the soap. There are Marines and Army soldiers and airmen, and we're all in this little tiny room, packed way past capacity, and we're watching *Sesame Street* like a room full of zombies. That's how I know we're all zombies—because despite our double occupancy of the room, there's hardly a sound.

Everybody's got travel fatigue. Switching time zones, numerous stops all over the world (no direct flights here!), sleep coming in incremental waves between cramped airplane seats during those few moments where you're able to forget how uncomfortable you are.

Cedar chips. Everything here smells like a hamster cage. Different countries have different smells—I've traveled enough to know—and Turkey smells like cedar chips. This is strangely confirmed for me by three independent voices in the crowd commenting about the way the country smells like cedar chips. Or at least this region does. Or this Army base. Or something.

We're watching *Sesame Street*. Elmo is dancing with a big elephant in a tutu yelling "Let's dance!" and is breaking into some John Travolta disco shit. It's one of those moments when everybody wants to change the channel but nobody does. No one wants to be the one to stand up and risk changing it to another show that nobody wants to watch. At least with *Sesame Street* you've got the zany antics of an elephant in a ballet tutu—doesn't get much more entertaining than that. I look around. I'm sure everyone wants it changed. I decide to risk it all, and I stand up and make my way past extended legs hanging into the aisle and start to change the channel.

"Don't change that!" barks a Marine gunny sergeant from across the room, scowling at me.

I nod and tiptoe back to my seat and sit back down.

Sesame Street it is.

After a few days in Kyrgyzstan we arrive at Bagram Air Base. Today is the first day of May—only 364 days to go! It's already ridiculously hot, but everyone who's already here is telling us that this is only the pregame show. They say we won't know what hot is until July hits.

Bagram was a Russian airfield that has since been mostly de-mined and turned into America's primary base of operations in Afghanistan. Ragged rough thorny mountains rise on all four sides on the horizon. They are leviathan wonders of wickedly carved granite, standing firmly against gravity and the forces of the Universe. An asteroid could fly into them from the far reaches of our galaxy, speeding at breakneck cosmic speeds, and bounce off these iron beasts. The air is also hot. It's very hot. It's May. I figure it's supposed to be hot.

Here at Bagram we do our in-processing. I hate in-processing. There's always in-processing in the Army. They inform us where the chow halls are, and the Internet sites (from which I'm now e-mailing you), and the phones, and the PX, where we can buy snacks. They're all listed on a map that I can't quite orient myself to, so I leave the briefing no more illuminated than when I came in.

We're taken by Halliburton folks to a tent city on the edge of the base, where we set up inside on cots. We're given some basic instructions and released for the rest of the day. We've got a layover for a few days while our betters figure some things out. I use the shitter, which I find is literally overflowing with feces. The word "literally" has been overused. When most people say it, they don't even mean it; they're still exaggerating. But here I literally mean to use the word "literally," as in "there literally was overflowing feces."

No; I'm exaggerating.

It wasn't actually coming out of the toilet. But it was still bad.

Ryan, Diego, and I take a bus into the heart of the base and are amazed at the place. We immediately made public and private apologies to the Army for calling it incompetent while back in garrison in Hawaii. The place is a monument to—well, not necessarily efficiency, but to lots of work having been done in a short period of time. It's an entire minicity for seven thousand soldiers complete with all the requirements of a city: trash collection, supply points, showers, toilets, and food. And everywhere the telltale signs of intense Army stuff going on: barricades, barbed wire, guns, and lots of busy trucks driving back and forth.

We stock up on soda pop at the PX. My bags are going to be loaded down with ammo and Coca-Cola. In the chow hall, a local Afghan national has been hired to record the number of foreign service soldiers who are eating so that their respective countries can be appropriately billed for the meal. Our soldiers, the new ones, the ones just off the plane, point and laugh at him. He's an oddity. An actual Afghan—the type of person we're supposed to kill.

"Wow, look, it's an actual Afghan!"

"Can we pet him on the head?"

"No, this is a non–petting zoo! You don't pet the Afghans! They are wild animals! In fact, every single last one of them is scheduled to be put down!"

"Down with the Afghan animals! They make lousy pets, anyway," another said as he petted the little Afghan on the head and poked his finger in the poor man's ear.

The Afghan, who understood English perfectly well, only frowned at us. He hates us. But we didn't make him hate us. He hates us because of hundreds of other soldiers he's dealt with in the past.

We head back to our tent city. Upon arrival, we find out about the old Haji in the sleeping rocker!

"You haven't seen the old Haji on the sleeping rocker?" everyone exclaims.

"No," respond Ryan, Diego, and I with more than a little envy. You see, we too want to see the old Haji in the sleeping rocker, although we don't yet know why we should want to see such things.

"The old Haji man in the rocker is this little old guy on this corner in the middle of the base! He's got this old AK-47, and he'll let you take a picture of him with it with you standing next to him for a dollar! And for two dollars? For two dollars he'll get down on his hands and knees and let you take a picture of you holding the AK to his head like you're going to blow him away!"

Anyway, Mom, so I'm here. For whatever that's worth. In a few days we're going to a place called Ghazni, which is the area of responsibility for our battalion, the 5/2. So Alpha Company, Bravo Company, and Charlie Company (Cougars!) are all being set up in these little bases in the area around Ghazni along with a bigger battalion base somewhere there. It'll just be my platoon and second platoon, because first platoon is being sent to guard an embassy in Kabul or some damn place. Ghazni is like, I think, the third or fourth or something biggest city in Afghanistan, and they're telling us that it's one of the hottest places for combat in Afghanistan at the moment. I don't mean to worry you, but from what they're telling us it's not sounding good, and it appears I'll get what I signed up for. Send me lots of food please, and tell everyone that I love them. I'll write when I can.

Love,

Johnny

Chapter 17

THE FIRST TWENTY-FOUR HOURS
AT FIREBASE COUGAR

This is it.

Ten minutes until we are to land in the wilds of Afghanistan. In a place we can't yet visualize. Our only conceptions are framed by *Newsweek* articles that spoke of a lawless mountainous land of danger. Aside from a couple of older soldiers who rotated in on the tail end of Bosnia, none of us have been in danger before. And not a single one of us, save for our platoon sergeant, Sergeant Derrens, two years away from retirement, has fired a weapon in an attempt to kill somebody.

The helicopter abruptly descends, and everyone stirs, sharing last looks that seem to belong to an already bygone moment in our lives when we were safe and secure. My mind conjures up images of us landing in a hot zone, gunfire kicking up dirt next to our feet as we try to disembark from the chopper. I realize my weapon's not even loaded. Someone told me to load my weapon with ammo before we left, but I had been playing "Age of Mythology" on my laptop and forgot. Fuck. I can't keep forgetting shit like that. I make a mental note to remind myself to load my weapon with ammo from now on.

Then the helicopter bumps slightly, and we can feel the wheels touching down.

I see open vacant desert at the rear end of the chopper, where the ramp is already lowered. Everyone moves in accelerated slow motion, and I crawl quickly over a mountain of gear, getting my rifle's sling stuck several times on odd ends and baggage straps. I stumble off the top of the pile of bags, my helmet falling over my face, and rush outside into the exhaust of the Chinook's engines. It's like sticking your face in an oven. We cringe from the heat and try to keep the smell of burning fuel from reaching too far down our throats and gasp for breath as we stumble into the desert, looking around nervously, not wanting to be the one guy that fucks up. Two Blackhawk gunship escorts whirl about overhead, providing security.

"GO! GO!" screams staff Sergeant Stephens, and I go running wildly and furiously in one direction, only to be interrupted by Sergeant First Class Derrens yelling at us to run the other way instead. We run back and forth, unsure of where to run to, but we run as hard as we can.

Finally, we collapse on berms of dirt, lay our rifles in front of us, push our loose helmets back off our brows, and make a pathetic security pattern for the chopper. And then I notice Afghanistan for the first time.

It looks just like Colorado, like the rocky hill prairie with very slight mosquito-bump hills that connects Nebraska to Colorado, and it seems to go on to infinity. It's only in the deep distance that the shade of mountains, made miniature so far away, can barely be seen.

On a hill to my left, some local Afghans in robes and head wraps gather and clap, laughing and smiling as they watch us pull security. My face flushes with embarrassment. Jesus, can't somebody shoot them or something? They can't laugh at us; we're U.S. soldiers! Finally, word passes down that we can start unloading our ridiculous quantities of baggage.

I turn to see the 10th Mountain Division's Firebase Apache, a literal re-creation of the Alamo but without the church. It's a pathetic-looking fort with four rickety guard towers on each corner and clay brick walls that stand about ten feet high, all of it surrounded by concertina wire. It belongs in some deranged version of the Old American West, the sad frontier fort where time ticks slowly and dust is a bit heavier. The 10th Mountain soldiers stand on the ramparts overlooking the dirt landing platform out front, laughing at our seriousness.

The entire base is nestled snugly in rolling hills of orange and brown dirt topped by sparse yellow patches of desert grass. In one di-

rection, rolling hills seem to stretch to Wisconsin. On the distant opposite horizon is the teeming mazelike dystopian metropolis of Ghazni,
located in southeastern Afghanistan a few hours drive from the Pakistan border. Bracketing the base are two small villages code-named
Denver and Dallas, each a picture-perfect snapshot of the type of white
clay brick villages you'd expect to see Jesus riding a donkey out of in
Biblical times.

We frown. The Afghans and the U.S. soldiers continue to laugh at us
as we lift our gear. Our backs burdened with duffel bags, our rifles slung
at odd angles around our necks and bouncing off our bodies, our hands
filled with cheap Kmart plastic storage chests and luggage, we walk up
the slight incline through a barbed-wire mesh to the entrance of Firebase Apache.

"You better hurry the fuck up! You don't want to get shot!" someone cries out from the rampart walls.

At this, several of the new arrivals start a small double-time shuffle
as fast as they can under the weight they're carrying, which only causes
howls of laughter from the 10th Mountain soldiers. Someone shouts,
"Look there's Osama!" "You missed him! You missed him!"

Inside the front gate, we struggle to get to the middle of the base,
an empty courtyard of gravel. We drop our bags, exhausted from our
small walk. The altitude will take some getting used to. I feel like a glad-
iator entering the arena for the first time.

The soldiers in the guard towers smoke cigarettes and stare at us
with angry eyes. And then the 10th Mountain Division soldiers begin to
appear, slowly emerging from their tents, and down from the ramparts
to inspect us personally as we stand in formation. They are windblown
and filthy, wearing uniforms that haven't been washed in months, and
their faces are caked in dirt and mud as if they stopped caring long ago.
Dear God, what have they gone through to get in this condition?

Our company commander is immediately requisitioned by the existing command and takes off with two lieutenants while the sergeants
bark orders for us to pick up our gear. They move us back and forth
from tent to tent, and then back to the center. An hour later, nobody is
sure where we're supposed to be.

A young cocky 10th Mountain soldier with a New York accent slips through our formation and grabs me by the arm and asks, "You the RTO?"

"Uh, yeah," I mumble.

"Come with me," he says.

He darts behind one of the tents. I follow, and he immediately starts his well-practiced explanation of duties, which probably means that as soon as he passes the torch he can pack his things.

He lifts up a blanket underneath one of the rampart walls and points to a big box of batteries, "These are for the ASIP radio, down there, behind the latrines." He points to a series of wooden stalls at the rear end of the base. "Next to the shitters, on the other side of the shitters. Use those ones for the satcom, these ones for ASIP. Don't mix them up. Discharge your batteries before using them, and toss 'em in the burn pit."

"Um, yeah, uh, sure," I reply nervously, already overwhelmed as I dig deep into my pockets, trying to find my notepad and pen. He grabs me by the collar again and drags me farther down the edge of the tents, deeper into the base.

He points at the sky and says, "Declination 285 degrees for satcom; don't ask me why, because battalion base is . . ." He twirls me around in the opposite direction. "Battalion base is over there outside of Ghazni, but you point the antennae this way." He whirls me back around again. "Forty-five degrees elevation on the antennae."

He grabs me by the collar again and drags me farther into the base, and I ask, "Um, what were uh, what were those first batteries for again?"

We stop abruptly behind a small chow tent at the back of the base, where soldiers who look as though they hate life are washing pans in large buckets of water sitting on the ground. He says, "I almost forgot! Frequencies! 56750 is internal company frequency, 57660 is battalion net, and 57110 is fires net, but you won't ever use fires because they're actually on battalion's frequency, but that's how you have to program your radios. For satellite radio you're going to use 113. That's for fucking everybody, though! Everybody! That's the whole of goddamn

Afghanistan, so don't use it! Medevac is 117, but you don't use 117. If you have to call in a medevac call it on 113, but for medevac it's 117."

I scribble as intensely as I can and pause to ask, "Um, what's this satellite radio you keep talking about?"

He ignores me, saying only, "We good? Great; have fun."

"Wait! Wait!" I ask, the desperation in my voice both pathetic and sad.

"What?!" he asks. He sighs and turns back around, giving me only a few seconds to sell him on the possible legitimacy of my question.

"Uh, are there any SOPs, any standard operating procedures that I need to know about as far as patrols or missions; I mean, I don't even know what we actually do here. Is there one RTO a mission or two or . . ."

"The radio?" he responds quietly.

"Yes?" I say.

"Turn it on when you go out. That way you can call the base." He pats me on the shoulder and goes inside the chow tent, leaving me alone with my incomprehensible notes and mental confusion.

"Rico!" I turn to see Ryan running at me. "Where the fuck did you go? Lieutenant Michael is looking for you. You gotta go out. You got a mission, man."

"What?! We just fucking got here!" I exclaim, agitated as all hell.

Ryan shrugs. "Hey, I'm not in fucking charge; go complain to someone else. Go get your shit on. There's some Taliban guy in the next village over, and we're going to get him!"

Ice dumps into my heart and pushes out into my veins.

A frosty chill follows the arching networked vessels of my body, slowly consuming me in a growing anxiety.

And when I'm fully saturated, when there are no sober reserves left in my toes or other far-reaching appendages, then fear sets in.

I'm not ready for a combat mission. I need to unpack my clothes, set up my little area somewhere, get something to eat. Then, in a few days when I've adjusted, then we can talk about going out on combat missions.

"But I don't know what I'm doing! I don't know where the radio is!

I mean, I just got here! I just got here!" I keep saying it over and over as if the profound power of the concept that I just arrived will somehow be enough to change reality.

But even as I say this I move through the tents back to the center courtyard where I had dumped my gear and put on my flack vest and helmet.

To make matters worse, while I'm on the mission, the rest of the soldiers will choose their cots and carve out and define their small areas of space within their tents, and I'll come back to find that I've been given the leftover, some broken cot with only a few inches of space.

We march out the front gate, where the guard puts on his gloves and rolls the barbed wire aside, and start over the rolling hills to Dallas, a shimmering maze of white compounds interspersed with palm trees, that is just a thousand meters from our northwest guard tower.

Two 10th Mountain soldiers walk ahead, laughing and joking, their weapons slung on their backs, looking at each other instead of at the roads and buildings in front of them. The nine of us follow, creeping up in tense jerky movements as our rifles move back and forth at the ready, covering the street and then the rooftops and then the open doorways we pass. We stay close to the walls, bound up in buddy teams, who spring up to a position and then drop abruptly on the ground to provide security for the next group of guys.

A few local Afghan men walk by in their long flowing body dresses, staring while offering a smile as our weapons bear down on them, ready to take them out. We stare at them intently, not quite able to believe that we are suddenly in the third world among real native Afghans. We take an instant dislike to them. They smell bad, they have bad teeth, and their smiles seem too smug. But then, we were trained to dislike them before ever arriving.

The 10th Mountain soldiers take us through dizzying turns of lefts and rights and through alleys and finally into a courtyard, where, separated from all the other interconnected buildings of the village, a lone ranch-style house sits at the end of this Afghan suburban cul-de-sac.

It's a clay brick home, surrounded on all four sides by tall walls, which deny visibility to the interior courtyard. Outside the red front gate, a donkey slowly chews on some hay as it swats flies with its tail. For the second time that day, the thought occurs to me that Afghanistan is some twisted episode of the American West, but one where time goes by too slowly. We have somehow time-warped into a bad John Wayne movie. There's even a well in the middle of the courtyard. The only thing missing is the Mexican having a siesta, leaning back against the building with his sombrero pulled low over his brow to stop the sun.

I take cover on the side of an alleyway wall and crouch down on my heels, my senses alert and my breaths deep, long, and hard, although I've only been walking. Lieutenant Michael pokes his head over a dirt berm, his rifle at the ready as he surveys the scene. Sergeant Santiago barks orders to his soldiers to cover various alleys and to keep an eye on the rooftops. Lieutenant Michael motions for me. I sprint across the small open courtyard and dive into the small culvert behind the dirt berm, breathless and nervous.

This is it.

This is what I've trained for.

But have I really trained for this?

What about all the times I pretended to be dead because I was tired of training? All the times I volunteered for yet one more office detail to get me out of the field so I could get some fast food and change into some dry clothes?

And then the horrifying truth hit me.

I wasn't trained at all.

The Army had attempted to train me but I refused it. I had subverted their training. I hadn't taken it to heart. I hadn't paid attention. A little bit, but not really. Not enough to suddenly be in Afghanistan hiding behind a dirt berm outside the house of a known Taliban leader.

I envision machine guns opening fire on us at any moment from any one of the buildings that surround us in this densely populated village. There are alleys and streets everywhere, each created almost haphazardly with no apparent sense of planning, each a potential avenue for what I imagine to be an old rusty Toyota with a machine gun mounted on top, about to come screaming around the corner, and driving it will be very angry Arabs.

I hate angry Arabs.

Angry Arabs scare me.

Lieutenant Michael motions for the hand microphone, and I untangle it from underneath my arm while he frowns at me, waiting impatiently.

It takes me a long time to untangle the hand mike. I have it completely wound up and twisted around a loop in my tactical vest. This is another one of those mental learning curves, one of those notes to file away for later review.

Load my weapon with ammo.

Make sure the radio hand mike is free.

Finally, freeing the hand mike, I hand it over. Lieutenant Michael whispers, probably unnecessarily, into the radio: "Cougar Base, this is Hunter-6. We are in Objective Dallas and in position. Over."

There is a pause before Cougar Base responds: "Roger, Hunter-6, this is Cougar Base. We read you. Keep us informed of all activities. Over."

I scan the faces of my fellow soldiers. Devon is behind his machine gun covering an alleyway, looking around nervously, overwhelmed by his sudden immersion in a biblical village. Ryan, covering Devon's rear down the opposite fork of the alley, repeatedly looks over to Sergeant Santiago for guidance. Cox, nose to his rifle as he was taught, is on the corner of a building at the right of the courtyard, covering the convergence of road and dirt and yard that all end with him.

The 10th Mountain soldiers walk past us and sit in the open on the berm that we're hiding behind. They take off their helmets and look back at us, amused.

"I thought she was banging that E6 from Alpha Company," the first one says.

"Nah, man, she was banging a lot more than him. She was banging the whole fucking company," the other responds.

"Sergeant," Lieutenant Michael interrupts from his dirt berm, crouched down in a weird, sideways, almost fetal position. "What's the plan for this guy?"

The 10th Mountain soldier looks at him, confused, for a second. "There's no plan, sir. This is just where he lives. In fact, there he is right now." Inside the Taliban's home, a man appears at the doorway and waves. The sergeant waves back. "We're not allowed to arrest him."

"Really?" Lieutenant Michael says, somewhat confused.

"Well, we don't really know if he's Taliban. We think he is. He might be. Who knows? Doesn't really matter," the second sergeant says, picking a weed up off the ground and putting it in his mouth as he relaxes on the dirt berm, his hands behind his head, his rifle on the ground.

Lieutenant Michael gives the "all clear" to Sergeant Santiago and climbs up from the berm. "So what type of operations are you doing here, then?"

"Oh, we gotta shitload of operations," the first one says.

"Yeah, we gotta shitload of operations," the second one concurs.

"Like we have this little walk—oh, I'm sorry, I mean this patrol that we do. We walk about a mile up the road from the base, see if there's any Taliban on the road, and if there's not, we turn around and walk back to the base."

"Then there's another patrol that we do," the second one continues. "We walk in the hills about a mile behind the base, and if there's no Taliban hiding in the dirt behind the base, then we walk back to base."

"I was under the impression this was, I don't know, an intense area," Lieutenant Michael says, with more than a little suggestion in his voice about how he wishes them to respond.

Both sergeants think about this for a moment and then say, almost in unison, "No, no; there's nothing going on here. Uh-uh."

The first one then offers, "Well, sometimes these ranchers, like ranching or whatever the fucking verb is, ranch their sheep, oh yeah, they'll come within a half kilometer of the base, and once or twice, we've had to fire warning shots."

"And other times?" the second sergeant continues. "Other times? We'll go down outside of Denver or Dallas and do a vehicle checkpoint, and we might confiscate some"—he pauses, lending what he is about to say the optimum dramatic effect—"opium!"

Lieutenant Michael sighs, his visions of leading men into glorious battles where he'd be awarded prestigious medals of valor dissolving in front of his eyes. "How long have you guys been here?"

They think about it for a moment, although they both knew the answer, and then the second one says, "About a year. Yep, going on a year now."

"Well, anyway, this is where he lives," the second one states. "Let's head back."

Lieutenant Michael pauses angrily, kicks a pile of dirt, frowns, and says, "Rico, call up Cougar Base and tell them we're coming back."

I pick up the hand mike on my shoulder, this time beaming with pride that it isn't tangled up in my tactical vest, although no one notices this or praises me. The first 10th Mountain sergeant screams, "Jonesey! We're coming back in!"

There is a slight pause before someone behind the Taliban's house yells faintly, "Okay!"

I lie down on my broken cot in the corner, a casualty of the orderly, disciplined move into the tents which only had, at the last second I was told, turned into a total brawl.

The soldiers are cleaning their weapons as Sergeant Stein, a Louisiana redneck with a deep Southern drawl, marches up and down the center of the tent, yelling at men for making jokes.

"You think this is a fucking game, y'all? Y'all think this is a fucking game till one of you motherfuckers gets shot for fuckin' dicking around. We're in a combat zone now, men; we ain't got time to be playing grabass no more." Sergeant Stein notices me writing in my journal and kicks me in the leg. "That goes for you too, Rico. Just because you're RTO, just because you're Lieutenant Michael's boy don't make you special none. You get to cleaning that fucking weapon right now. We might get attacked tonight; you don't fucking know."

I sigh and pull out my weapon cleaning kit from under my cot and disassemble my weapon as I look over at Sergeant Santiago, who offers me an apology with his eyes.

The soldiers of the platoon are silent for a while, cleaning their weapons in the dim light of a single bulb. But all military orders have a half-life of approximately twenty minutes, so everyone soon begins to talk again, this time uninterrupted. They swap anxieties about combat and offer one another promises to do the right thing when the moment comes when others will be depending on them to save their lives.

"I don't fucking care, man," Mulbeck says. "I'll fucking save any of your fucking asses. Fucking you, too, White. Even you, White." White, the fat soldier who always messes up and whom everyone hates with an open tangible disdain, smiles silently. "That's just the way I was raised. Sure I'm afraid of dying, but that's what I trained for, you know? That's what I fucking trained for. If it's my time, it's my time."

"Whatever happens, guys, I just want you to know that I loved all of you," Private Ryan says.

"Faggot!" someone calls out.

"I'm serious!" Ryan pleads. "We've had our ups and downs, but we're all here now, and we've got to do what we've got to do. We might not all come back from this deployment. I don't know. I can't see into the future. But I love you guys. Seriously, I love you guys."

Sergeant Santiago and I lock eyes, quiet in our secret knowledge that perhaps Ghazni isn't going to be everything that we have been told it would be.

Satisfied that the weapons are properly cleaned, even though they were thoroughly cleaned every day for the past week, Sergeant Stein says, "Second Platoon has guard tonight. Everyone's getting up bright and early; we got us a patrol real early in the morning. I don't know what time it's at, but it's early, so I suggest y'all get some fucking sleep."

And with that he turns out the light, indifferent to the soldiers who haven't finished putting their weapons back together.

In the pitch-black night I snuggle into my broken cot, which tears a bit more as I rest my weight against it.

It is going to be a long year.

I force my eyelids open. It's three o'clock in the morning, and no sooner have I fallen asleep than the light flips on with Sergeant Stein screaming and kicking everybody to get up.

"Listen up, you little fucks," Sergeant Riley says. We're in the chow hall, which at the moment is our makeshift briefing room. An easel with paper and markers is next to him as he gives our operation order. Sergeant Riley is the tender loving father of three boys back home, but through his alter-ego identity as a U.S. soldier he is dripping with extraneous aggression and a constant nervousness. He's always on edge and flips out over every small infraction and detail, but fortunately for his soldiers, he also rarely remembers these infractions and is quick to get back into a good mood. He reminds me of a child who has a temper tantrum and then all it takes to change his mood is a cookie. He's a big guy with a wild, long-haired flattop that goes nuts when sweat is applied.

"Okay, what is our mission?" Sergeant Riley asks. "Come on, somebody fucking answer me. What—am I fucking talking to myself here?"

Ryan forces back a yawn as he snaps the last piece of his body armor in position, raises his hand, and suggests, "To kill bad guys?"

There is a light pause before Sergeant Riley erupts on us, "Listen! You fucks better start fucking taking this shit fucking seriously! Because I'm not going to get a goddamn bullet in the back because you guys are too fucking stupid to take this shit fucking seriously! No, we're not here to kill . . ." And then he trails off, noticing the confused expressions of the eight soldiers sitting in front of him.

"I thought we were supposed to kill people," Darrenowsky states, confused.

"Yeah," Marciano concurs.

"Well, yes, that is what we do. We kill bad guys. You're right; we do kill, but our immediate mission . . ." And then he recites it from memory as it was drilled into him: ". . . is to deprive anticoalition forces movement in Ghazni province through presence patrols and security checkpoints." Sergeant Riley turns to the easel and starts writing this down and then pauses. "How do you spell coalition?"

I'm about to tell him when he realizes the marker doesn't work. He throws the marker down and says, "Fuck it, well, you know, it's just what I told you. So we're going to do a vehicle checkpoint, we're going to stop all the vehicles on the road, and we're going to tactically interrogate them in a professional fucking manner to see if they're Taliban. Key word being fucking professional. Any fucking questions?"

Ryan raises his hand. "How do I get out of this chickenshit outfit?"

Sergeant Riley points at the ground as a few soldiers murmur quick morning laughs. Ryan sighs and starts doing push-ups.

"Anyone else?" Sergeant Riley asks.

Marciano asks, "Where we doing this?"

Sergeant Riley reaches down, picks up his marker, and taps it on the easel a few times to get the ink flowing. Then he starts to draw a map on the easel board. "Well, we don't have any maps of the area, but they say that like, if this is Cougar Base, then we go out south, and there's a road that's pretty well traveled, like somewhere, like, if this is, if this circle is Dallas, and this circle is Denver, then it's like over here, behind this hill." Sergeant Riley pauses and realizes his map makes no sense and throws the marker back down. "Well, we'll find a fucking road and stop some motherfuckers, okay?"

"Jesus, we don't even have any maps?" Marciano asks me.

I shrug, not knowing what else to say.

In the movies, when combat soldiers operating in foreign countries were given mission briefs, there was always satellite photography and highly detailed plans.

We have dry markers and Sergeant Riley.

The jingle truck, a decorated miniature semi with chains dangling from every square inch of exterior space, drives in the quiet early hours of the morning when suddenly, on the road ahead, the headlights of a U.S. Humvee flip on. The truck comes to a screeching halt, and armed U.S. soldiers are everywhere.

And now the frigid early morning is quiet except for the rough idling of the diesel engine and the quiet click of Army boots on pavement as Sergeant Riley and I approach the driver's-side door and the window rolls down. Our local Afghan interpreter, clean-shaven and dressed in an L.A. Raiders jacket, who is quite high on opium, asks, "Are you Taliban?"

The driver of the vehicle is a small man with timid features and scared eyes. He has dirt on his face, and his clothes are stained with sweat and grime.

"No," the driver says.

"Do you know of any Taliban?"

"No."

"Have you seen any Taliban in the area?"

"No."

Staff Sergeant Riley considers this and then suddenly breaks into an anxious scream. "Fucking liars! Fucking goddamn liars! Get the fuck out of the vehicle!"

The Afghans sit in the truck, immobile but visibly shaking in fear. Their refusal to follow English orders only infuriates Staff Sergeant Riley, and soon the passenger and driver doors are opened and they are forcefully pulled from the cab.

Soon there are eight Afghans on the road in the calm cold of predawn light, blinking in confusion, squinting in the glare of the headlights. In the blackness beyond the reach of their vision, they are vaguely aware of soldiers wearing night vision goggles and moving about their vehicle. They hear doors opening and closing and shouts in English, which they don't understand, that seem to travel a long way in the empty desert.

Through the interpreter I ask them a series of questions: Name, village of birth, father's name, where they are coming from, where they are going. I write it all down with fingers numb from the cold as I hold a small flashlight in my mouth. The early mornings are a bitter cold that has no business being in the same country as the miserable sauna sweat-stained afternoons preceding them just twelve hours earlier.

"Darrenowsky, search these fuckers and send them over to Marciano," Staff Sergeant Riley shouts before walking over to check out the truck. "Make sure you check everything!" he says to the rest of the soldiers searching the truck.

Staff Sergeant Riley turns back around to see Darrenowsky and Marciano laughing at a scorpion on the side of the road. Darrenowsky flips it over with the barrel of his rifle, both of their backs to the Afghans. One of the Afghan passengers of the truck, curious about their find, peers over their shoulders.

"Jesus Christ, man!" Riley screams, his voice already going hoarse. "Did I fucking tell you to watch them? What the fuck are you doing? Look, Habreem over there is fucking wandering down the road, and Mohammed Fucking Mohammed is right fucking behind you!" Staff Sergeant Riley kicks Marciano in the ass as both Marciano and Darrenowsky run back to the Afghan passengers and berate them and shove them around as punishment for their own inattentiveness.

I move on to the third passenger, who looks up at me with eager bright eyes, his bad yellow teeth grimacing as if he anticipates that my question will cause him pain. His eyes keep darting over to the jingle truck, where loud booms and slams are emanating from deep inside as the soldiers search for weapons or drugs or something. He cringes each time he hears another boom, probably imagining the loss of an invaluable resource, perhaps his only source of income.

Truth was, nobody has told us what we are looking for.

"Ryan!"

Ryan, who is off to the side pulling security in a field, answers, "Yeah?"

"What are we looking for?"

Ryan thinks about this and then says, "I don't know. They never really briefed us on what we're looking for."

"We'll know it when we see it, huh?"

"I guess."

The interpreter looks up at me to see if I have any more questions, but I tell him I don't.

Ryan says, "I'm going to go back and stare at my field. If I turn my back to you guys I can close my eyes and nobody knows I'm sleeping."

"Yeah, all right," I reply.

One of the passengers of the vehicle moves to the side of the road and squats down, and Darrenowsky runs up on him, shoving his rifle in the man's face screaming, "GET THE FUCK UP! DON'T FUCKING MOVE!"

I sigh, move over to Darrenowsky, push the muzzle of his weapon away from the face of the trembling Afghan. " Darrenowsky, he doesn't speak English, and he can't both get up and not move at the same time, and finally, he's taking a piss, man. He's okay."

After the truck has been thoroughly searched, and whatever cargo it has been carrying—rice or matches or bicycle parts—dumped all over the road, Staff Sergeant Riley lines the passengers up and shakes their hands in turn. The interpreter translates for him: "Thank you for your cooperation. We're searching for Taliban. We're here for your security."

"Are you sure none of you are Taliban?" Sergeant Riley says calmly, almost cooing them with sweet talk.

It's the Taliban honor system.

You don't have to give yourself up as Taliban unless we ask you nicely.

All the Afghans state very emphatically under the bright light of the flashlights mounted on the ends of the rifle muzzles pointed at their faces that they are not, in fact, Taliban.

As the sun rises behind us we drive back across the flat desert and ascend slowly into the slight prairie hills up the dirt road that leads to our base.

I'm in the backseat, nodding off and then catching myself, while Sergeant Riley sits up front in the passenger seat cursing the Afghans, "I know that fucking asshole was fucking Taliban. Fucking pisses me off. We should have been allowed to shoot him on sight. God, those fuckers are hiding something. They are all fucking liars."

I turn to the Afghan interpreter, whom we've decided to call Jerry because none of us can remember the Afghan name he told us, and offer a slight apologetic smile. Jerry smiles back and then turns and frowns, staring out the window. He hates us; I can tell. I would hate us too.

"Jerry, why the fuck is this country so fucked up?" Sergeant Riley asks from the front seat. "No wonder you guys are still driving fucking donkeys and don't have electricity, because this is one fucked-up country."

Jerry says nothing.

"Do you want to come to America, Jerry?" Sergeant Riley asks. "I guess that's a stupid question. I mean, why would you want to stay here?"

"This is my home," Jerry says. "I am proud to be Afghan."

"You're proud to be Afghan?!" Sergeant Riley laughs. "Man, come to America, Jerry. We'll hook you up. You can sleep in my yard. Get you a job at 7-Eleven or something."

I'm in the shitters staring at the small image of the naked woman that I downloaded onto my Palm Pilot. I'm jerking off as fast as I can. A line of soldiers is outside waiting to use one of the three makeshift wooden toilets, each of which holds a soldier jerking off. The smell of the large pile of feces in the metal canister a half foot below my ass is making me want to vomit as flies buzz in my face, but I desperately need a few precious minutes of alone time, a physical release. A momentary period of relaxation, however brief, so I can reenter the fray more collected.

The small Palm Pilot image not doing it for me, I switch tactics and start thinking of my friend Amanda as I swat at a few flies trying to get into my mouth. There's a knock on the door.

"It's in use!" I scream almost like a girl, shrilly and high-pitched.

"Rico, is that you?" It's the calm friendly voice of Sergeant Santiago.

"Yes," I say reluctantly after a slight pause, knowing that eventually I'll have to leave through the door, although the idea of crawling out underneath the latrines next to the shit cans does cross my mind. But then where would I hide? There's nowhere to hide at Cougar Base. You can't hide on a base the size of a movie theater that houses one hundred men.

"Quit jerking your meat. You've got guard, and it started two minutes ago."

I sigh. Jesus Christ; this shit is really nonstop, isn't it? It was just a mere ten minutes ago that we rolled back through the gate from our morning vehicle checkpoint.

"No one told me this, Sergeant," I yell back.

"I'm telling you now," Sergeant Santiago says from the other side of the door. I can tell that he's stressed out and the last thing he needs is an argument.

"Jesus Christ, Sergeant! I haven't even eaten breakfast yet, and I got like two fucking hours of sleep last night!" I yell back.

"Get to the fucking front gate, Rico. Everyone's in the same boat. Everyone's busy."

His footsteps fall away as I sigh and pull up my pants.

I collapse on the little bench in the shack next to the front gate with my arms crossed over my chest, pouting. Sergeant Kibbul spits some chew as he looks down the dirt road leading up to Cougar Base with his usual wise, contemplative look. An interesting look, in that he is neither wise nor contemplative. He always seems to me like a weasel with squinty eyes, angling for the next play. A thin Hawaiian-looking guy who actually comes from Kentucky, he's one of those guys who is well liked and popular for his jokes and humor but seems to regard everybody coolly and without empathy, as if they are only a potential resource.

"How's it going there, Rico?" Sergeant Kibbul asks sarcastically.

"This is bullshit. They can't keep running us nonstop like this."

"Oh, they can and they will. Have you seen the patrol or guard schedule yet? Take a look. You'll laugh. It's fucking funny. Fucking hilarious. We've got patrols leaving here nonstop. Over to Denver, over to Dallas, up the road, behind the base in the dirt hills. Cougar Base, open twenty-four hours a day, seven days a week. We never close. Captain Zimmerman feels that it's very important that we're off to a good running start and that his soldiers are busy. God forbid we have free time."

The bitching has already started. It isn't just Sergeant Kibbul; it's everybody. All the privates and low-level sergeants who can afford to get away with it are already complaining about operational tempo and sleep. Complaining is what soldiers do best.

"I haven't even gotten to eat yet," I tell him, looking for some sympathy as I peer down the road beyond our base. All is quiet and still except for a light wind stirring the dusty road. Two Afghans in the distance are walking a donkey into town, and farther out a slow-moving truck is pulling out of Dallas. It seems that Afghanistan is forever trapped in the pace of a quiet, lazy Sunday afternoon.

"Well, let me tell you," Sergeant Kibbul says, spitting out some more chew juice. "You didn't miss anything. A half scoop of boiled freeze-dried egg and half a bagel. It was quite delectable." Every once in a while Sergeant Kibbul throws in a big word that seems out of place, rarely caring whether it is used correctly.

A figure approaches us on the road, just mounting the slight rise in the distance.

I turn to Sergeant Kibbul. "What's our SOP for this?"

"You don't need no goddamn SOP. Just go out there and stop him and bring him up."

I put on my helmet and grab my rifle and walk out to meet what I could now make out to be a tiny, wrinkled old man.

Sergeant Kibbul calls out after me, "And be sure to search his Haji motherfucking ass!"

I immediately feel sympathy for the old man, who pauses in the middle of the road and raises his fragile limbs in order for me to pat him down. I walk slowly next to him, keeping his pace as I move him into the guard shack, and point to the bench, where he timidly takes a seat.

Sergeant Kibbul hands the man a bottle of water. "Want some water there, buddy?" To me he says, "I called an interpreter on the radio. He'll be down shortly."

The man nods his appreciation, pops the cap, and swallows hard, some water going out on to his chin. His Adam's apple bobs up and down as he gulps the water.

"Guess you're kinda thirsty there, aren't you, buddy?" Sergeant Kibbul has one knee up on our bench, his rifle somewhat aimed at our new guest. "Let me ask you a question there, buddy: Why is it that your country is such a fucking shithole? I mean, can you tell me why? I would just like to know why."

The man babbles in a Dari dialect.

"Hey, you don't have to tell me, buddy," Sergeant Kibbul drones on. "You know what I think? I think we should just nuke every goddamn one of you, just put you all in a big hole, and throw a nuclear bomb in there and then get the fuck out of the way. Whaddayathink about that, huh, buddy?"

The man looks at me in confusion and mumbles some more in Dari.

"Oh, you agree! You agree! Well, that's just splendid, then!" Sergeant Kibbul turns to me with a big smile. "This motherfucker agrees with me! He wants to nuke his own people! Well, as long as we're all in agreement, I say we just go and get it started. What do you say?"

The interpreter, one we've named David, another young urban Afghan who dresses as a Westerner, suddenly dips his head into our holding area. We quickly discover that the man is the landlord of the property on which Cougar Base sits, that he is paid only twenty-five U.S. dollars a month in rent, and that the 10th Mountain soldiers told him to come back and take up the matter of a raise with the 25th soldiers when they arrive. A few calls go back and forth on the radio until finally Captain Zimmerman enters the guard booth, sighing, angry that he has been taken from more pressing matters.

The interpreter presents the land ownership documents that the old man brought with him and explains. "He, uh, he own this land, this land, uh, Cougar Base belong to him? And he uh, let, uh not sell, but uh, not buy to, but uh, rent? He rent to 10th Mountain? He's only being paid twenty-five dollars U.S. a month and was told by 10th Mountain that they would pay him one hundred dollars U.S. a month?"

Captain Zimmerman smiles and replies, "Tell him we'll give him what we want to give him. How about you tell him that?"

The interpreter translates this and gives Captain Zimmerman the response. "He say this not fair, that he was promised by the 10th Mountain . . ."

Captain Zimmerman interrupts. "What's he going to do? Take it from us?" And then to the scared old wrinkled Afghan, "You wanna evict us? Go ahead and evict us. You wanna evict the U.S. Army? Go ahead and try it. You're lucky we pay you at all." Captain Zimmerman sighs and folds his arms in disgust. "I've got work to do. I don't have time for this shit."

Captain Zimmerman leaves. Our interpreter shrugs apologetically at the local and leaves him in our care as he exits following the captain.

Our unhappy landlord sits solemnly in our shack, staring morosely at the ground.

I feel bad for the old man. Is this really the best way to go about making friends in this country? Harassing random drivers and telling old men to fuck off? Would an additional seventy-five U.S. dollars have killed the military budget?

Sergeant Kibbul starts berating the man. "You fucking Jew bastard. Greedy fucking Jew. You want more money. Goddamn you're a fucking greedy Jew."

As the old man starts to leave, I desperately look around the shack for some conciliatory prize I can offer him. "You can take some water if you want."

I collapse on my cot and look at my watch. It's not even noon yet. We haven't even been at Cougar Base twenty-four hours. The heat is stifling. Every time I swallow I choke on the dry air. It's as if some furnace is on and the windows are shut. The tent is mostly empty. Everyone's on guard duty or on patrol. I look over at Ryan lying on his cot. "What have they had you doing all day?"

"Oh, I've been on tower three for seven consecutive hours. I watched dirt for seven consecutive hours. Then I went on a nice little patrol by this riverbed, down on the back side of that hill? Well, I'm sure you'll see it. Yeah, we pulled security in a dried-up riverbed. For like three hours. I saw a camel. Mostly just more dirt. Guard the dirt."

And as Ryan is talking to me I fall asleep.

Two minutes later I'm waked up by Sergeant Pauley. "Rico, get up, you've got a patrol."

With the mess tent in use, we're now on the side of the shitters blinking in the hot sun at Sergeant Pauley, a small, understated, former Ranger who is our company's drug testing officer and also a rumored user of several illicit substances, a habit made easier by his position. He smacks the gum around in his mouth and reads quickly and indifferently from the easel board: "Purpose, to deny anti-Coalition forces mobility within the Ghazni region through presence patrols and observation. Standard. Cox, what's the standard?"

Cox sits with his eyes closed, trying to nap. He lifts his head and shrugs indifferently. "The standard? To do it to the standard? To not fuck up? I don't know."

Sergeant Pauley considers this and accepts it. "Good enough; the standard is not to fuck up. So, men, don't fuck up."

As Sergeant Pauley drones on the absurdity of our mission in Ghazni begins to register. We haven't been on the ground for twenty-four hours, and already I am unable to control my incessant need to question orders.

And Sergeant Pauley just keeps talking. We're going to guard a god-damn ditch.

Sergeant Pauley scans through the binoculars as he lies on the berm of dirt. Cougar Base is behind a rise in the prairie land about half a kilometer back, and we're in a small, dried-up ditch that runs between two small hills. The break between them looks out over Denver.

I'm next to him, my pen and paper in hand, fuming angrily through my nostrils. The rest of the squad is purportedly pulling security around us at various points along the ditch, but not a single one is paying attention. Private Marciano is making little piles of dirt and drawing in them with his finger. Cox is sleeping, pretending to be watching for bad guys sneaking up on us from behind.

"Fifteen hundred, we've got two men on bicycles, both wearing brown garments and turbans. One appears late forties, the other maybe late twenties."

I pretend to write this down and say, "You don't think this is legitimate, do you?"

"Why wouldn't it be?" Sergeant Pauley responds, resting for a moment as he drops the binoculars.

"What possible intelligence value could this be? What—you think some analyst is going to look at this and go, 'Oh! Gee! Two guys in turbans on bicycles. Something's up!' "

"One boy leading a donkey away from town, time, fifteen oh one. He's wearing an orange jacket."

I pretend to write this down, too. "You need to think for yourself, Sergeant Pauley. You don't really think that they know what they're doing, do you? That's one thing I've learned in this life—it's bullshit all the way to the top. I guarantee you the captain and the first sergeant are in the tent right now, just coming up with random shit to keep us busy."

Sergeant Pauley scans the road leading to our neighboring village and says, "Well, Rico, this is the Army. We don't think for ourselves. Fifteen oh two, one man, one donkey."

"That's the problem!" I'm agitated now. "Nobody in the Army thinks for themselves. If you don't think for yourself you can't be innovative or adaptive. The best organizations are innovative and adaptive."

"Well, when you're done with the Army, you can feel free to go get a job at one of those organizations, Rico. Same time, two little girls, purple dresses both of them."

I give in as I shake my head in disgust and start writing down the description.

Sergeant Pauley looks amused, realizes I'm on one of my frequent rants, and suddenly points his rifle at me, "Stop thinking for yourself, Rico! Stop it! Right now!"

I laugh and say, "Okay, okay; I'm not thinking for myself!"

"Yes you are! I can tell! You're still doing it!"

Sergeant Pauley thinks for a second and then says, "You know what we should do? I've seen three Afghans on the road with weapons. We should just say that one of them shot at us and we had to kill him. Nobody would question us. Who's interested? Rico?"

"I don't really want to murder anyone," I say, still angry over being given another bullshit patrol.

"Cox? Marciano? Darrenowsky?" Everyone shrugs or grunts. "Goddamn you all, doesn't anybody want to shoot someone?"

My report for the day is as follows:

The wind lightly crawls.

The desert bakes in the warm sun.

In Denver, there is light traffic in and out of the villages as peaceful Afghans wearing various clothing of various colors go about their business.

It is maddening.

And then Sergeant Pauley says, "Purple shirt, brown pants, time fifteen oh two."

It's two hours later, and I'm back in the shitters flexing my legs and rapidly stroking despite the pounding on the door and the voice that's screaming, "Hurry the fuck up!"

An eye peeks through the warped wooden slats that compose the shitter wall, followed by fingers. "Do you want me to sweet-talk you? Will that make it easier for you? I can sweet-talk you if you want me to." My own psychological development on the Freudian scale being stalled at the anal stage, all my life I've been particularly averse to being bothered during private time in the bathroom, and I contemplate the likely consequence if I decide to chew off his prying fingers.

"Fuck off!" I scream, kicking the door. The spying eye and fingers disappear. "I got guard in ten minutes!" I shout. "I can do this! I can do this!"

Outside there are soldiers laughing.

A fly is buzzing the inside of my stall, rotating between my nose and my earlobe.

A bead of sweat rolls down my forehead and hangs precariously on the edge of my nose, deciding whether to fall.

The smell of shit is overpowering.

I can't do this. The conditions aren't right.

And then I breathe deeply. I block out all extraneous noise and clear my senses. I channel Tyler Durden and put myself in my mental power environment, a quiet library. And my power animal a raccoon, appears. And it's peaceful and *nice.*

And then it happens. Better masturbation through meditation. I relax into the back of the wooden stall and sigh peacefully as I grab some toilet paper to clean my mess.

Suddenly, it's okay that I have guard in ten minutes.

Chapter 18

THE FOLLY OF WELL-MEANING PEOPLE FROM PLACES WITH NAMES LIKE OHIO

Dementia settled in after about a month. Every day, patrols went out, and for a month nothing happened. And when we weren't on patrol or guard duty, our aggressive tensions were slowly dissolved and replaced with apathy as we sat in the same cots, in the same tents, day after day, sick with the fantasies of our lost luxuries.

The firebase consisted of only a few tents, an ammo collection point, and the wooden shitters, which were being used in ever-increasing frequency for activities that had nothing to do with going to the bathroom. It didn't help that we hadn't showered or bathed in a month. Most of us had worn the same uniform from our first day at Cougar Base. A uniform so slick with sweat and stink that it'd peel off like a bandage.

So we sat in our cots, remembering all the food we used to eat.

"Do you remember Chile's? Awesome blossom. An awesome blossom onion ring platter with ketchup and barbecue sauce."

"No, chicken soft tacos from Taco Bell," another would counter. "Chicken soft tacos and a large iced Pepsi with foam at the top."

For a U.S. soldier, the dry-run time from feeling total indifference to a McDonald's cheeseburger to feeling complete anxiety and a frothing salivating lust at the idea of a McDonald's cheeseburger is exactly one week. Three weeks after that, a McDonald's cheeseburger is on a par with getting to bang Pamela Anderson.

The excitement I once felt about arriving in a so-called combat zone was replaced with the horrific reality that my deployment consisted of nothing but never-ending hours of tedious guard duty and mind-numbing boredom. I justifiably feared that my brain would atrophy from too much pornography and too many bad Hollywood movies played over and over on portable DVD players.

Sergeant Santiago, who before arriving in Afghanistan had been the image of stern soldierly resolve, was reduced to humping unsuspecting soldiers in their cots before racing across the tent to retreat and giggle wildly. Private Marciano, who in previous weeks had gone to the shit-ters to jerk off only a respectable three to four times a day, was now making it an hourly event. He had become infatuated with the feeling of heavy breathing and tense muscles pulling on erect taut sensitive parts while his eyes gazed at page after page of bouncing big breasts and moaning lips licking off protein facials. Specialist Cox smoked two packs a day and slept fifteen hours, eating almost nothing except the Twinkies my mom sent that I'd occasionally throw at his inert, sleeping form. They piled up in the curve of his body on top of the Army pon-cho he used as a blanket.

And then later, after the mail had been dropped by a convoy of U.S. Army trucks from the nearby battalion base, we were suddenly kicking and punching and tossing the care packages that well-meaning people from places with names like Ohio sent us.

"This is fucking bullshit!" screamed Private Mulbeck between little-girl giggles that escaped his rosy cheeks as he drop-kicked a package into the ceiling of our tent after finding some old Western-themed nov-els that any sane person would obviously realize held no value with an infantry soldier. "This is the shit my grandpa reads!"

Sergeant Santiago went into berserker mode, transferring his wild kinetic energy targeted first at destroying a box that offered him good Christian praises into pretending to pull out his hair and falling onto his cot with racking convulsions.

Specialist Diego was tossing shampoo and toothpaste against the wall, saying in a dry monotone, "Ohhh! Shampoo . . . yeah! I'll use that! Oh wait, we don't have any showers!"

We were all worked up into a real frenzy. We really were.

And Private Hugh, who knew nothing of theological logic, yet proclaimed close personal ties to Jesus, tried to rip the Virgin Mary bubblegum trading card off my dog tags because I had been idolizing a cum sock, claimed to be a biblical artifact that had belonged to Jesus.

Private Hugh said I didn't deserve to be protected by Jesus fire, since it had already been predetermined that I was going to hell. I danced around the tent on the cots, threatening horrified onlookers with the actual event of licking the cum-stained sock. It had been a depository for Diego's wayward sperm, which in turn had been inspired by the stolen picture of Private Ryan's sister.

Before dancing around the tent with the cum sock dangling near my tongue, I ransacked an "Any Soldier" care package that had been put together by some church and kicked the contents across the room in a mock simulation of rage over the caring strangers whom I'd never met, who were sending me unsalted peanuts instead of porn and cigarettes when the bubblegum collector's Virgin Mary trading card fluttered to the ground.

I made an immediate dive for it, as did Private Hugh, who rightly feared my desecration of the Holy Mary. Specialist Diego, though, made the catch and proceeded to auction the coveted card. Hugh offered him a *Penthouse* and cheese-and-cracker packages. Fortunately, my mother cared about me more than Hugh's mother did, and thus I received more care packages and had more to use for barter. I purchased the Holy Mary trading card with two issues of *Hustler* and a dog-eared copy of *The Catcher in the Rye*.

Sergeant Santiago broke up laughing as he read a letter from a 7th grade class of students forced to send letters to Any Soldier. "Dear Soldier! How are you! My name is David. I am in the 7th grade. Did you want to go to war? Do you have guns over there?" Sergeant Santiago crumpled up the letter, pegged Private Hugh with it, and began air writing a response. "Dear David! No, I didn't want to go to war; are you fucking stupid? Are you in the special needs education class that they keep all the retards in?"

Everyone burst out laughing and grabbed letters from Sergeant Santiago, and soon all of us in the entire tent were sitting on the edges of our cots, taking turns reciting and listening to the poorly written letters sent to us by the well-meaning children of America.

"Dear Soldier. How many kids your daddy got up in your house? My daddy got seven kids!" shrieked Private Ryan between howls of laughter as he turned away from the letter and mimicked in his best black voice, "How many kids you got up in yo' house!"

"Dear Soldier. My birthday is next month. Did you know that? My uncle is in the Army, maybe you know him, his name is Michael!" *No, I didn't know it was your fucking birthday next month, you stupid fuck! Why the fuck would I know some dumb-ass shit like that!*

"Dear Soldier. Have you had to kill anybody?" *That's all I do all day long, kid—kill. I'm a natural-born motherfucking killer!*

"Dear Soldier. Are you safe? I sure hope so." *Yeah, I'm safe, kid, real fucking safe. I'm especially safe every time they start shooting at me. Yeah, I'm real fucking safe, kid. Thanks for asking!*

And then, as the evening wore on, the trash bags came and hauled away most of the things the well-meaning people from places with names like Ohio sent us, along with the empty boxes and wrapping and Styrofoam peanuts. My fellow soldiers, all tuckered out from the day's wasted energy, sat down to huddle closely around a small five-inch portable DVD monitor to watch *Swiss Family Robinson* while quietly munching on the cookies and crackers and snacks that people from Ohio had sent.

When the next shipment of mail came and no one had sent us Any Soldier care packages, we took it extremely personally and as indicative of a low type of national character, a representative sign of the apathy of a nation that just didn't care about its soldiers who were on the front lines of war, who were standing up against evil, and terrorists, and other bad things.

Chapter 19

FATTY BOY RYAN AND
THE SODOMIZING TALIBAN

Ryan sits up on his cot across from me and tosses the letter he received behind him, saying, "Fuck . . . that . . . bitch."

I look up. "What's bothering you?"

"My fiancée just broke up with me. I don't believe it. She just Dear John lettered me."

Ryan, who looks like a young Harrison Ford, has been engaged to a beautiful blonde. Also in the Army, she had been deployed to Iraq during the time we had spent preparing for Afghanistan.

"Really?" I say, trying to sound more sympathetic than I am.

"What pisses me off isn't that she broke up with me, but all the pussy I missed out on this entire last year being faithful to her. Everyone else came over here full on their pussy and sex reserves. I came in empty, and now I've got a fucking year to go." Ryan, being pretty successful with the ladies, spent the past year in Hawaii teasing himself about all the ass that he could have had if only he had given in. "Fuck!" Ryan shouts, collapsing on his cot, and burying his head into his pillow.

"I've sure got some fucking strange toe lint in my toes," I say, somewhat distractedly.

"You a little bored, or what?" Ryan asks.

"Little bit. I can't handle this shit. I feel like I'm going crazy. This is worse than prison. We're confined to a space just as small. The food is just as bad. The only difference is they have television and a gym."

"You have to find something to do that's productive while you're over here, or you really will go crazy," Ryan says.

"What are you doing that's productive?"

"I'm going to go and jack off right now," Ryan says, looking around his cot for the porno magazine.

"I could learn origami. How to make the paper unicorns and shit? That'd be a neat trick to come out of Afghanistan with. Maybe I could order Swahili on tape and come out speaking Swahili."

"Write a book," Ryan says as he gets up to look around, now completely perplexed regarding the location of his porno.

Of course! It's that simple! I should write a book! All the soldiers from Iraq are selling their books, whoring out their experiences. Why can't I do the same? I could whore out like no one's business.

"What will I write a book about?"

"Write about me. I want to be immortalized as a war hero," Ryan says. "Write about how my parents want me to take over a failing health food store when I get back to Michigan. It's depressing. I want to share my depression with the rest of the world."

What only I and almost no one else knows is that, while everyone else is saving their deployment money, most coming out at the end of the year with anywhere from ten to twenty grand, Ryan is secretly funneling most of his money to his parents, who are in some tough times. Hide it as he often tries, he is a real sweetheart.

"Splendid idea!" I flip my notebook past my letter home to Mom and start writing. I begin writing a manuscript entitled "The Adventures of Fatty Ryan in Afghanistan."

After two chapters in which Ryan is being sodomized by Taliban, however, I quickly grow bored. Ryan says, "Write about us. The soldiers. A book about the war."

"What war? I don't see any war; do you see any war?" I look under my cot and call out, "War? War? Are you here, war? Where are you?"

"A war memoir doesn't have to be about combat. It can be about the quiet unsung heroes behind the lines. The enlisted men that make up the Army, the real heroes of America."

Down at the other end of the tent, Devon is humping Cox's leg as I say, "I don't think I can write that type of book."

"Write a liberal's perspective on the Army," Ryan suggests. Ryan, like me, is one of the few liberals in the infantry. Surprisingly, Ryan can switch modes from joking frat boy to seriously concerned liberal. "Write about us, the unsung heroes of America. The brotherhood that exists between men in combat."

"I don't like any of you, though," I say.

"Well, maybe you should get to know us," Ryan says indifferently as he stands to leave, porno in hand.

He has a point. It couldn't hurt to get to know the soldiers I'm serving with. Back in Hawaii I lived in an off-post apartment, and my friends were outside the Army, and at work I was almost always separated from the rest of the soldiers doing specialized office duty. I didn't really know the people I was serving with at all, then or now.

It's time to find out if they truly are the shitbags I imagine they are.

Sergeant Santiago lies on the dirt berm, looking through binoculars, and says, "One orange shirt, one brown shirt."

"I'm not writing it down!" I say defiantly as I chew on a weed and toss my notepad and pen to the other side of the ditch in a lame gesture of defiance.

Sergeant Santiago offers me a stern eye, which is his gentle rebuke. But then gentle rebukes are all that he can ever give me. The others? He could make them do push-ups until they puke and scream at them and holler and do everything he is supposed to as a noncommissioned officer. Sergeant Santiago is the epitome of the professional soldier's leader: he is disciplined, in good shape, and a good leader, who enforces the standards and makes his men follow the rules.

Except me. In me he's found a private kindred spirit that he couldn't articulate. He can't stand the look of exaggerated exasperation I give him when he attempts to enforce rules that I know to be ridiculous, so he allows me considerable latitude. Underneath his pro-Army slogans and necessary statements of motivation, he is really a subversive, who loathes religion and social tradition and all forms of irrationality. It takes a subversive to draw out a subversive. He can't help but smile at my endless pathetic and meager attempts at rebellion. In his eyes I am like a kitten attempting to be tough. And that makes me cute.

"You're so fucking cute when you get angry!" Sergeant Santiago says, laughing. "When you're trying to be tough? You're all skinny and everything, so no one could ever really take you seriously as any type of threat, but you act two levels outside of your weight class? That's cute!"

I can only respond, "Fuck off."

Santiago laughs and says, "Rico, this is the Army. Just follow the rules. Your orders are to write down the clothes that people wear. You do it. You don't question."

"Look, basic organizational theory dictates that a proliferation of rules results only in rule nonenforcement and subversion. This is true of police departments with police officers, college students in a university, employees in any organization. When you have too many rules, the rules themselves cease to become important, and a hierarchy develops between rules that really need to be followed and rules not so much. If the Army's proliferation of useless rules is to ensure that rules are followed, I would say that they're having the exact opposite effect."

We both turn our backs to the village and sigh in unison.

"Rico, I've decided that I've wasted the last six years," Sergeant Santiago intones dryly.

"Keep going; I'm trying to get to know you guys," I say as I start writing down his statement.

"I didn't know our casual conversation was going to be transcribed. And here I thought I was just creating small talk."

"Yeah, well, I'm not quoting you on everything."

"Quote this. When I was ten I would wrestle my sister and get a boner. I enjoyed getting a boner from wrestling my sister."

Sergeant Santiago has the peculiar habit of saying such shocking things in those rare moments of downtime when he isn't playing the professional leader.

He'll sometimes pontificate over which of his future children he'd favor. A soldier in the tent will explain that he is supposed to like all of his children the same, but Sergeant Santiago knows the horrific truth that nobody else has the balls to verbalize.

He takes a certain pride in being the sole claimant of unclean thoughts, so when someone produces the follow-up question about how to tell which one to favor more, he'll typically respond with some casual statement like "Well, it'll probably be determined by which one gives me the best head."

The more the crowd groans and grimaces and pretends to be sanctimonious and clean, the more he'll up the ante. The thing of it is that he can't stand phonies: the religious leaders who refuse to admit they masturbate, the politicians who refuse to admit they have affairs, and the common soldiers who refuse to admit they have ever not pleased a woman or ever lost a fight.

The more lies the people around him tell, the more brutal the truths he tells. He goes crazy with the truth to account for all the goddamn phony liars. He is some type of truth-telling savior, here to save everyone from their lies by offering enough of his own truths to cover everyone.

This is another reason we are friends. We both hate contrived gestures, whether they be sentimental, moralistic, or machismo. I responded with tulip cover sheets for our weapons folders, he responded with brutal, wince-inducing honesty.

He is honest about his fears in having a new family. A week earlier he was on the ramparts of Cougar Base crying with his wife on the satellite phone as she gave birth to their first child, whom he wouldn't meet until it was almost a year old. Just days later he was in a ditch sharing his anxieties. In the infantry, this male-to-male sharing of intimacy and emotions is rare.

"I don't know if I'm ready to be a father. In fact, I know I'm not. I'm not ready. I have a child, a human being, and I'm not ready. What if I fuck up my kid raising it, and she turns out to be a child molester or a psychopath?"

"You've got a girl. Clinically speaking, child molesters and psychopaths are normally boys. You're probably safe," I tell him.

"Well, what if she turns out to be a slut or a prostitute or something? There's a real possibility I could fuck this kid up!"

Despite his raw honesty, which freaks out many within the platoon, he is widely regarded as the good sergeant, the general theory of sergeants being that each platoon has a senior good sergeant and a senior bad sergeant, the lower-ranking sergeants being barely one step above private. This theory has evolved out of watching Oliver Stone's *Platoon*. Sergeant Santiago is the Willem Dafoe sergeant, the sergeant who, although he can be a dick at times when it was necessary and called for, is also the first to worry about the welfare of the men. Sergeant Stephens and Sergeant Riley, the platoon's other two senior sergeants, are our platoon's Tom Berenger characters, the sergeants who vocalize to their soldiers that they don't give a shit about them and will kill them if they fucked up.

Sergeant Santiago is our platoon's sister-rubbing-boner-receiving good sergeant.

Cox loves being deployed.

Absolutely fucking loves it.

It gives him a chance to sober up.

Here he is, on the far side of the world, pulling guard on alien landscapes in a faraway land that most people would never have the chance to visit in their lifetime.

Cox screams into the quiet, still prairie that stretches to infinity behind guard tower number three, "SOMEBODY SHOOT US! SOMEBODY SHOOT US! PLEASE FOR THE LOVE OF GOD TRY AND KILL US!"

He collapses in frustration, resting his head in his arms and relaxing his vocal cords for a second, and then says, "We got fucked, Rico. We got fucked. We should've gone to Iraq. I get letters from the folks back home; they say to me, 'At least you're not in Iraq.' It's like I'm not sacrificing because I'm not getting shot at or something. This having nothing happen is worse than being in fucking the heart of Fallujah with the shit going down. At least those dudes roll back, and they've got respect. We roll back, we got pity. I thought there was supposed to be some fucking Taliban offensive. Some fucking offensive. These guys suck."

"So," I ask, relaxing against the wobbly wall of tower three, which doesn't feel as if it will hold up much longer. "Why'd you join the Army?"

Cox, a young, handsome Russell Crowe–looking type of guy, thinks and says, "I had to get out, guy. L.A. was killing me! It was the boooze!" He always dragged out his enunciation of the word "booze" and followed it with laughter. "Just couldn't stay sober, and all those fucking phonies in the music world—man, you don't even know. None of these people here, these people here in our platoon, in this firebase, everyone thinks I'm this bar rat, this boooozer. But back in L.A., man, I was the shit. It was all about the music, man, the piano. You dig, daddy-o?"

Cox was a musical prodigy in L.A. and attended some very prestigious music schools before drinking killed his classical music career. From there he fell to playing seedy lounges on the wrong side of town and Carnival cruise ships. And from there he fell all the way to the U.S. Army and Cougar Base in Afghanistan.

He joined the Army in the hope of sobering up. In retrospect, even he admitted that was the equivalent of a recovering sexaholic finding work in the porn industry.

Between patrols, Cox tells me, cigarette in hand, that he is headed to the big city to be a failed musician. "I'm thinking of going back to New York, but then New York's a hard fucking city to starve in, man. A hard fucking city."

Cox's genius is that he was already planning his future of poverty.

He fascinates me because he's built his identity on the idea of the failed musician. He imagines the future and finds romance in the idea of being a lonely drunk. Yet, he isn't just some wannabe drunk. He is inspired. At the bar, when separated from our fellow Army soldiers, he can talk at length about the music composition and music theory and how that makes some sort of strange geometric mathematical sense out of the world. He can talk intricately about the latest scientific exploits and how their application matters to the world. He is ridiculously well read, able to discuss Steinbeck or Hemingway—and not just *The Grapes of Wrath* but everything that Steinbeck wrote. In Afghanistan, he is most often found on his cot rereading *Crime and Punishment*, a book he claims to have read more than ten times. He is well traveled; he's been to Japan and England and exotic ports throughout the world. He appreciates the finer things in life, like good wine and fine films.

"I've got the plan, Rico. The all-intensive, all-purpose, all-contingency plan; right? I get back from Afghanistan, I'm not going to hit the boooze anymore. I'll get back into my music, start writing again, start playing again. You know? Find some clubs in Honolulu or some shit, start playing a few gigs, get back in the game, you know? Get out of the Army, head for the Big Apple, go and be a failed starving artist there—but at least I'll be playing." And then, more to himself, "God, I got to get back in the game."

Here he is in Afghanistan, planning his second stint in poverty. After our return to the States he'll tell me in a bar patio overlooking a lake near the base, "That was the happiest I'd been in ten years, man. I truly laughed. Emotions over there were real. I was sober. Getting shot at was the best. The fucking best. Better than sex. Better than Mozart." And then he'll give me that long quiet stare of contemplative internal mental mechanics that let me know there's more to say but he doesn't want to give it up until he has a few more beers.

Cox starts humming me one of Mozart's symphonies as he explains its intricacies. "Now listen to that! Listen to that! That changes with the harmonics of the first set, see? And then we go . . ."

I smile and stare out into the desert and I pay halfhearted attention to my music lesson.

What I like about Diego was that even as he contemplates blowing his foot off, his demeanor still suggests a positive, uplifting attitude toward life. Diego is one of those rare individuals who is able to take jaded cynicism and turn it into contagious, positive, inspiring laughter. He is an emotional alchemist. He'll leave you smiling and in turn take your angst from you and add it to his own growing pile of future dementia.

"You realize how insane this is?" he asks. "I'm standing here think-ing whether or not to blow off my foot, and I'm thinking that blowing off my foot is the best option? The irony of this type of existential dilemma occurring in shit-hole moments in shit-hole countries . . . you always just think your moments of epiphany will be more important, you know? That they won't come standing two feet away from a big pile of cow dung."

He looks from the messy pile of cow dung, swarming with flies, to the land mine near his foot. He is lost in the tragicomedy of his own moment.

Of course, Diego views most of his life as a tragicomedy. A put-upon intellectual, misunderstood by the world and surrounded by a mass of idiots. The interesting twist is that, in Diego's particular situa-tion, I mostly concur with his evaluation.

Diego is seemingly the world's last Boy Scout.

The guy who in the middle of a liquid-infused bender still refuses to take advantage of girls.

The suffering Catholic who feels guilty about his whore-themed in-spired travelogue of Eastern Europe.

The quintessential cynic who still cannot bring himself to give up or not care.

He is that nice guy who will talk with you and send you on your way feeling better about yourself and the world, not knowing that he hasn't exorcised your bad emotions; he's simply absorbed them into himself for your benefit.

They drop me and Diego off on the perimeter to pull security while Lieutenant Michael and his element go into the interior of the village to find some elders. Diego, who fancies himself a deeply religious per-son, is giving me a full summary of the whores in Eastern Europe as if he were a food critic. "The Romanian whores, they're willing to at least pretend that they're enjoying themselves, so that definitely puts them above those bitches in Yugoslavia."

It was then that Specialist Diego almost steps on the land mine and starts relating to me a strange and curious bylaw that even now I sus-pect is modern-day urban Army legend rather than fact. If you are the recipient of a Purple Heart, many states have laws offering free college education for your children. Diego calculates that with the rising costs of tuition, even if you only have two children, a Purple Heart is worth at least sixty thousand dollars. And that is if your children are not especially gifted or motivated and attend a mediocre college. Imagine if they attended Harvard or some other top school?

Diego thinks that a missing foot is worth sixty grand. Of course, Diego is, like most in the Army, a minimum-wage kid. He struggled with college; the pretentious academic community was too much for him to stomach. So he rebelled against things he was not fully aware of or able to articulate, and he joined the Army as a flaming liberal. No respectable middle-income or upper-income person back in the States would sell off a foot for sixty grand. But these minimum-wage Army kids are willing to start selling off their body parts. They are injury whores.

"You could be wrong about the whole free tuition thing. What if it's total bullshit?"

"Maybe," he says, staring down at the ground. "Purple Heart would still be cool either way. The thing that sucks is that I noticed it. You see, I was actually going to walk out there to take a piss, and I could've stepped on it, but I didn't. I decided to smoke this cigarette first, and now I've lost my opportunity. You can't purposefully do it. It has to be by accident."

Some guys are just born unlucky.

It wasn't an antitank mine or anything. Nothing that would erase all evidence of your existence. Instead, it was of the more popular "ankle biter" variety. The thinking behind ankle biters is that it is more effective in reducing the enemy ranks to have it blow off only the bottom of your leg or your foot. When someone blows up completely, they are already dead, and you just leave them there and fight on. But when someone blows off their leg and is on the ground screaming in pain, you not only took him off the battlefield but take anywhere from two to three others as well, who now have to care for this person and tend his wounds and evacuate him to the rear.

Diego stands there, transfixed with the idea of blowing off his own foot. He quickly creates a pro-and-con list that all the expert psychologists say indecisive people should do. The cons would be that it would hurt and that he would no longer have a foot, or he may even lose a good section of his leg. The pros would be that he would get out of Afghanistan, get out of the Army, get a Purple Heart, get free tuition for his children (assuming the rumor is true), and probably be paid some type of disability, which would allow him to do nothing for a great many years.

And he'd have a really cool story to tell the folks back home. In his momentary perspective, it seems that the pros vastly outweigh the cons. The Army has many excitable slogans, one of which is "Pain is temporary; pride is forever." It is supposed to motivate you to get through tough courses like Ranger school. Diego too has a slogan: "Pain is temporary; disability payments are forever."

"If I am permanently disabled, that's like free access to a life reading Nabokov while relaxing in hammocks for the rest of my life. Still, though," Diego says, scratching his chin in contemplation, "the whole 'no foot' thing is a slightly big deal if you think about it. But then, from another perspective, if I contemplate my foot, my foot's existence, I realize it's largely a useless appendage to me. I hate running. I'm never going to run another day in my life once I'm out of the Army. And there are all types of great prosthetics available these days. What with the war in Iraq and all, the Army surely has access to the best prosthetics people money can buy. It's not like I'd be paralyzed or be confined to a wheelchair for the rest of my life. It's just that I'd have to learn to walk differently."

There aren't many opportunities in life for minimum-wage kids. There aren't lots of places to make money. A deployment is one. Sometimes you are lucky if you can get deployed to Iraq or Afghanistan in a combat zone, because you'll come back with those credit cards paid off and cash for a new car. You have to take gifts where you can find them. Stepping on a land mine is another one of those rare opportunities.

"Well, little puppy, you going to bark all day, or are you going to bite?" I ask.

Diego thinks about it for a while and then says, "I'm scared. I'm not going to do it." He frowns and sighs at his own weakness.

"Just what I thought," I say. "A spineless bitch."

Private Mulbeck curls his lips back and laughs. My eyes are always drawn to the way he curls his lips back as he laughs.

"So what do you say in your higher-up world, Rico, when you see somebody you like? What you say? 'May I court you?' All formal and shit?"

We're all between the clay rear wall of the Camp Cougar Alamo and three rolls of concertina wire.

Ryan has a clipboard and is busy scribbling notes, wearing glasses borrowed from Hank to make himself look more studious to our interview subjects as I ramble on into a small mini–tape recorder, pretending to be a distracted scientist who is too preoccupied with my own thoughts to notice the test subject in front of me.

Ryan puts his finger up to his mouth and in a hushed whisper says to Mulbeck, "You'll have to be quiet. This is a formal interview setting now, and everything is on the record."

"This is Private First-Class Richard Mulbeck, age twenty-six, recently divorced with one child but already madly in love with someone he's met recently on the Internet. Completely typical. Mulbeck, what were your motivations for . . ."

"Do you say, let us go drink some chilled wine and attend an art gallery together?" Mulbeck asks, interrupting me.

"No, no, you dumb ass," I reply. "Now, if you don't mind?"

Mulbeck puffs up his collar in readiness and sits up straight against the clay brick wall, his hands folded in his seat like a proper young gentleman. And then suddenly there is a small hiccup of giggles, and he asks, "What about fucking? How do you ask a bitch if you want to fuck? Do you say, 'May we make love now?'" Mulbeck laughs obnoxiously at his own comment as his top lip twitches and curls.

"I can't work under these conditions," I state, and pretend to walk out of the meeting in anger. Ryan smacks Mulbeck on the head with the clipboard and threatens to stop the interview until a state of serious approach is obtained. Mulbeck apologizes and promises to do better and again regains his composure.

"Dick, Richard, buddy, here you are in Afghanistan. The ass of the world. What were you thinking? Just what were your motivations for coming to Afghanistan and for joining the United States Army? Go!" And with "Go!" I stick the tape recorder dramatically under his mouth.

"Well, I wanted to get Saddam, you know, and you know, I just want to kill these sons of bitches because they attacked my home, you know? And you don't attack my home and get away with it, you know? And I'll probably be stop-lossed to go to Iraq next, but that's fine, I don't care if I get out when I'm supposed to, I'll just go and kill Taliban there, too."

There is a slight pause as Ryan and I exchange glances, and Ryan says, "Would you excuse us for a moment?"

Mulbeck looks perfunctorily curious as we lean back and Ryan whispers in my ear, "I don't think he knows the difference between Iraq and Afghanistan." I nod my confirmation of our mutual fears and lean forward again.

"Mulbeck," I say. "I'm going to ask you a series of questions. Just answer the best you can."

"Go for it."

"Okay, question number one. Bin Laden was a member of which international terrorist organization?"

"The Taliban. Right? Wasn't it the Taliban? Yeah, it was the Taliban."

"Okay, question number two."

"Was I right?"

"We'll get to that later. Right now, it's question number two time. Okay, question number two. Is Saddam Hussein a member of Al Qaeda?"

"Yes. Right? Yeah, he was, that was that uh, that group, that group he was a part of, it was Al Qaeda, it was him and bin Laden, they were like uh, a captain and first sergeant."

"You just said bin Laden was part of the Taliban."

"Right. Oh. Well, I mean, yeah, he was, well, it was like he was a part of both. It was both."

"You do know what country we're in right now, don't you?"

"Afghanistan!" Mulbeck states firmly and somewhat appalled before looking at both of us to confirm his answer, as if he himself has his doubts.

I just nod to Ryan and say, "We're finished here."

Ryan tries to lead Mulbeck away, and soon they are wrestling on the ground as I say into my tape recorder, "Sadly, Mulbeck is not the first soldier I've known to not even know the difference between Iraq and Afghanistan. This is indicative of a larger, almost pathologic political ignorance within the Army."

From the ground underneath Ryan's shoulder blade, Mulbeck cries out, "Pathologic what? What's pathologic?"

Oblivious to their wrestling, I continue, "It's very common for soldiers to believe that weapons of mass destruction have been found in Iraq, or that rather than a debatable linkage between Al Qaeda and Saddam there was a long-ago verified and assumed linkage. Taliban and Iraqi insurgents to many soldiers are interchangeable; all that matters is that they are enemies of the United States. In this way, the U.S. propaganda in creating a climate of fear and a diffuse never-ending enemy in a post–September 11 world has worked remarkably well."

"Okay, Rico, I got it," Mulbeck states from beneath Ryan's struggling limbs. "The world and Afghanistan have reached a period of uh . . ." He struggles to come up with intelligent-sounding words that he can attempt to satirize. "A period of uh . . . stability, yeah, stability that has required a United States presence." He pauses, not knowing where he is going with his statement, and says, "I'll tell you what. I'm going to write me a poem, sell it to a college or some shit, and make a million dollars and retire, and then put a bar in my living room."

"Yeah, that's completely out of left field. But hey, thanks for that, man. Thanks," I say as I sigh to myself.

"Uh-oh, Johnny's working on his book again," comes a grating voice that drags and slurs on itself in incomprehensible southern Louisiana redneck drawl. It's Sergeant Stein, who takes a seat with us against the crumbling wall.

"What you writing about now, Johnny? 'Bout how you'se a liberal and you want to marry John Kerry and Bill Clinton and have gay sex with them all?"

Sergeant Stein is my nemesis. He is the embodiment of everything I despise, not just about the stereotype of the Army personnel but about people in general. He has been the sergeant directly in charge of me for too much of my time in the Army. He constantly fills comfortable relaxing silences with talk and is now an overweight soldier bragging about his days in the Marines when he was fit. Every sentence is about how he could "whup" somebody's ass. He was irrational, forming opinions and proffering them without any backing, and then he gets upset when people disagree with him. He is the type of guy who thinks it's funny to contribute to a serious discussion on whether or not to allow gays to marry by saying, "God made Adam and Eve, not Adam and Steve!" To which he then endlessly laughs, making even the opponents of homosexual marriage in the room roll their eyes and feel embarrassed. He is basically just a thirty-two-year-old man still swapping stories and hoping to impress people with details of how he got some girl's panties off many, many years earlier in the backseat of a van after both had drunk a bottle of tequila.

But mostly I despise him for his potty language. Perhaps it's because I was stalled in the development of my anal fascination stage in Freud's hierarchy of psychological advancement, but I've always been bothered by explicit language regarding people's bowel movements.

"POOP!" A big saucy smile comes to Sergeant Stein's face. "Man, I gotta go let me out a big poop! Big slimy greasy poop! Got a nine-inch turtlehead the size of my pecker coming out right now!" I grimace while Sergeant Stein uses his hands to illustrate the size of his poop.

I'd understand the fascination with poop descriptions if it were a rarity, something that only a few people have had experience with, like some rare disease. But for some reason, Sergeant Stein always seems to have to go to the bathroom and always has to describe his thoughts about his going to the bathroom, both before and after the actual event.

"You want to go take a shit with me, Johnny?" Sergeant Stein asks.

"You can put that in your book. How impressed you are with the size of my poop."

"I'll pass," I reply, trying to ignore him.

"Ohhh, I pissed Johnny off. Now he's annoyed."

"I'm not annoyed; I'm just trying to think." I'm very fucking annoyed.

"All right, give it to me. What's the question?" Sergeant Stein asks.

"The question is . . ." Ryan pauses as he tosses one cigarette and starts another. Afghanistan has a habit of creating chain-smokers. "The question is, why did you want to join the Army?"

"Oh shit," says Sergeant Stein. "Rico's asking them liberal-thinking questions again. Hey, let me get one of them cigarettes from you, girl." Ryan hands him a cigarette. "I'll tell you what we need to do. What we need to do is fucking just nuke this entire goddamn place. Just fucking nuke every last one of these motherfuckers."

As Ryan laughs, mostly at Sergeant Stein's stupid comment, I say, "That doesn't even answer the question. Sergeant Stein, that's a fine and valid opinion, but it wasn't what we asked."

"I know! But it needs to be said! These fuckers here? These fucking Haji motherfuckers here need to be shot dead. I just want to kill fucking Haji. There! There! That's my um, my uh, motivation for joining the Army. I want to kill fucking Haji!"

Without another word I stand up and wander away.

"Hey boy, you think that's bad?" Sergeant Stein yells to me, completely confounded that his interview is over.

"You know," Devon says, breaking the long silence and looking around to make sure no one in the courtyard below is looking up into the tower as he takes his helmet off, "I could eat a thousand puppies right now." Devon frequently offers the most ridiculous comments with a dry delivery that one can't help but laugh at.

"That has no relevance to my book whatsoever," I say, looking up from my notepad, in which I am scribbling ideas.

"Well, it's true!" Devon stammers. "Puppies are tasty. You better watch yourself, or I'm gonna end up shooting you someday," he continues before giggling incessantly.

Devon is a blond, bright-eyed nineteen-year-old who still maintains the ambiance and sheen of childhood innocence and a sense of fun about the world. It is easy to see what he looked like as a little boy. He's the perpetual comedian, always laughing and giggling, having a good time regardless of the situation.

His few moments of seriousness occur when he contemplates his future, which he is able to approach with enough seriousness to be appropriately nervous about, but without the discipline to settle on any single course of action. He grew up poor, with aspirations larger than his world allowed him.

"Rico, I'm thinking now of doing that, um, that international banker route. I want one of those jobs that are advertised in the back of *The Economist*, like financial planner for the African Development Community of Tanzania or some shit like that. So what do I need for that?"

"Shit, I don't know," I say, looking up again from my notebook. "I guess if you want one of those jobs advertised in the back of *The Economist*, go to one of those schools advertised in the back of *The Economist*. One of those international MBA programs."

"Yeah," Devon says, deep in thought. "The other thing I'm thinking about is stuntman. I want to jump out the window and fall ninety feet to the street below!" he says, suddenly standing up and mimicking the violent crashing of himself through a window, followed by a dramatic fall and a pavement death, before abruptly sitting back down with his hands folded in his lap and his legs crossed like a pristine dandy little boy.

"That's very good; I'll put you in for an Academy Award," I say, smiling.

Suddenly, Devon takes an uneasy serious turn, and the smile melts off his face. "I'll tell you one thing, Rico. I'm never going to be afraid again. I'm suddenly over here, and now I'm here for a year, and I realize that right before I left there were all these things I was afraid to do. I think back at my life and all the things I've been afraid of, and it makes me sick. Why should I ever be afraid to approach a woman? I'm going to let a woman intimidate me?"

"There's no reason to!" I state, angry as all hell. Upon our return to Hawaii, Devon will become the pickup master, bedding different girls each weekend.

"Exactly!" Devon fervently agrees. "Why should I care what other people say when they want me to lead my life one way and I want to lead it a different way! It's my life! I'm the one who's going to die out here!" And then, as an afterthought, "Maybe, if anyone ever bothers to try and kill us."

"There's no reason to!" I'm still angry. "So, next question. What gets you through this out here? Granted, it's early in the deployment, but day to day, long days, little sleep—what in your life gets you through it?"

"You're going to think I'm being funny, but I'm not. Masturbation."

"Masturbation?"

"Masturbation. No matter what, I'll always have masturbation. A girl can break up with me, the Army can suck, I might not get sleep, but eventually I'll be able to masturbate again. And that makes me happy just knowing that masturbation is out there waiting for me at some point in the future."

"In masturbation we trusted, huh?" And then, as an afterthought I add, "I like seeing the more serious side to you. It's a nice change of pace."

"I have a huge serious side," Devon states quietly. "You just can't trust it with everybody, you know? People in the infantry, if you ever show a serious emotion or fear, they remember it and file it away for the future to bug you about that one thing and press you on that one thing, just to fuck with you to see if you'll break and get pissed. It's not that I don't have a serious side; it's just that I'm cautious," he says. "The reason I trust you is because you have a colony of chipmunks living in your ass. I always trust people with chipmunk colonies in their assholes."

It takes a moment for me to register this nonsense as Devon busts out laughing at his own pointless humor.

My platoon sergeant, Sergeant Derrens, relaxes in his chair, anticipating my easy line of questions. "So why do I love America as opposed to any other country?"

Sergeant Derrens is the quintessential straight shooter. Rigid and dogmatic in his conservative moral doctrine, he's also the type of guy who either betrays or complements his externally perceived image by his quiet mention of his secret casual aspiration to be a social worker. A longtime foster parent, a tender husband and loving father, to me he is the glorified World War II–generation soldier reincarnated in our era. He is religious but keeps it quiet and close to the vest. He runs a disciplined platoon, requiring the soldiers to perform their duties and work hard (work being something he advocates accomplishing in the quickest, most effective way possible—an aberration in the Army system). But when the chores are complete, he laughs, relaxes, and encourages his soldiers to play and have fun. He is always referred to as our father, because although he punishes us, he also protects us, frequently taking the responsibility and blame for platoon errors in an attempt to protect his soldiers. He is also only an E7, a rank disproportionate with his years in service, caused by his inability to hold back honest appraisals from his commanders, and flat refusals to accept orders perceives as being detrimental to the soldiers in his care. None of which endeared him to his superiors.

"I know you're going to come up with all these reasons not to like America and why I should like other countries, so I'm just going to say, because this country is mine. It's that simple," Sergeant Derrens says.

I have become fascinated with the responses to the question of what motivated people to join the Army. For most soldiers it was an afterthought, because they failed in their first or second choices and retreated with their tails between their legs to the U.S. Army. For others it was the call of adventure and the opportunity that just maybe they'd get to kill somebody, a perennial favorite of testosterone-laden teenagers with no outlet for aggression or for testing themselves in a safety-conscious, politically correct society. But for a precious few, like Sergeant Derrens, it was about patriotism. Sergeant Derrens has his college degree. He has continued to do this and has made a career out of it because he believes in protecting Americans. His aspirations are really that noble.

"What can I say," he continues. "The world is a scary place, and someone has to protect Americans. I can do the job as good as any other."

I'm suddenly ashamed of my own selfish motivations for joining. I pretend that protecting people, my fellow Americans, also factored into my decision. Sergeant Derrens blows me away with his innate all-around goodness.

This is also the problem. Everybody states some variation of this response. They can be boxed into corners and forced to admit foreign policy blunders and acts of aggression initiated by the United States onto other countries, forced to admit that freedom as we define it in the United States is also available in a great many European nations. But ultimately it keeps coming down to "Because this country is mine." Sergeant Derrens repeats his claim, this time with more urgency, perhaps hoping I'll eventually say something.

"Sergeant, if the only justification for your devotion to country is that this one is yours, then so what? This one is yours, and that one is his, and that one over there is hers. If everybody is just responding to their environments and adopting that as what they fight for, then what's the difference between anybody's point of view? Where's the external validity for one person's idea over another? Don't you think it's important to have external validity? I mean, you're willing to die for America, aren't you? If you're willing to die for America and her ideas, shouldn't your faith in her have external validity, some ultimate truth, something more than just that this is where you were born?"

Sergeant Derrens stares at me with an amused smile. He's frequently amused by me, especially when I get all serious and riled up like this. He shrugs. The question doesn't bother him.

"Sergeant Derrens," I continue. "By this rationale, if you were Palestinian, then you'd fight for Palestine because that's where you were born. You'd fight for Afghanistan because that's where you were born. There has to be an external validity to an idea, a justification for one side that's so apparent that it's obvious to external observers who is right and who is wrong. Don't you see? Your own justification for

American nationalism is, in itself, an argument against American patriotism!"

"I don't care!" Sergeant Derrens says, laughing. "This is my home. I guess if I was born in Palestine I'd fight for them, too. But the thing is, I'm not. I'm here. So this is where I fight."

"So do you even examine the situation you're being sent to fight for? What if we invaded Canada? You'd fight then?"

"I'm a soldier," Sergeant McDonald explains to me gently. "I go where my country tells me to."

"But what if your country is wrong?" I ask, somewhat confused.

Sergeant McDonald shrugs. "Sometimes they are. I don't agree with everything the U.S. does, but this is my country, and I support her through thick and thin."

I'm on my cot in the tent, trying to sleep, but I'm disturbed by all I've heard. Strange that I should be so bothered by inspiring and motivating statements regarding patriotism and love of country. I hope that our supposed enemy, the Taliban, who are supposedly somewhere here in Afghanistan and whom we are supposedly fighting, have more than nationalism burrowed in their dislike for us. I hope there is some stream of logical reasoning that allows them to come to their conclusion, some piece that I have missed. I don't want to consider the reality that they are mostly ignorant illiterate peasants who are fighting America simply because they were told we are a part of an Axis of Evil and because some religious inspired leader who believes in some God tells them that we are the enemy.

The idea that two sides of any group could and would engage in warfare, killing innocents and each other for reasons that are completely interchangeable and almost entirely dependent on the randomization of geographic placement at birth, is frightening. If everybody simply adopts the ideas of their environment, then what does the right or wrong of any conflict truly matter? The same participants fighting the war would just as easily fight for the other side if they had been born into a different environment. The simple fact that they were not, and it was as it was, did not seem to add special significance or meaning to an otherwise empty claim of interest in the notion of war.

America did have an external obvious and widely regarded legitimacy, at least with regard to its mission in Afghanistan. A known attacker used the nation-state of Afghanistan to plan and carry out his attacks against us. This was a situation in which global moral justification was in the bag. We had avoided the pitfalls of initiated aggression, which immediately suggests the role of the bad guys. At least, that's how it was in World War II and when Saddam took over Kuwait.

Yet, no one talks about it in those terms. No one talks about ideas. It's just because this is their country.

And Afghanistan is Habreem's country, and Iraq is Mohammed's country, and Palestine is Nazeer's country. Everyone's got a country. So fucking what?

My mind reels with the enormity of the number of soldiers I imagine dying throughout the course of civilization for causes that they would've fought against and died for had they simply fought for the home turf.

Humans can't be trusted with weapons. We need some alien race to fly in and put us on a probationary period. Give us back our weapons when we've evolved a little bit or at least thought things through a little more.

Yet, here we were, out in the middle of the desert, trusted with bombers and guns and explosives, being sent out to kill people who had never met Osama or agreed to harbor him but were linked only by six degrees of separation through Taliban party lines.

Absurd.

It was all absurd.

The whole damn world was absurd.

TWO GRAND AND A MOTORCYCLE:

A LETTER TO MOM

Dear Mom,

How is Rusty the cat doing? Is he still escaping outside a lot, or is he mellowing now that he's getting up there in kitty years?

The Taliban has completely dispersed. They are an echo, a whisper from some village elder. A rumor you hear here and there. We are so different from this culture that it is almost impossible for us to collect solid intelligence, mobilize, and effectively act on it. Everything happens slowly. You go to many villages before you get any solid intelligence.

The Pentagon, or Afghanistan command, or whoever the fuck, has finally given us a mission. Instead of doing patrols in a one-mile radius around our stupid little base, we now drive for entire days to remote villages where we basically just interview everybody and try and ascertain conditions in the village so that we can hopefully try and track Taliban movement. To be honest, though, we have no fucking idea, because everyone lies to us and we know that we have no idea.

We go into all these villages doing these assessments and asking questions about democracy: Are they registered to vote? And they always say yes, but they aren't. They nod their heads and say yes to everything, which we write down as a positive answer, but it doesn't mean anything. Their "sphere" is their village and their immediate countryside and province, their tribe. That's their world. So when U.S. soldiers come in talking about elections and handing out slick election pamphlets that look like they're advertising a disco, they simply nod and be agreeable, because what else are you going to say to thirty guys armed to the teeth?

What's fun is that the village assessments are done by myself, my lieutenant, and a civil affairs guy, so I'm on a three-man team getting to speak to village elders in remote regions of Afghanistan who have never even seen Americans before. Well, they have, but the Army has lost like a year's worth of reports about visited villages, so we never know if we're visiting a village for the second time or the first time. We just pretend everybody is being visited for the first time.

What's interesting is that almost all the locals in this surrounding region supported the Taliban. Yet, when we go on village assessments, they always pretend to be so pro-USA.

Lieutenant Michael gives grandiose speeches about America and Afghanistan working together as one nation, one people, a brotherhood united, for a better future. He talks about the children a lot, about making the world better for the children, for their children, for our children, for all our children, so that our children can one day play together as friends in a safe and prosperous Afghanistan. (For the record, I plan on never bringing my children over to Afghanistan.) And while he raises his voice to sing the praises of international unity and cooperation, he grabs the feeble fist of the village elder, clasps it with his gloved hand, and makes solemn promises about all the wonderful things the United States will do for them.

He makes promises. Lots of promises. If they cooperate, if they stay away from the Dark side of the Force, wells will come. And food. And schools. And clinics.

And these are all lies.

Sometimes, if the village has been visited before, they say U.S. troops already came through and made the same promises six months ago. To which we reply that those guys were lying, that we're serious this time.

Which is a lie.

We're a bunch of goddamn liars.

> Love,
> Your Son,
> Rico

P.S. Apparently there's an open bounty out on U.S. soldiers. You get two grand and a motorcycle from the Taliban if they kill one of us! Neat! I never imagined I'd be worth two thousand dollars *and* a motorcycle!

Chapter 20

WATER BOTTLE TORTURE TECHNIQUES

It's the quiet early twilight hours of morning before the sun has yet to show, when soldiers are expected to be awake and prepare for the day. These are the quiet moments when the day does not yet have momentum or warmth to it. When groggy dreams are shaken from heads, and squinty eyes still try to hold on to pleasant dreams that quickly become mental vapors. When weary legs of waking soldiers are slowly slung over the sides of cots. I stare at the last vestiges of night through the open slat in the tent. The sun will rise very soon. I'm a nocturnal person and always have a pang of regret when the sun rises and the moody silent atmosphere of nighttime is replaced with the open visibility of sunlight. I prefer the obscurity that darkness provides. I wonder what this says about my life and my character.

"Wake the fuck up, everyone!" Sergeant Riley says, breaking the calm of a perfectly tranquil moment of quiet self-contemplation. "Captain wants everyone front and center. That means right fucking now, fuck-faces!"

Captain Zimmerman gathers us in the motor pool, a large gravel area in the middle of the base. Our company commander climbs onto a pile of sandbags as we gather around blinking in the morning sun. Every time he speaks to us it seems that I'm blinded by the sun.

After two months in country, he has decided that Ghazni is not a combat zone. There is no active enemy presence.

And his soldiers have been bad. They have taken to actively running local Afghans off the road. More than a few Afghan bicyclists riding on the shoulder of the road have heard the blaring of a horn and turned to find an up-armored Humvee bearing down on them, causing them to flip headfirst into drainage ditches as the sound of laughing U.S. soldiers flies by. In other instances, during routine village patrols, soldiers have been screaming at cooperating locals, aiming their rifles at them.

"Men, this isn't Vietnam. This is never going to be Vietnam," he says as a parent would speak to a wayward child. "We have to curb the aggression a bit. This is a peacekeeping operation! We're rebuilding a nation here, not destroying it."

After all the cadences during company runs back in Hawaii to chop up the little Afghan children and to kill their mothers with bullets.

After all the speeches in the rain by the battalion commander while "Eye of the Tiger" played on loudspeakers behind him, telling us that we needed to prepare for war. For war, men! War, I tell you!

After all the brainwashing in basic training, where you'd cry out chants of "Kill!" and that it is "Blood that makes the grass grow green!"

After all the infantry training that was entirely dedicated to battle drills and maneuvering squad-sized elements under fire and honing our target practice with endless firing ranges.

And suddenly we are supposed to revert calmly to a peacekeeping force? Something we had never trained for? Well, I can revert real easily, but I wasn't aggressive like the rest of these guys.

After the speech, back in the tents, the noncommissioned officers pretend they have been telling us the entire time to cool it, telling us they don't want to see anything but civil behavior out of us, or we'll all be in for some serious hurt.

This lasts for one week until a soldier in Bravo Company at a base similar to ours on the other side of Ghazni has his leg blown off by an improvised explosive device (IED) planted on the side of a road.

Suddenly, we're going to raid a village that has actual bad guys, where actual shots may be fired.

So once again we find ourselves in front of the company commander in the motor pool, clustered around him as he stands on the sandbags telling us that we aren't peacekeepers, we're not international social workers, we're fucking goddamn infantry killers! We need to stay frosty, sharp, on the edge! We can't get complacent or relaxed!

Back in the tents, the sergeants pretend that they had never told us to cool it or to calm things down and that they have always maintained an opinion of high intensity.

We drive into the village preparing for war.

Ryan is in the back of the truck with me, where he maniacally locks and loads his weapon over and over again to hear the sound of the bullet chambering. "Rico! We're gonna kill some motherfuckers today! Finally! Let's fucking kill someone! Goddamn!"

He slaps hands with Cox, who screams, "Let's bring this shit on!"

I've remembered my ammunition this time.

I'm proud that I've remembered my ammunition.

I'm a little apprehensive today, though. Some days you want combat; some days you could put it off for another day or so. Today my tummy hurts. I wonder if they'd consider delaying the mission for a day or so until Specialist Rico's tummy feels better.

As the soldiers around me work themselves up into a frenzy, I stare out the side of the truck, grimacing as I hold my stomach. My body shakes and jerks back and forth and bobs up and down with the uneven terrain. I feel really ill.

It's another quiet, lazy Sunday morning in Afghanistan when the U.S. Humvees speed through the village and come to a screeching halt at various intersections, blocking off the main roads. The Afghans come out from their homes to watch as the U.S. soldiers dismount with intensity, running and screaming.

Wait, hold on; everyone hold on.

Captain Zimmerman and the first sergeant carry on a discussion as soldiers look around in confusion.

Everyone back on the trucks. Everyone get back on.

The soldiers climb back into the trucks, and the trucks move forward as the drivers scream in confusion to the sergeants on the ground who are guiding them to their new positions.

The word is given, and the soldiers jump out of the trucks—this time with a little less intensity.

The first sergeant just decided the trucks would be better positioned facing outward in case we must rapidly retreat, instead of facing inward toward the village.

Get back on the trucks, you fucking faggots! Get the fuck back on the truck! Yeah, I'm talking to you, shithead!

The soldiers get back into the trucks, and the vehicles reposition themselves slowly, moving in reverse in small increments in the narrow streets lined with clay walls, moving forward a bit, then straightening the wheels out, and then going into reverse again, for what seems like an eternity before the trucks are finally positioned correctly.

The Afghans watch, amused, wondering what strange military tactic this is. The U.S. soldiers jump out and walk to their various security positions.

We secure the area until the Americans in the T-shirts and the beards and baseball caps with the sunglasses arrive. Arguments quickly ensue between the soldiers about whether or not they are CIA or some top secret Army intelligence unit. The men of the village are put in the center of a courtyard and guarded by two soldiers, who argue over who has smoked the other person's cigarettes, while the possible CIA operatives pull men at random out of the collection point to the side of a building.

The possible CIA operative screams at the man in English while a scared and nervous Afghan translator who doesn't like the way his countrymen are being treated quietly translates into Pashtu, his hatred for us obvious on his face.

"WHERE THE FUCK IS THE MAN WHO MADE THE BOMB?" the possible CIA operative yells for the second time.

The Afghan man looks up pleadingly to his fellow Afghan, our interpreter, and babbles incoherently in his native language for thirty seconds.

The possible CIA operative smacks him in the face with the water bottle he's drinking from, pulls his gun, and puts it to the man's head, screaming, more at the interpreter than at his detainee, "TELL HIM YES OR FUCKING NO! IF HE SAYS ONE MORE GODDAMN THING BEYOND YES OR NO I'M GOING TO SHOOT HIM IN THE FUCKING FACE!"

The interpreter stumbles over his own words. He is now visibly trembling, pleading with the detainee to only say yes or no. The detainee doesn't understand and starts a whining pleading diatribe, which infuriates the possible CIA officer, who smacks him in the face again with the water bottle and screams, "I'M ABOUT TWO GODDAMN SECONDS FROM SHOOTING HIM IN THE FUCKING FACE! YES OR FUCKING NO!"

We watch this as Devon, leaning against a wall, offers me a cigarette. I reach for the cigarette, but Devon slaps me across the face with his water bottle, laughing hysterically. "I TOLD YOU TO SHUT THE FUCK UP, RICO!"

"Hey, Devon, let me get a drink of water."

Devon pulls the water from my reach and slaps me across the face with it one more time, now on the verge of hysterics. "I TOLD YOU TO SHUT THE FUCK UP, RICO!"

I grab his water bottle. "It doesn't even really hurt that much. It's a strange tactic."

"Don't you fucking question our tactics," Devon snarls at me. "These tactics have been tested on terrorists all across the world. You don't know shit about our tactics!"

"Yeah?" I toss his water bottle into a feces-strewn muddy cattle staging area immediately in front of us.

Devon immediately stops laughing and draws up a sincere and sad look on his face, "My water. You son of a bitch. I'm going to kill you for that, Rico. You'll die before this deployment is over. Friendly fire, Hooah?"

"Hooah."

Back at base, in the motor pool, disturbed that the soldiers are now hitting each other in the face with water bottles, Captain Zimmerman has a mass formation to remind us that we are here to help the Afghan people, not to kill them. So it is time to quit thinking like brutes and start thinking like civilized people. We are here to help, not to hurt. Pretend, he tells us, that we have joined the Peace Corps, not the U.S. Army. He reminds us that we have been over two months in country, and not a single bullet has been fired.

So, the next day, of course, a bullet is fired.

Kind of.

We're trying to find the village of Gar Geshawan, and we're completely lost. We've driven straight through some farmer's field, up the side of a mountain, down a valley, and past a village. Now we are in an empty field, and where the town is supposed to be there isn't a town. Our convoy of six vehicles is strung out over a half mile, with the rear ass of our convoy still back by the village.

I'm in the lead convoy vehicle with Lieutenant Michael beside me bragging about how his life will ultimately be that much better than the life of anyone who's enlisted because he was a West Point graduate and an officer, when the last vehicle in the convoy calls me on the radio.

"Um, someone's shooting at us," Sergeant Pauley says calmly over the radio.

"Roger," I say. "Wait one." I turn to Lieutenant Michael, who has stopped bragging about his West Point experiences and is now arguing with the private driving the vehicle, telling him that he has taken a wrong turn. "Sir," I tenderly offer, trying not to interrupt.

Lieutenant Michael gets excitable, as he sometimes does, his lap a mess of maps and satellite imagery, and turns to me and yells, "Shut up, Rico! Not now!"

I hate it when he yells at me. That's one thing I don't like about the Army. Everyone's always yelling.

I purse my lips and wait patiently and then realize how absurd it is to follow a command to be quiet when we're being shot at, so I blurt out, "Sir, we've got shots fired!"

Lieutenant Michael stops arguing with the driver. After a long pause he realizes the reality he has been waiting for but until now has not heard. Then he asks calmly, "Well, who says we have shots fired?"

"Sergeant Pauley."

There's another long pause. "Well, where are the shots coming from?" He starts craning his neck around the inside of the Humvee as if he could see the shooter through the metal walls and equipment that are piled up high all around us.

"Sergeant Pauley," I say into the radio. "Where are the shots coming from?"

"We've passed him now; that was like thirty seconds ago," Sergeant Pauley calls back.

"We've passed him now, sir; that was like thirty seconds ago."

Lieutenant Michael shrugs and starts arguing again with the private, when the second-to-last vehicle being driven by Sergeant Stein calls up to say that we have more shots fired and dammit to hell if they aren't getting tired of getting shot at back there and would we mind very much if they shot back. Again, I interrupt and say, "Sir, we've got more shots fired. They want to know if they can return fire."

"No! No one returns fire! Someone needs to isolate where the shots are coming from."

I put a call out on the radio net for everyone not to return fire, to just take getting shot at, and ask if anyone knows where the shots are coming from. But no one does.

Lieutenant Michael thinks a moment and then says, "Drive forward. They'll stop shooting eventually."

And they do.

Chapter 21

THE RUSSIAN BASE

"Here, hold this," Devon says as he hands his rifle to our prisoner, who is standing off to the side sulking because he has been arrested. Devon lowers his sunglasses over his face, grabs two of the AK-47s that we've recovered, and holds them in either hand as he freezes his mouth in the midst of an imagined scream.

I take his picture.

Devon rushes over to see the picture and, not liking it, has me take a few more action shots before he put the AK-47s back in the pile of seized weapons and grabs his rifle back from our prisoner, who at this point is turning it over in his hands trying to figure out how to use the damn thing, and says, "Gimme that, you son of a bitch!"

We received the call at Cougar Base early in the morning. Battalion had a legitimate bona fide mission for us. On the outskirts of Ghazni there was an abandoned Russian base, where, according to numerous reports, there were illegal caches of weapons.

The ripple of excitement was tangible. Even the guys who had the day off were offering to go, trying to swap with the guys who were supposed to be working that day.

After a filling breakfast of grits and boiled scrambled eggs, our convoy of five Humvees leaves Cougar Base early in the morning. It reminds me of getting up early as a child when my grandparents drove me to Iowa City to visit the Adventure Land theme park. It is just another early-morning road trip, and I am happy and excited to have something tangible to accomplish. An actual mission. This isn't just driving around the countryside randomly talking to whomever we could find; now we have a purpose, a destination, and a task.

Our convoy heads toward the distant city of Ghazni, which until then has always just been a small blur on the distant horizon during the day and a pathetic handful of city lights at night.

We are in shock as we enter the city. As the third or fourth largest city in Afghanistan, it is a teeming, overflowing mess of claustrophobic streets and wayward alleys. The streets are open sewers, and piles of garbage litter the intersection. The buildings are not just the clay brick buildings of the villages but actual three- and four-story cement buildings, each in some level of decay or destruction, as far as the eye can see. And the ripe smell of rotten fruit and feces reminds me of the monkey cage at the zoo. It is what I imagine the impoverished quarters of Calcutta or Delhi look like. It is worse than the worst slums I have ever seen. It is worse than Managua in Nicaragua, or downtown Saigon. At least those countries can still attract the occasional global corporation to set up shop somewhere in their cities. Afghanistan has been banned from the global friend's marketplace—something that is evident by the conspicuous lack of advertisements for a single brand-name product or service. Everywhere there are motorbikes and donkeys and old rusted Toyota pickups, and as we roll through the town, horns blaring, moving everyone off the road as we plow through deep into the urban nightmare, we become the immediate and instant center of attention.

Finally, as the town starts to thin itself out, we arrive back out in the desert. We are out of the prairies now and into the foothills of the mountains. We pass a beautiful mansion where Afghan men with machine guns lounge in the courtyard. And finally we come upon what, at that point, is the largest junkyard I have ever seen. It was the Epcot Center and Universal Studios of junkyards. Rusted tanks and gutted airplane husks, long since blown up and abandoned, for as far as the eye could see. This was the epicenter of a fierce battle during the Russian occupation.

In the distance are two ancient obelisks at the foot of the mountains, remnants of the era when Alexander invaded Afghanistan and found it a more civilized culture.

Our Humvees pull into the center of the junkyard, and we step out slowly, overwhelmed by the piles of junk everywhere. A weapons cache could be anywhere. There are two small two-story buildings on the perimeter of the junkyard, one wall already falling into debris. And inside of one, on the top floor, in a little darkened, soot-seared, trash-strewn cubbyhole on the top floor that I imagine only trolls could live in, we find the four men.

They wear mud-encrusted military uniforms, much too short for them, that have holes in the elbows and knees. And they blink and wince, painfully averting eyes not yet adjusted to the light as we pull them out by their thin skinny malnourished arms and throw them down in the sunlight.

They tell our interpreter that they were on duty here and were the forgotten property of an Afghan general whom none of us had ever heard of and whom they themselves did not remember ever meeting. They were told to guard the junkyard and have been on guard for months now.

They're disciplined; I'll give them that. I complain if I have guard duty for more than six hours.

We ask them if they have any weapons here at this "base." They stated that there are none.

So when Cox kicks a door open two minutes later revealing piles of AK-47s, we decide to place the one who lied to us under arrest.

Which is why Devon and I are guarding the one who lied while Devon takes action photos with the seized weapons and I try desperately to remember where I put the important-looking notebook we discovered that Lieutenant Michael told me to hold.

A hundred meters to our front, the rest of our platoon is loading hundreds of discovered mortar rounds into the back of a big Army truck for transportation. An explosives and ordnance disposal officer from battalion is explaining that they probably won't blow. He isn't entirely sure. So Sergeant Santiago and Cox and Ryan hold the mortar rounds delicately, quick to hand them off to the next person in line.

"Rico, I need you over here," Lieutenant Michael tells me through the radio hand mike attached near my shoulder.

"Roger, en route," I reply.

A moment later and I'm on the other side of the junkyard with only Lieutenant Michael and another explosives ordnance and disposal officer. They've discovered a door that leads underground and are trying out their best action-movie door kicks, to no avail.

It's always a lot easier to kick in doors in the movies.

I start kicking around the debris where I was standing and uncover two sheets of plywood that cover a large hole in the ground.

"Up here!" I yell as I find a rock and drop it down the black hole.

If it hits bottom, it makes no sound.

"Wow!" Lieutenant Michael exclaims, excited at the find. "Wow! This is an extensive underground network of something. Wow. Maybe we should try blowing the door open." He thinks to himself for a moment about what the U.S. Army possibly has that could blow open a door and then says, "Bet a grenade would do the trick."

"No, sir," the EOD officer tells him. "We're the only ones authorized to blow doors."

"Okay, then you blow the door," Lieutenant Michael replies.

"Unfortunately, we're not allowed to blow anything," the EOD man replies.

Lieutenant Michael has me call up to battalion to report our find and ask permission to use a grenade to blow open the door. Battalion responds that there will be no use of grenades. Someone could get hurt.

I stand over the rim of the darkened pit, spitting into the bottom, as Lieutenant Michael walks around me in small concentric circles attached by the tether of the hand mike while he argues with battalion: "Well, we are in the Army. The Army uses grenades. That's the nature of the Army. To use grenades and guns to blow things up."

Battalion responds that although we are in the Army, they are still afraid that someone will get hurt, and they're trying not to use weapons if at all possible. In fact, battalion isn't even sure if they want us collecting the arsenal of weapons that we've found. Again, weapons and all that . . . it sounds messy.

This was the new twenty-first-century U.S. Army. The non–weapons-using Army.

Lieutenant Michael hands the mike to me in disgust and grumbles about why they bothered to send us out here in the first place and tells me to stay here while he goes to find Sergeant Santiago and Sergeant Stephens to inform them of the situation.

I collapse on my back, putting my hands behind my head. I stare at the sky and at what looks like a civilian airliner flying by far overhead, and wonder if the people inside have any idea that they are flying over the worst place on the planet at this very moment in time.

And then the EOD officer screams at me, "RICO! GET THE FUCK OVER HERE!" And then he screams something in Dari and "DROP YOUR WEAPON!"

My heart jump-starts in my chest, and I leap up and run to the EOD officer, who leans against a nearby crumbling wall, facedown to his weapon, his weapon aimed at something. He grabs me by the back of my vest and shoves me into the wall and points into the distance. I follow the line of his arm to the tip of his finger, and in the distance I see it.

There is another small building, half of which has crumbled to the ground, turning the inside and the second floor into an open-air atrium, and there are Afghan soldiers scrambling. One of them is at the edge of the opened second floor with his rifle, turning back to yell at his fellow soldiers. The EOD officer whispers in my ear, "He just pointed his weapon at us. If he points it again, take him out."

The EOD officer runs off screaming for help, when I remember that I'm the one with the radio. I dig my knee into a sharp piece of rock and shift my entire perception, my entire world, to the small immediacy of what I can see through my rifle's scope at the end of the muzzle. The red dot from my rifle's aiming system bounces up and down wildly at the second floor as I struggle to control my breathing and steady my hand.

I force myself to breathe slowly. I tuck the butt of my rifle into my shoulder to steady my arm. Slowly the red dot stops bouncing and locks onto the Afghan soldier at the edge of the second floor. The thumb of my opposite hand, just like clockwork, flicks the selector level on my rifle from safe to semi, and my right hand's trigger finger moves to the trigger of my rifle, applying pressure. One more millimeter's worth of pressure, and my rifle will fire. I'm a good marksman, and my weapon is very accurate.

In my new world, in my new frame of reference—the second-floor world that's surrounded by a black eyepiece and a red dot that now bounces only between head and midsection of the body—I see the Afghan soldier with the rifle turn back to stare at me.

He sees me.

Somehow he sees me.

He has to be at least three hundred meters away, and I'm behind a berm, but sure enough he sees the rifle being pointed at him from behind the distant wall.

He hesitates. It is the indecision of all famous last moments. I can imagine him sweating, wet with adrenaline and anxious with fear and excitement, which can make one's judgment sloppy.

And he starts to raise his rifle. He applies both hands to it—one hand on the pistol grip, the other hand underneath the barrel—and he starts to raise it from above his knees where it has been pointing down at the ground.

I want him to lift it. If the rifle's muzzle rises past his knees, that's it. I'm going to blow his dirty Afghan brains out all over that dirty Afghan room.

I can't get this stupid silly smile off my face, but I'm elated to finally have the opportunity to be able to kill someone.

And then the thought occurs to me. I can get away with killing him right now. He has a rifle in his hands. No one would question me. No one would know that in the small universe that exists only through my scope, he has never raised his rifle past his knees.

Am I really that type of guy? Am I really about to murder someone just for the opportunity? Jesus, the Army really has gotten to me. I thought my education and advanced life experience had inoculated me against all the infantry killer training bullshit, but apparently it hasn't.

I don't know if he's a bad man. He technically hasn't attacked us.

He's only doing what any soldier would do when he discovers other soldiers invading his place of responsibility. He's probably just nervous. He probably doesn't know what to do. Maybe he doesn't want to hurt us at all. Maybe he just raised his rifle so his comrades will think he is doing the right thing.

And where the fuck exactly are his comrades? Are they running up at me right this second but I am too blind to see it because my world is consumed with the dirty indecisive Afghan on the second floor?

No. No. I'm not going to shoot. A lot of the soldiers in my company are itching so much for a fight, for a chance to shoot. A lot of them might take this opportunity for their confirmed kill. But that's not me. I'm better than that. I'm not that type of person.

And that's when I decide to pull the trigger.

And that's also when I hear the squeal of vehicles and the blaring horns. My head twists from the private world of my indecision to the road in the distance. A caravan of expensive black SUVs with tinted windows and little diplomatic flags fluttering off the hoods speeds up the twisting dirt roads out of the desert and toward the junkyard. It's that same caravan of black SUVs that you always see in the movies belonging to a drug cartel leader in Mexico or maybe the president of the United States. I turn back to the building to see the man's comrades I was worried about race toward the caravan. The indecisive soldier on the second floor disappears. He seems to sink into the floor, obviously running down a flight of steps.

The moment is over.

I berate myself for not having the strength of my convictions. For my poor discipline and follow-through.

And then the U.S. soldiers arrive. Sergeant Santiago crashes breathlessly into the berm next to me, yelling, "What do we got!" And then Cox and Ryan and Devon are all around me, their rifles next to me, and in the distance Lieutenant Michael and the rest of Sergeant Stephen's squad.

And I suddenly become overwhelmed with the feeling of brotherhood I had been missing. This is what it is like to feel a kinship between soldiers. These courageous men who sprinted to my location to help me out of a possible sticky situation, who are ready to maybe kill with me and die with me.

The Afghan soldiers who were in the building now wait out front for the caravan like angry children anxious to tell on us.

The caravan pulls to a stop, and a large fat man in a polo T-shirt and aviator sunglasses, smoking a cigar, steps out. He starts speaking to them, and they start pointing to us.

Fucking goddamn tattletales.

Lieutenant Michael taps me on my back and jumps over the small protective wall, and I join him. He turns back to Sergeant Santiago and says, "If something happens here, take everyone out." And then as an afterthought, "Except me and Rico."

We walk through the junk. Taking a cue from us, the fat Afghan in the polo shirt with the sunglasses and the cigar walks forward to meet us with another one who is in uniform, although his uniform is straight and clean and of a proper size. It's that same third-world dictator uniform you always see on third-world dictators, overly ceremonial and pompous, trying to compensate for their lack of membership in a real military.

The fat Afghan extends his hand and, in perfect English, explains that he is a general, that this land is one of his military bases, and that we are unlawfully taking his weapons and detaining his men. Lieutenant Michael refuses to recognize the general's authority because he has not been recognized by the Karzai government.

Realizing I just might be in the presence of my first Afghan warlord, I produce a big smile. I've always secretly hoped I'd get to meet one. I wonder if he'll give me an autograph and let me take a picture with my arm around him.

"You cannot take from me these weapons," the fat Afghan general says.

"Yes I can," Lieutenant Michael argues.

"No you can't," the fat Afghan general replies.

"Yes, I can."

"No, you cannot."

"Yes, I can."

"No, you can't."

"Yes, I can."

I can't believe that such grade-school negotiations could be connected to words like "Afghan warlord" and "military base" and "weapons cache."

This goes on for a few minutes until Lieutenant Michael has me call up battalion to report the latest situation. We all sit on stacks of tires and burned-out tank hulks as we wait for those back at battalion to scramble to find someone of high enough authority and rank to make a decision.

Finally, I get a call. I turn the hand mike over to Lieutenant Michael, who frowns.

There is a slight pause before Lieutenant Michael stands up, extends his hand to the fat general, and says, "I'm sorry to have bothered you. We'll be leaving now, and we'll release your man and leave your weapons."

We drive back to base. After a satisfying dinner of a scoop of rice and a small boiled pork chop, we regale those at base with exaggerated versions of the day's events. With no night patrols or guard duty scheduled, I collapse on my bunk in the small green Army tent and go to sleep.

I awake late at night in the darkness of the tent. I can make out the absence of Sergeant Santiago's sleeping form. And then I hear whispering a few feet away outside the front flap of the tent. It's one of those titillating conspiratorial whispers that knows a secret. I start to wake up, aroused by the idea of dirty little secrets and gossip under the cover of darkness. I feel for my sandals and put them on and walk across the rocky ground, my arm outstretched to the edge of the tent, feeling my way until I get to where the moonlight illuminates the entrance.

Outside Sergeant Santiago sits on a pile of the sandbags that surround our tent. "What's going on, Sergeant?" I ask.

Sergeant Santiago is visibly excited, almost trembling as he speaks in hushed whispers. "Tomorrow they're dropping a helicopter full of National Guard guys to take over Cougar Base, right? We're moving to this place called Tarin Kowt, where the Marines are in this huge fire-fight with over one hundred Taliban, and they're pulling us over there to support them. I don't know the details yet, but they did this airfield seizure, and they got hit hard, and it's fucking going nuts over there! We're . . . fucking . . . going . . . to . . . war!"

My mouth hangs open as I imagine a massive army-on-army conflict that engulfs the mountains while mortars and fire ring out from all sides. The future has suddenly become delicious with anticipation and excitement.

THE VALLEY OF THE SPIDER:
A LETTER TO MOM

Dear Mom:

Remember that big Marine offensive we were supposed to take part in that we missed out on because they couldn't find any helicopters to fly us there? Well, now we're finally leaving the Army base in Tarin Kowt after a month of playing cards all day to head off into the mountains to our south to chase after the remnants of some Taliban or something.

It's a small snakelike line of blue cutting a swath through the crisp raw mountains. A valley of green spreads forward from the blue river, which acts as a critical vein of life, giving energy to an otherwise lifeless and barren and unforgiving landscape.

We sit in the mountains above the valley in a blocking position . . . waiting. Bravo Company and the Marines are supposedly pushing Taliban toward our location. I'm not sure how this is supposed to work. There seem to be too many uncovered fields and unguarded mountain passes. How will they be filtered to our position? Why wouldn't they just go in a different direction? I don't really understand how big operations work, what with flanking positions and crap like that.

Yet, in the middle of the night we hear the echo of gunfire on the other side of the valley. And every morning the new reports: "Bravo Company killed five last night." So we wait.

It's very frustrating to be this close to it all and still not be able to participate. This is the reason half these guys in my platoon joined, and it's driving them crazy not to be able to do anything. I think some are secretly relieved, though, that they get to keep sitting everything out.

The valley itself is the size of a medium-sized city, a forty-minute drive from end to end and surrounded on all sides by massive, jagged, craggy mountains.

During the day we go into the valley to do raids. The first morning we raided this compound. Forty heavily armed soldiers rushed inside, beating down the door and screaming at the occupants to get down. Interpreters were running around trying to keep up with all the shouted commands. We tear the house apart searching for weapons that we know we won't find amid the cries of children and the wailing of the women. I really feel like shit, but the women are always home; they never go anywhere, so every compound we enter there's just these screaming women that act like we've just raped them.

At the front of this one house inside the compound is a huge sheep with matted fur, its back broken, flies buzzing on its face, half crippled and twitching. Its intestines are coming out its ass, it's covered in piles of its own feces, and little toddler children are playing in the mess. It's the most disgusting thing I've ever seen. I know it's the third world, but Jesus Christ, don't they have enough sense to not let their children play in dying sheep guts and shit?

Then, when we're done with the compound, this new man out in the field starts running from us. Our commander tells us to fire warning shots, and this is interpreted as "shoot to kill." We go chasing him and shooting at him through farmers' fields, but miraculously he never gets shot and actually eggs us on by flipping us the bird and running off laughing. He easily outruns us.

Then one of our bullets goes astray and takes out a man's cow. I'm sure they love us for that. Cow just falls over dead. Too funny.

The next day we raid another compound to find a woman and her screaming children. This woman has a daughter who she says is possessed and is severely mentally ill, screaming, screeching, and coughing excessively. The woman keeps her locked up in a rarely used corner of her compound.

It creeps me out to think that deep in rural Afghanistan, while everyone in the world is living normally, there's this mentally ill teenaged girl locked in a rear room of some obscure compound.

Anyway, we knock down her walls and destroy her home, only to find nothing. When we leave, we apologize but state it was for her own good. It was scary, though; the entire time we searched her house we kept hearing this horrific screeching ghostly wail from the back room where her daughter was locked up.

Yesterday we were supposed to do a Medcap. This is where doctors come out to treat the sick, but the doctors never came. Which is unfortunate, because the sick all show up. One guy had a leg that was obviously infected and super gross and about ready to fall off. We gave him a bandage and an apology, and sent him on his way.

Then at night, or on guard days (on alternating days the two platoons switch off guard duty and mission duty), I sit high on this God-forsaken mountain, burning up. Midsummer in Afghanistan is the hottest I've ever experienced in my life. Yesterday at lunch I heard a hissing sound coming from my gear and realized it was my water boiling inside my canteen! Let me tell you, nothing goes with MREs (Meals Ready to Eat) like boiling-hot water!

The ants down here are ferocious! And huge! The size of spiders! And they bite and they are everywhere! You look and see a few, then refocus your eyes and see thousands in the same spot! We have no tents or sleeping bags with us, so we sleep freely with the ants!

At night we all listen to Specialist Devon's silly fictional stories about the Valley of the Spider that we all live within. And in the distance . . . gunfire. And so we wait for them to be pushed to us.

On the radio we hear that seven trucks of our battalion's equipment got blown up en route to our new base in Tarin Kowt. Ryan and I laugh about the morning before we left for this mission. We were walking to breakfast when a seven-story cloud of smoke billowed up a few hundred meters from the chow hall. Huge explosion! We both looked up casually and resumed our conversation.

Next day:

Today we do a village assessment, and it about breaks my heart. Again we tell them about wells, clinics, and seeds for farming . . . then the village elder says, "Please don't tease us. We are a very poor, very hungry people." The major doing the assessment pauses, and his eyes flicker. He knows what I know—that most likely nothing is going to be given to them. Yet, we make empty promises.

I've mixed thoughts on the Afghan people. On one hand, they seem so kind and friendly. People who don't have enough to eat give us tea and food. They are always quick with a smile and a laugh. Yet, on the other hand, these are still people who kill women openly for infidelity. Who let their children play in dead sheep carcasses and feces. This is definitely worse than any of the poverty I've encountered in Southeast Asia or in Central America.

I'm also bothered by their lack of initiative. We go into villages, and inevitably they want us to build them a well. They are hungry, yet almost always they are found during the day doing almost nothing. What simply bothers me is that for a people supposedly so poor and struggling to survive, few of them seem very concerned about it. I'm just curious how some countries in two hundred years can go from frontier living with few modern marvels to outer space and other countries can in two hundred years advance not at all, and still live as if they were in the Stone Age. And that's what it is like. Ever wanted to see what the world looked like when Christ was alive? Come to Afghanistan. It hasn't changed.

I'm also confused about the U.S. role here. In some ways we've made major changes. Many areas are now safe to travel in, and the Taliban are hard to find. Yet, we also do stupid things, like not communicating with the Marines so we end up hitting the same targets. The U.S. supplies the Afghan army with weapons, then when we see them in Afghanistan we take the weapons away from them because one side of the Army doesn't know what the other side is doing. Our new base is rented from one of Afghanistan's most brutal and violent warlords. One officer told me we pay him a million dollars U.S. a month. That's nice—us giving Afghan warlords a million bucks a month. We do business with him but seize opium when we find it. Supposedly, we are also supposed to be doing drug interdiction. Yet, HE'S OK. Well, I guess it's just politics as usual. What are we supposed to do? Create more enemies to fight?

I don't see Al Qaeda or Taliban developing out of religions or ideological fundamentalism. I think it's economics. These people are dirt poor. There's no work, no school (and as already discussed they don't seem to initiate their own self-improvement). So they turn to religious fundamentalism as a response. Something that explains their suffering and gives them purpose. Most of the Taliban we're fighting had nothing to do with those higher-ups who decided to give sanctuary to Bin Laden. These guys are just poor farmers who belong to the same political party as guys who offered sanctuary to our enemy. So why do they attack us? Because we're out in force trying to find and kill them! I'd probably try to kill us too!

Maybe, though, by killing these low-level Taliban we are making the country less fertile for the future extremist factions who could do us some harm. And maybe by tearing down the walls and raiding the homes of innocent people we are still offering up a visibility that will deter potential low-level Taliban from staging in that area. I don't know.

Donkeys . . . I've decided that donkeys are universally cute. Really cute. So cute that donkeys defy any arguments of preferences being relative. When you pet their noses, they blink their eyes and bashfully look away as if embarrassed. And when donkeys hee-haw, they have their mouths and lips curled up as if they are smiling. Boyfriend and girlfriend donkeys rest their heads on each other's rumps and fan each other's faces with their tails. And kid donkeys, the size of an average dog, trot around with big smiles on their faces and floppy, dangly, long donkey ears. Too cute.

Next day:

It's been hot out here. Every day it's over 115 degrees in the shade. We've either been kicking in doors every day or handing out Play-Doh and tote bags at villages.

Last night the stars were beautiful. I saw eight shooting stars.

Big mission today. Today we go forward of the Valley of the Spider to set up a forward operating base, which is farther out from our Valley of the Spider forward operating base, which itself is a forward operating base of Tarin Kowt, which itself is a forward deployed operating base . . .

The NSA (National Security Agency) has been picking up cell/satellite phone calls from this remote compound out in the middle of nowhere by a guy that we really want. We're going to go and get him.

Next day:

Well, still waiting to go on the mission discussed at the end of the last section.

Funny . . . last night under the stars a conversation started about the old show *Golden Girls*. Is Bea Arthur still alive? Has anyone heard? Not the type of discussion I would've ever expected to have in Afghanistan while staring up at the sky.

Next day:

Back from the mission . . . The raid was a bust. Nobody was there. We were looking at the satellite imagery upside down, so it was a good thing no one was there because everything ended up being backwards, so our assault teams and perimeter security teams were all jacked up. To get there, though, we had to drive our Humvees through a river. We got stuck, and the vehicle filled with water. I was submerged from my waist down in water before we got out. Then we went swimming in the river on our way back.

We had brand-new Humvees before we left to come out here, but we burn through them! They are all already almost deadlined. We go up and down straight vertical cliffs. The thing you have to realize is that in Afghanistan there are no roads. Everything is off road. We go through two extra tires a day from our constantly flat tires.

Tonight is quiet. No noise throughout the valley. It's quiet. The stars look special when viewed from the perspective of night vision goggles.

My new nickname is "Precious." It's because I have an electric pink toothbrush, and when I sleep at night, instead of just sleeping facedown in the dirt with no protection, I put a rain poncho out first to lie on. Apparently, in the world of the infantry this makes me something of a dandy. Hence, my new nickname—"Precious."

It's quiet today, and the sun beats down. I make the rounds of the camp. No one is moving. Up on one ridge they are sleeping under the Humvee listening to the one AM radio station, which comes from Kabul and plays lame seventies disco rock. On the opposite ridge they sleep under a makeshift rain poncho and respond to "what's going on?" in a series of guttural grunts. And the heat beats on, and the ants crawl and time crawls. I think Johnny Cash has a song about hangover Sundays. This seems something like that.

Later:

An uneasy sleep.

You think you're awake, eavesdropping on a conversation between the second squad leader and your platoon leader, where they're spreading incendiary gossip about the second platoon, but when the call shouts, you realize you have been sleeping for probably an hour or so. "Rico! Get up! Someone's on the ridge!"

You rush around in darkness, scrambling for gear, fighting the "just woke up" haze that surrounds you. You throw a bulletproof vest over your T-shirt and grab your rifle and chase shadowed forms of soldiers running up the side of the mountain. You can't see anything; you hear only the stumbling feet of soldiers as they step on loose rocks.

Winded, you sprint up the side of the mountain. You're in that mode where the adrenaline is starting to seep into your veins in small spurts, giving you momentary injections of energy. You just keep imagining suddenly seeing the telltale cracks of light and sound that would mean someone is shooting at you. Later, at the top, you peer into the darkness with adjusted night eyes and curse yourself for leaving your night vision goggles down below at camp. The sky is suddenly lit overhead as a luminescent mortar round turns the whole hillside into flashing temporary flickering daylight. You peer intently into the edge of your new field of illuminated vision. Nothing.

But there are so many huge rock outcroppings. The top of the mountain is not smooth and pointed. It's made up of little valleys and weird towering rock formations and thousands of places to hide. Lieutenant Michael and I find ourselves at the farthest forward point up the mountain, far above everyone else. After a little while, peering out in the darkness at the top of the world, we decide to go down. I cover my platoon leader as he makes his way down, so I'm the last man on the mountain.

Below me they are scanning the mountain with thermal sites, and that's when I get the call on my ICOM radio: "Rico, there's someone behind you on that mountain; get down now!" They've picked up what they think is the heat signature of a man behind me. I panic. I rush down the mountain. My gait turns into a perpetual reckless slide down loose gravel and rocks, which slide before me like a miniavalanche announcing my arrival at the bottom, exhausted from my descent. The man behind me? He's gone—ran off, they say, into the upper tiers of the mountain. I collapse on the dirt in my dripping wet sweat-stained T-shirt, peel out of my body armor, and fall asleep on a mound of rocks a short distance away.

Anyway, that was last night.

Today we leave the Valley of the Spider. The enemy was never pushed toward us. It's time to go home to Tarin Kowt, Camp Ripley. Before we go, we get out satellite imagery of one more compound. I hate satellite imagery. Crayon drawings would be better.

Then we go to the compound. A village elder comes by and tells us that he knows where the head Taliban guy we're looking for lives. But we can't raid the place, or the Taliban leader will know who told on him, and he'll get killed. We promise not to raid the place. And then, what do we do? We raid the place.

We probably just signed this guy's death warrant. Don't trust the U.S., I guess.

We find an empty house with lots of Taliban documents and audiotapes. But that's it. And now we're starting to load up the vehicles, so I gotta go.

Peace out, homies!

Love,
Johnny

Chapter 22

THE WASTELANDS OF AFGHANISTAN

We stumble wearily in the darkness down a long serpentine driveway, with large walls of metal fencing covered with barbed wire on both sides of us. Blinding floodlights track our movement, and behind them we can make out the subtle shades of towers standing over us. Afghans in military uniforms, smoking cigarettes and armed with AK-47s, stare at us as we move past the attached Afghan National Army base.

We make a sloppy uneven formation in a courtyard and squint in the darkness, trying to get a feel for our new home. Sergeant First Class Derrens, Sergeant Riley, Sergeant Stephens, and Sergeant Santiago have been on the side talking to some men in baseball caps and shorts and T-shirts. Then they come over to address us.

"Welcome to Firebase Dizzy," Sergeant Derrens says. He gives us a small speech that barely registers in our tired brains. He says that he expects us to perform at our very best. That we're with the U.S. Special Forces now, the Green Berets, and that we weren't going to embarrass him.

The month after our return from our mission in Tarin Kowt with the Marine offensive, we baked in the sun at an Army base called Camp Ripley, playing cards all day until the end of summer before being told to pack up and prepare to move out. We had worked ten days all summer since leaving Ghazni.

Cougar Company is being sent to Oruzgan Province, a deadly region devoid of any semblance of law and order and also devoid of any U.S. Army presence save for two small Special Forces teams operating out of the firebase we have just landed at. The rest of Cougar Company, along with Lieutenant Michael, has been air-lifted forty kilometers to our north to mark some new territory for the U.S. and set up a new firebase.

We're in the village of Deh-Rawood, Oruzgan Province, the birthplace of the Taliban and the same province where Osama bin Laden met with Mullah Omar in the weeks immediately preceding September 11, 2001. We have come home to the birthplace of the September 11 plot, and the idea leaves a romantic tickle of resonance and importance in my head.

The base, someone tells me—although I'm not sure whether to believe him—is an old Taliban village that has been taken by the U.S. Special Forces. Tall protective walls of Hesco baskets—five-foot-tall cubed meshes of chain-link fence filled with rocks—are now stacked three high. Razor wire and mines have been put up around the perimeter of the base, along with five large cement towers that offer a pentagon of protection.

We're led down a series of alleyways and enter a small room stacked with bunk beds that reminds me of a five-dollar-a-night youth hostel you might find in Central America. I spy a rat scurrying across the cement floor as I drop my gear. I can hear the Chinook helicopters that gave us a ride taking off in the distance.

We're marched up to the rear guard tower of the base, which overlooks a massive sloping valley and a village off in the distance.

And all throughout the valley we see the flashes of muzzle fire.

Tracers arcing back and forth show the trajectory of fired rounds in the far distance as the local Afghans try to kill one another.

We hold our breaths and take it all in.

The Special Forces soldier who is giving us the tour sucks on his cigar and says, "Welcome to the wastelands of Afghanistan, men."

Chapter 23

CONVERSATIONS WITH
A NONEXISTENT RADIO

"WAKE THE FUCK UP!"

I hear the voice, and my body jumps up before my mind gets a sense of itself. Somewhere in the back of the command hallway, a metal trash can slams into the wall and bounces off the floor with a metal vibration that hurts my ears. Brian, my kitten, jumps off my sleeping form and runs off, quickly abandoning me.

This is the intense startling jump-start of the heart when the eyes, half asleep, notice the alarm clock, which states you're two hours late for work, or when you're in Afghanistan and you've been caught sleeping on radio guard, as I just have.

I abruptly turn, broken from a deep comatose sleep that made me drool, my heart still in my throat, to see Ryan enter the command hallway behind me. He is pretending to be a drill sergeant, his chest appropriately puffed out, inspecting the mess that I have been marinating in over the past few days.

He knocks over a shelf filled with overturned coffee cups that holds piles of ground coffee. He kicks an already overturned trash can that is overflowing with candy and snack wrappers. He knocks over a teetering tower of old VHS tapes, which had been a midnight-hour artistic endeavor to make into a pyramid.

"Good God, man, what have you been doing in this place?"

I blush, momentarily thinking myself a proper gentleman, and straighten the boxer shorts and T-shirt he has caught me sleeping in while I was on radio guard. I brush cracker crumbs from my shirt and hope he doesn't notice my two-day beard growth and berate me for it. The early morning sunlight in the room accentuates the thick dust that coats everything. The wretched stale scent of body odor intermingled with stale coffee permeates the room.

We have been at Firebase Dizzy for four weeks, and the cooler late September air brought a much-lusted-for respite from the summer heat. And here the soldiers revel in the luxurious life of the Special Forces firebase, which includes e-mail and phones and round-the-clock food and showers and laundry service and televisions and movies everywhere. Removed from the company chain of command, Sergeant Derrens has relaxed the rigid rules of dress and behavior as reward for the soldiers' rigorous and disciplined guard rotations and daily patrolling. Although beyond our walls it is chaotic and violent, with tracers lighting up the night sky, thus far our patrols have found only quiet desert and courteous locals anxious to comply with searches and the random traffic stop.

"Is this how you're spending the rest of the deployment? How much sleep have you been getting every day?"

"About twelve hours," I respond, looking down at my bare dust-stained feet, somewhat ashamed.

"Twelve hours of sleep a day—and when you're not sleeping, you're watching movies?" Ryan motions to the television behind me, which is playing a 1980s Chevy Chase film on VHS. "Pathetic."

I try to explain to him that I have been caught up in the momentum of apathy. That I had started out wanting to do well, that I had good intentions at one point, but they dissolved day by day and . . .

"This is bullshit," Ryan states firmly, having arrived at his conclusions. "I slept ten hours yesterday, and I thought I was getting away with murder. But this slovenly environment . . . you lucky fucking bastard, how do you do it? I can't believe Sergeant Derrens lets you get away with this."

"He doesn't know; he's in Kandahar," I reply.

"Is this what you want to tell your grandkids that you did in Afghanistan? Forgot to take showers and watched movies all day?"

Ryan angrily exclaims, his voice betraying the jealousy he feels for my position.

I scan the disheveled room.

"Maybe we need some bad guys or something. I don't know," I say, starting to offer more before my words trail off in indifference. "What are we here for again?" I ask, turning from the room back to Ryan.

"Terrorists."

"Oh, right."

A week earlier, Private Mulbeck, who takes every opportunity to praise the Confederate flag and remind everyone that he doesn't give a fuck about nothing, slouched in the beach chair as he watched an old Jean-Claude Van Damme movie and said to me, "I don't give a fuck."

"Yes, I'm aware of that. But do you realize that I'm supposed to construct an operations center out of four dried-up markers, seven paper clips, some old glue, some monkey stickers, and three crayons? Do you realize this? How the fuck is it that we have monkey stickers here but no pens? Can someone tell me how this happens?"

Sergeant Santiago, who was playing solitaire on the platoon laptop as he organized his iPod music, stated, "Monkey stickers are a top priority for the war on terror. It was one of the lessons learned in Vietnam. That's why they lost the war. There weren't enough monkey stickers."

The only organization I achieved after three hours clearing out the command center, removing piles of garbage and mountains of old VHS tapes that Mulbeck pulled out of the trash, was to adorn a paper star with a smiley face that I cut out from red construction paper to indicate our firebase on the map. The checkpoints around our base were going to be monkey stickers, with a monkey holding up a banana to the observer as a big exaggerated thumbs-up. My plan had been to place the paper star and the stickers on the map that covered the wall, except I had been unable to find tape or glue, and nobody seemed to know exactly where on the map our base was. This was another one of those gestures like tulip weapon covers. Sometimes when life got too serious, it was best to respond with monkey sticker checkpoints.

The nonsatellite radio that monitored localized Army transmissions squeaked alive with a garbled voice. Mulbeck, completely disinterested, squeezed the hand mike and said, "Roger" before staring back at his movie and screeching, "Damn, that boy got fucked up!" after Van Damme beat someone up.

Every day and every night, one of the platoon's three squads would head out on a patrol while the other two squads pulled guard on the towers. Mulbeck and I had been given the assignment of permanent radio guard because we were the only ones certified to operate the satellite radio system that kept us in contact with our sister platoon at the newly designated Cougar Base and with Camp Ripley, the new battalion base in Tarin Kowt. The carefully guarded secret of our secret society of radio operators, however, was that our designation as operational experts meant only that we knew how to change the batteries and change the channel.

"Mulbeck," I stated in my dry monotone, which I hoped conveyed my annoyance.

"What?"

"Mulbeck!"

"What?"

I moved over to the television and flipped it off. This brought Mulbeck bolt upright out of his chair into a defensive fighting ninja position.

"You didn't even hear what they said," I yelled. "They just gave you their grid location, and you didn't even write it down. What happens if they get in trouble? We won't know where they're at."

I was especially worried because we had radio contact with our patrols over the nonsatellite localized radio for only approximately thirty percent of the time. The rest of the time they were out there alone. This fact didn't frighten just me; it frightened everyone. And everyone had taken me out to the vehicles to try and fix the radios to increase their range. I'd pretend to tinker with the radio for a few minutes. I'd tap the screwdriver on the side of the radio's metal casing, scrunching up my face to feign a discovery or solution, after which I'd have to scrunch my face up into another series of positions that attempted to feign a resulting disappointment from an idea that I'd never actually had that wouldn't pan out.

The truth was that I had no idea what I was doing. I didn't know how far the radios were even supposed to transmit. I didn't even know the most remedial basics about how a radio worked. As far as I was concerned, the radio's innards consisted of a series of trained mice that squeaked at high unperceivable frequencies that could be detected only by mice in the receiving radio, who would squeak in such a manner that it would come out sounding like the voices of United States soldiers.

Inevitably, I would end up shrugging my shoulders, saying that I had no idea. The Army had given me a forty-five-minute expert radio certification course before I was deployed. What exactly did they expect? This was forty-five-minute operational expertise in practice.

To which they would reply something like this: "You're going to feel real fucking terrible if someone dies because they can't raise base on radio."

To which I would defensively reply, "Of course I will! But that doesn't mean I know how to fix it just because someone might die!"

"It don't matter," Mulbeck said, brushing by me and flipping the TV back on before sinking back into his beach chair. "They're not going to get into trouble. This is Afghanistan, man."

I made sure that my knock on the door was heavy.

A tough intimidating type of knock.

When you were knocking on the door of the Green Berets, it just didn't do to offer one of my typical limp-wristed light slaps. In the background, on the base loudspeakers, the Special Forces soldiers were having their random occasional radio hour as they played Duran Duran and other eighties hits over the base loudspeakers.

The Special Forces combined barracks and operations center was a series of interlinked concrete buildings that constituted the center mass of the base. The door opened, and a ridiculously buff man in a wife-beater muscle shirt, surfer shorts, sandals, and a Yankees baseball cap frowned at me from underneath his beard, saying only, "What?" Next to him was their dog, a mutt whom they had spray-painted pink.

"Um, sir," I nervously stumbled. "Um, I'm from 3rd Platoon. Sergeant Derrens sent me over here to see if I could get some office supplies?" With Lieutenant Michael gone and the Cougar Company command element gone, Sergeant Derrens had put me in charge of the 3rd Platoon command center. My delegated task was to create some type of operational organization in the small building in the far corner of the base that we had been allowed to occupy as if we were an unwanted miserable tenant on public assistance.

The Special Forces soldier looked me up and down, and I looked away at the ground, unwilling to meet his eyes. Finally he said, "Follow me."

He walked me through the Special Forces command building, a confusing labyrinth of twists and turns and hallways and random rooms. Strings of beads and curtains acted as makeshift doors, and pictures of naked women adorned the walls.

Finally, we ended in a lounge of sorts, where two men sat on the floor propped up against the couch while they furiously tapped on video game controllers, their eyes glued to a big-screen television. Overflowing ashtrays and empty soda bottles littered the floor.

The soldier who showed me in said, "Dave, this soldier here needs some office supplies. He thinks this is Office Max or something."

Dave didn't bother to respond. He squirmed his torso as his character on the screen barely made his way past an obstacle, and replied, "What do you need?"

"Um, yes, well," I said, pulling out a folded piece of paper from my pocket. "Um, we could use some pens, you know, for writing. Uh, some thumbtacks, a printer cartridge, notebooks . . ."

"We don't have any of that stuff," Dave said before biting his lip as his character exploded. "Fuck it all to hell!" The soldier playing next to him laughed endlessly as his on-screen character continued forward in the game. Dave turned to me and said again, "We don't have any of that stuff."

"Okay, thank you very much for your time." I turned to go and walked straight into the chest of the soldier who had shown me in.

I was very impressed with the Green Berets. They were extremely cautious about handing out their office supplies. But that's the way it had to be. You didn't get to become a Green Beret by handing out office supplies at the drop of a hat.

Five days later I was on duty, monitoring the radio at about one in the morning, when the radio died. There were no more batteries. We were entirely dependent on our battalion airlifting us our supplies. And battalion wasn't pushing any more batteries out to us.

I had long been curious about what tasks were performed by our battalion headquarters. One thing I knew they didn't do was send out supplies. Every week I'd diligently prepare a supply request and send the order up to battalion. We'd eventually wait two months for a box of black ink pens. In the meantime, we were forced to start writing with crayons and random markers found in various stages of dehydration. We'd order a small box of pushpins for our area map, and instead we'd receive ten cases of strange greasing oil. We'd request parts to fix a vehicle, and instead we'd receive a large composition of parts that had nothing to do with the part that we'd requested. Our new strategy was to start ordering parts we didn't actually need in the hope that we'd eventually start receiving the parts we did need. We would steal AA batteries from our Walkmans to operate our night vision goggles. We'd steal medical supplies earmarked for the local Afghan population to treat our own soldiers.

My entire Army experience was of being ill equipped for whatever task was at hand.

Without the batteries the radio blinked off, and our communication with the outside world was mostly severed except for the finicky and sporadically working satellite phone with the broken antenna that wouldn't hold a charge no matter how long you plugged it in.

The next day Doc Walker asked, "Where's the radio?" He motioned to the empty desk, where I had a hand microphone attached to an empty Styrofoam cup with peeling tape. Doc Walker was uniformed in his flowing Afghan-man dress and had a raging little mess of a bloody nose. His head was tilted back below the cut in his shoulders, causing his spine to bend.

"How can you prove a nonexistent variable?" I asked. I bent his head back farther as I applied crumpled-up printer paper to the bleeding. I saw his spine buckle a bit more. I was hoping to see his spine snap. "I can't prove that something doesn't exist. You can't prove that something didn't occur." I was still stupefied by the battalion's request to offer evidence that we did, in fact, not have two satellite radio units. "I mean, I can understand a mistake being made over how many we have. But if I tell you we only have one radio, you have to accept that. What the hell am I supposed to offer as proof that we only have one? Take a picture of an empty table and offer the absence of a radio on the table as photographic proof of the nonexistence of the radio? You need to bend back a little bit more. You're not helping me at all here."

Doc Walker, our resident platoon medic, who had gone native, had been bloodied in a morning brawl in the sick call line, where the local villagers started a small fiasco, pushing and shoving one another to get into our base. Doc Walker and his group of medics pushed back, and before long a melee broke out that resulted in Doc's bloody nose. He came into the operations building, where I was pulling a diligent shift of radio guard on a radio that did not work, monitoring battalion traffic that could not be heard. Doc was complaining about the type of moral character that was seemingly inherent in the locals, that ill-bred sort who pushed and shoved to become first in line. They had to be put down, shown their place, he had come in stating, defending himself to accusations that had not been made. You never want to encourage a violent sick Afghan, he said. Those Hajis are no good, he had concluded through a pinched nose, swallowing some of the blood, which went down thick like mucus snot.

"Don't you have any Kleenex?" Doc asked as he dropped his back onto the radio desk, which was empty, knocking over my Styrofoam cup and relaxing his spine in the process.

"Don't worry, Doc! You'll live yet! As God as my witness, you'll live yet!" I stated firmly with a stern resolve worthy of a Hollywood World War II medic as I forcibly shoved a sheet of printer paper up his nose. "I have an idea!" I shrieked suddenly. "I could take a picture of the radio that we do have, the one that doesn't work, and send that to them and tell them that it's the one that we don't have! They ask for proof of the radio we don't have; I'll send them a picture of one and say, 'This is the radio we don't have!' Wouldn't that be hilarious?"

"Where's the radio?" Doc Walker asked again calmly, not responding to what was now my own howl of insane laughter.

"I told you—it doesn't exist," I said, backing up into the room and scanning our scarce supplies for some type of blotting agent that would work better than crinkled printer paper.

"No, the one that does exist," Doc replied.

"Oh, that one," I said distantly as I tore open a plastic knife-and-fork set that I'd found behind the coffeemaker. The plastic knife-and-fork set came with a napkin. "We don't have any batteries," I continued. I replaced the crimson-stained printer paper with the softer dinner napkin, quickly replugging his nostril, which made a little "pop" sound and gushed blood. "It's sleeping in my cot," I intoned as I finally leaned back against the wall, exhausted, but satisfied that my patient would live.

"What are you doing up then, if the radio isn't working?"

"I'm monitoring the other radio," I said, pointing to the empty desk.

"I thought that radio didn't exist," Doc replied.

"It doesn't!" I said, exasperated as all hell.

The previous night I had promptly announced that, since we had no radio, and my only job was to monitor the radio, I was therefore going to bed. The sergeant of the guard on the night shift, Sergeant Wu, reminded me of my first general order in the Army. The one that you have to repeat endlessly in loud bellowing yells in basic training, doing push-ups for slight infractions in its recanting to drill sergeants. It had been one of those silly conversations in which I was being discreetly guided toward developing the correct conclusion.

"What's your first general order?" Sergeant Wu stated.

"I don't remember," I replied.

"Sure you do," Sergeant Wu continued. "What's your first general order?"

"I shall not leave my post, nor will I leave my post without the proper relief of guard to relieve me of my post?" I offered hesitantly. It had been a long time since basic training.

"So what does that mean?"

"That I'm not to leave my post until I get someone to replace me?" I asked without any hint of sarcasm, truly and seriously struggling for the answer.

"And where's your position of duty?" Sergeant Wu responded in even tones, which made him sound as if he were teaching wise proverbs to an eager class of philosophy students in ancient Greece while sitting side by side with Socrates or Plato.

I mused over this for a while and then cautiously said, "Here?"

"Yes," Sergeant Wu said simply, as if I were a dumb deaf mute to be placated. He mouthed the words fully so I could attempt to read his lips because of my apparent lack of hearing. "Yes, this is your place of duty. Now what time does your relief come on at?"

I glanced at my watch. "In six hours."

"Then in six hours you can go back to bed."

Sergeant Wu walked around the operations tent, stirring his coffee while staring at various objects that offered no sane person any discernible or even momentary entertainment value. I pondered the implications of such a line of questioning. Finally I suggested, "But Sergeant Wu, the radio has no batteries. There are no batteries on the base camp. My job is to listen to radio traffic, but there's no radio traffic to listen to."

Sergeant Wu nodded his head forward so that he could look at me straight, his glasses on the bridge of his nose now facing the floor. "Yes, but this, this is your place of duty." He offered a slight smile and left me to my contemplations.

I prodigiously affirmed my duties in the hour after his departure. I sat intensely in the quiet, ready to pounce should I hear our call sign emanate from the radio that did not work. I knew that I would not hear our call sign, but in fear of being in dereliction of my duty, I pretended that it was a feasible thing to hear at any moment.

When the morning shift came to relieve me, long after I had removed the radio from the operations building and placed it in my bed,

I refused to relinquish my position. I took on a sarcastic dedication to my job and stated loudly to one and all (the morning traffic of sergeants and privates who entered the operations tent mostly for the coffee I had prepared) that I would not be leaving my radio guard shift until batteries arrived at our base.

"That could be weeks," Ryan told me as he stirred his coffee.

"If it's weeks, it's weeks. So be it. This is war, man. I don't have time to play games. If I lose a little sleep over it, big deal. Greater men have lost more for their country." It was after Ryan had left that Doc Walker came in gushing blood all over my floor.

All afternoon I kept handing out sticky notes to various passing soldiers, relaying messages for Sergeant Wu that God had called and he needed to get back in touch with him. They'd glance at the sticky note and then up at me, all spread out on the wooden bench, the hand microphone that allowed us to speak into the radios next to my ear, the hand microphone attached to a Styrofoam cup. "Could you pass the message?" was all I would say.

I killed a chunk of time pretending I was stabbed. I'd sit doubled over at the wooden table writhing in pain, gasping for last breaths until someone entered the operations building. Then I'd hand them a sticky note with my last dying breath and ask them to pass on the message to Sergeant Wu that God was calling for him. I'd point lamely behind me to my Styrofoam cup as if it was a big hassle to have to answer it all fucking day long. Like I said, something about the Army made me lose all pretense of maturity.

Eventually, when Sergeant Wu came in around seven that night with a handful of sticky notes gathered from various individuals and stood over me quietly, arms folded, waiting for an explanation, all I could do was offer that I hadn't yet thought the joke that far ahead, and in fact I had no idea what God wanted to talk to him about.

I lasted only thirty-six hours before Ryan came in and found me passed out on the wooden bench.

Chapter 24

A PERPETUAL NEVER-ENDING TOUR OF DUTY

Amanda lurches drunkenly on roller skates through the courtyard with her blue bathrobe trailing in the wind behind her. Her face is lit with the glow of happy goofy nonsensical fun. Her perky but petite breasts protrude as enticing taunting shapes from the bathrobe. That's what I imagine.

My eyes squint, scanning the e-mail lines, focusing, concentrating, blocking out the background noise of my fellow soldiers, who are gathered around the terminal next to me hooting and hollering and loudly condemning the unattractive women who e-mail them on various on-line dating sites. Their mocking tone is on the periphery of my consciousness like some distant sound during a waking dream: "I like to have fun and hang out with friends and family! Bitch, shut the fuck up! You like to take my cock in your mouth is what you like to do!"

I keep seeing Amanda making out with other women at the club. She's drunk. She's introducing herself to men and kissing them. As I read her e-mail explaining her wild Friday night and her drunken bathrobe roller derby, I feel a quick tightening of my throat.

I'm jealous.

I sigh and move to the next e-mail. The flies swarm about my face. Firebase Dizzy is infested with flies. Hundreds of them fill the room, buzzing and flirting with my mouth and nose. The computer, old and decrepit, hums loudly like a washing machine on spin cycle. I spit as a fly dive-bombs my face. I wait for forty-five seconds as the blue bar slowly lurches forward and then retreats and then moves forward again as it loads my next e-mail. I spend a lot of time monitoring the blue bar. I look over at the waiting cot. There's a line of people to use the e-mail. We have only thirty minutes to use e-mail. And the blue bar is moving so slowly.

These are my evenings. Sitting in four- and five-hour blocks, staring at the ceiling, lying on the concrete floor or on the cot, swatting at flies, using the computer for thirty-minute increments after arguments about waiting and who signed on first and then going outside for a smoke and all the while listening to an ever-changing cast of soldiers at the next terminal sign on to their online dating services and disparage the quality of women who contact them. Some have moved onto the next stage, the phones. They sit in the corner whispering quiet laughs as they try to persuade their women to send them naked photos. Many succeed.

I have an online profile. I'm talking to women online. But I never succeed in asking for nude photos. I don't even ask. It seems rude. Instead, we have nice respectable conversations in which I slowly learn about them and ask them interesting and thoughtful questions that they say are interesting and thoughtful.

What do I want from everyone?

Do I want to be inundated with grateful love letters acknowledging the sacrifice of my wasted year in Afghanistan?

No. Whenever anyone offers me a compliment or thanks me for being over here, I quiet up and don't respond. Or I make some sarcastic comment designed to make them feel silly for showering me with praise.

Mostly, my e-mails don't get a reply.

Next e-mail.

Eric went to a movie with Sean. It was a really good movie, and I should go and see it. Everyone e-mails me about all the things I should be doing that I'm missing. Parties, movies, great nights at the bar, road trips, camping trips. It's a perpetual year of missing everything.

The guys next to me are making fun of a woman with crooked teeth. All these guys are married or have girlfriends. What are they doing online anyway?

There's an article on the MSN home page. "Bush says a resounding no to reinstatement of the draft." People e-mail me about this. Seems some people back home are worried about the draft. *God, no, don't let us have to go into the Army!*

I'm glad Bush doesn't want to reinstate the draft. It's about time for him to do something right. The very concept of the draft, of people being forced to fight the often unnecessary conflicts the United States puts itself into, is abhorrent.

Hey, buddy, don't worry about it. You stay back in the States; I'll go to Iraq too, when I'm done in Afghanistan. In fact, I'll stay past the three years I volunteered for and ruin my life further and ruin all my plans so you don't have to go; okay?

Diego taps me on the shoulder. Sergeant Stephens has some news for all of us short-timers who think we're getting out.

Ryan, Diego, Devon, Cox, and I all sit at the picnic table, anxiously awaiting word. Sergeant Stephens is wired to the underground rumor networks, having friends scattered to all corners of the Army, and is often our source of late-breaking news. He is our CNN. Sergeant Santiago sits next to us, taunting us that we are all going to be kept in the Army perpetually. "You can't die here! You know why you can't die here? Because you're going to Iraq! You're supposed to die over in Iraq!"

I feel bad news coming. It's like a distant storm, when you feel the rain in the air before it starts to fall.

Sergeant Stephens comes out of the operations center with a big smile on his face. He always has a big smile on his face when he is the bearer of other people's bad news.

"So, fucking 5/2 is getting disbanded as soon as we get back to Hawaii. What this means is that they're going to send you to another unit to finish out your tour in the Army. What this means is that any unit you arrive at, they're going to hook you up with whatever brigade is deploying so they can fill up empty slots for the deployment first. And almost every division in the Army has some brigade that will be deploying within the next year of our return. What this means is that you all better start getting some combat experience soon, because you're going to need it when you arrive in Iraq."

I look over at Devon, Diego, Ryan, and Cox. They're silent, their mouths hanging open as they contemplate this news. Sergeant Santiago is taunting us and laughing at us. "Ha! Ha! You're going to Iraq! You're going to Iraq!" I want to shove some gravel down his throat until he chokes on it and shuts the fuck up.

Long ago, my mother told me an interesting anecdote about crawdads. Put a couple in a bucket and when one starts to climb out, the others will gang up and pull it back down. Instead of cooperative teamwork so they can all get out, or at least a few of them, they spend all their time ensuring that they will all suffer.

The Army is a lot like that.

Cox is the first to leave, saying, "Well, fuck it; I have a year and a half when we rotate back anyway. Thought maybe I'd get lucky. Whatever. I already knew I was going."

Devon has lost his sense of humor. I start to say something to him in an attempt to lighten the mood, and he shoots me a look as he stumbles off fuming. Devon's good mood in Afghanistan has been firmly rooted in his knowledge that he'll soon be able to attend college for any of the thirty different occupations he has been perpetually considering.

"Rico's going to Iraq! Diego's going to Iraq!" Sergeant Santiago shrieks, barely able to contain his glee that our future plans are suddenly ruined.

"The hell I am," I state flatly, suddenly angry.

"Hey, you signed on for it! That's a fucking eight-year contract; read the fine-fucking-print, soldier! You didn't sign on for three years; you signed on for eight years," says Sergeant Santiago, with a big smile on his face.

"Yeah, but my recruiter said that the eight-year thing would never happen. He said that had never happened and would never happen. That it was only for World War III."

"It's worse than World War III," Diego says calmly in a manner that almost frightens me. "This is the war on terrorism. This war doesn't end. It's like Orwell in *1984*. It's a diffuse enemy. It's Afghanistan; now it's Iraq; next year it'll be Iran."

"Doesn't matter; you signed it!" Sergeant Santiago cheerfully exclaims, acting now like a child.

"So I gotta be fair with the Army, but the Army doesn't have to be fair with me? As far as I'm concerned, the Army's in violation of its own contract. Thus, the entire contract is null and void," I say. I can't understand Sergeant Santiago's glee about our situation. He is supposed to be my friend. He even wants to get out of the Army.

"What has the Army done to you?" Sergeant Santiago sarcastically asks. "Was the Army mean to Johnny?" he says in a whiny caricature. "Did the Army make you go to Afghanistan and act like a man for once? Did they make you pull guard and make you do push-ups?"

I haven't felt as close to crying at any point within the past decade as I do at this moment.

"Well," Diego says, finally speaking. "I gave the Army five years of my life. And I'm glad I did it. But I'll be damned if I'm going to sacrifice another two years of my life at the whim of some fucking officer in the Pentagon who has arbitrarily decided that he thinks my life is his to sacrifice. I've got too much to do. Unlike the rest of you clowns, I have plans with my life, and I don't intend on wasting them here in the goddamn United States fucking Army."

"I don't think you have much choice in the matter," states Sergeant Santiago smugly, his arms folded, beaming a big smile from ear to ear.

"Sure I do," says Diego indifferently. "I'll just go AWOL."

Sergeant Santiago suddenly turns from laughing clown to angry drill sergeant, "What the fuck did you just say?"

"I said I'm going to go AWOL if I have to go to Iraq."

"You really would, wouldn't you—you piece of fucking shit!"

"If they extend me past my five years I signed up for, yeah. I'm really going to consider it."

"So you'd just throw your life away. Everything you've worked for, you'd throw away just like that."

Diego shrugs indifferently, "I've been all over the world, Sergeant.

There's lots of good countries out there that I consider to be just as good as the United States. I've always wanted to live in another country. This way it would force my hand. Might almost be a good thing. Be the impetus that I've always needed to leave. To tell the truth, I don't even put the United States in my top-five favorite countries."

Sergeant Santiago doesn't say anything for a moment and then angrily exclaims, "And you're a fucking traitor, too! Not only are you a coward! But you're also a fucking traitor to the United States!"

"Sergeant, first of all," Diego says, doing his best to remain calm and collected, "I'm not a traitor. I'm here, aren't I? I just consider the Iraq war to be immoral and unjust. I've always thought that way. I couldn't in good conscience participate in a war that I feel is morally wrong."

"YOU DON'T GET A FUCKING CHOICE! THE ARMY DOESN'T FUCKING CARE WHAT YOU THINK!" Sergeant Santiago explodes. He looks as if he wants to hit Diego but is barely restraining himself. Diego has crossed the line. Santiago is a subversive soul, but one who retains a loyalty unfamiliar to most soldiers. Soldiers suffer, but it's their job to suffer. He can handle criticism, even appreciate it, as long as it is within the context of continuing one's overall responsibility. But once somebody mentions going AWOL . . .

"And I don't care what the Army fucking thinks!" Diego screams back at him.

Sergeant Santiago is furious. He walks back and forth in half circles. "So you would violate a contract. That's the type of man you are. You gave your word that you would fight, and then you'd become a motherfucking coward! This after you signed up for the fucking Army while the Army's at war!"

"I signed up when we were going to war with Afghanistan! Iraq wasn't even in the picture! Who the fuck would've thought that we'd hit two countries, one after the other! I never would've signed up if I knew Iraq was even a possibility! I go back on my word to the Army, or I participate in something I don't believe in. To me, going back on my word is the lesser of two evils. That's why the world is so fucked up, why Nazis happened in World War II, because everyone's just following orders and fights without thinking!"

Sergeant Santiago starts to walk away and then suddenly turns abruptly and moves back toward Diego, his red face inches away from Diego's, throwing spittle into his eyes, "STAND THE FUCK UP AND GET AT PARADE REST! YOU'RE TALKING TO A NONCOMMISSIONED FUCKING OFFICER! GET THIS THROUGH YOUR FUCKING HEAD! YOU DON'T HAVE A CHOICE! YOU DO WHAT WE FUCKING TELL YOU TO DO! YOUR LIFE BELONGS TO US! I'M SO FUCKING TIRED OF WHINY BITCHES LIKE YOU INTERPRETING EVERYTHING AND ANALYZING EVERYTHING AND TRYING TO DECIDE WHAT THEY WANT TO DO! YOU DON'T GET A GODDAMN MOTHERFUCKING CHOICE, YOU COWARDLY PIECE OF SHIT SORRY EXCUSE FOR AN AMERICAN!"

Diego stands up straight, his eyes forward and holding back tears, his hands behind his back. All he says is "Roger, Sergeant" with tense lips and a firm immobile face. I stare straight ahead, trying to be inconspicuous.

Diego flees, leaving me and Sergeant Santiago at the picnic table. Everyone else gone, Sergeant Santiago is quiet. He calms down and sits and looks over at me and smiles and says, "Sorry, but there's no excuse for shit like that. I've got a baby girl at home I've never even met. You think I want to stay here?"

"No, I suppose not."

"It's not about us, Rico. It's not about us. And this generation of soldiers seems to have forgotten that. They join up for college money or because they don't think about it, and they raise their hand and promise to defend America, and then when things turn out differently than they had planned, they complain and whine and want to leave. I hate whiny fucking soldiers."

"Yeah, me too!" I say, hoping he has temporarily forgotten all the times I've whined incessantly.

"Look at the World War II generation," Sergeant Santiago continues. "We're sitting here doing jack shit, playing video games and watching movies, while they had to storm the beaches of Normandy. We've lost some of that valor."

"I think there were these soldiers in World War II though," I tenderly offer, testing the waters of his condition. "You just don't hear about them because there weren't the Oliver Stone movies that showed soldiers complaining and smoking pot in Vietnam."

"No, I think you're wrong."

"Okay," is all I can say.

It was too late for Diego, though. Diego stated that this supposed war in Afghanistan was secondary to his immediate and more important war with the U.S. Army. Of course, a war against the United States couldn't be fought directly. This had to be a covert war, using nontraditional tactics and strategies.

So Diego became a *civilian* recruiter. It became his goal to cost the United States over a million dollars. He had read an article about how important it had become for the Army to retain seasoned veterans. The article stated that the cost of recruiting a soldier was approximately fifteen thousand dollars when you factored in recruiters' salaries and rent for recruiting offices. The cost of basic training when you factored in drill sergeants' salaries and training ammunition and food and initial uniforms was almost one hundred thousand dollars per soldier. All of this, to say nothing of sign-on bonuses and college money. Every time a soldier left and the Army had to train a new soldier, the costs were enormous. But to play it safe, to be sure he would cost the United States Army a million dollars, Diego figured he would have to entice ten people who were going to reenlist to become civilians instead.

Sergeant Pauley, knowing that Diego had been to college and worked in the real world, wanted to know what he thought of his chances of being hired by a police department. He thought that the skills he supposedly had after being trained to kill would make him a shoo-in. Diego knew that police departments weren't looking for soldiers, but rather social workers, and that they'd be more attracted to an English major who could write and communicate and deescalate situations than to a gung ho soldier who had an itchy trigger finger. So, of course, he immediately told Sergeant Pauley that it was an excellent plan and that surely he would be immediately hired by a police department of his choice, even without a college degree. In fact, Diego told him, he'd be surprised if they don't ask him to go to S.W.A.T. right away.

Private Mulbeck thought that maybe he could get an associate's degree at the local community college in Oklahoma and become a combat journalist. Diego told him that he had several friends in college who had become combat photojournalists and that most media outlets cared little for your skill with a camera or your ability to convey emotions and capture ideas with pictures, but rather cared only that their cameramen had seasoned experience in a designated combat zone. He was a sure thing, Diego told him. Best bet is to get out of the Army and enlist in a community college journalism class with a side interest in photography as soon as fucking possible.

Diego saw himself as a prophet. He gave rousing speeches on the picnic table outside the operations tent on the evils of the Army, "Do you want to live as an indentured servant for the rest of your life? Your own life as a martyr to whatever war the Army wants to fight next? Never being able to live where you want to live, to dress how you want to dress, never to exert control over your own life? Don't be fearful of the choices the civilian world offers you! It is not a thing to be feared, but a liberation!"

During dinner, when younger soldiers asked him about the civilian world, he downplayed the difficulty of making it in the real world and pretended that it was an easier place than in the Army, "Oh yeah, first year out of the Army, you'll be making at least twice as much as you make here. Definitely. Without a doubt, man. Without a doubt. And that's without college."

The thing of it was, the soldiers in our platoon were very fearful.

They were scared.

Not of Taliban and Al Qaeda. Not of being shot.

They were scared of the world outside the Army, of being a civilian. Most had joined at anywhere from eighteen to twenty-one years of age and had already spent a few years in the Army. Now, approaching their midtwenties and contemplating their future opportunities, they were very afraid.

What would they do? How would they make money?

They had made good money in the Army—not as much as they would have made had they already graduated from college and entered the workforce, but money that would be hard to make in their first few years as a civilian while they went to college or learned a trade. And many already had children of their own and new cars with high monthly payments that they were able to afford because the Army provided for their housing and health care. Even though so many of these soldiers hated the day-to-day work that they had to perform in the Army, and despised the Army as an organization, they slowly convinced themselves when it came closer to reenlistment time that it wasn't that bad, and they tried to forget how much they had previously complained about the whole mess.

They had vague plans to own and operate ranches or to start bars or dance clubs or to speculate in the stock market and retire early. But they held general equivalency degrees and high school diplomas that had been barely obtained. They were keenly aware of their insecurity about how to achieve these goals, and they bit and chewed on this anxiety openly and frequently, asking for information, advice, and suggestions whenever possible.

Diego found his ten converts to the civilian world. He figured he cost the Army a million dollars. He could have had eleven, but he had thrown one back like a fish that's too small to eat.

Private Damien was a quiet inner-city kid who wasn't known for his intelligence, but he was "squared away" in that he always did as he was told and never created problems. Private Damien had been very poor and had come from a series of foster homes; he thus took to the comfort and security the Army provided him rather intensely. He had just gotten back from Kandahar and was now in rare form, bragging about the current offer on the table: a ten-thousand-dollar reenlistment bonus for four years. He was smiling from ear to ear, just beaming at the idea of ten G's. That was a lot of money to a kid like himself. He felt he was doing all right for himself in the Army. He had some money in the bank, a new car, and, most important, a place to live and food on the table. And he was staying out of trouble.

Then Diego entered the room.

"Ten thousand dollars for four years? After taxes, what's that? Two thousand dollars a year? You're going to sell your fucking soul for two thousand dollars a year? Jesus, man, you must have fucking low self-esteem if you consider yourself that goddamn worthless! For fuck's sake, you could make two grand with a part-time job for a few months as a civilian. No reason to bend over and take it up the ass for the same price! You realize that while you're cooling your heels in the Army, all the other people your age are going to college and in about six years will be making twice as much as you? More than a million dollars more than you over the course of their lives? Damien, listen."

Diego got down on his knees so he could look Damien in the eyes as he was sitting on his cot. His face had grown slack, and the joy had leaked out. Diego took his hands in his own and said, eye to eye, "People who stay in the Army for life? They're pathetic. It's sad is what it is. Very very sad. Get the fuck out and do something with your life. Go to college, rob a bank, do whatever the fuck you want. But for the love of God, don't waste your life in an organization that doesn't give a shit about you. Because that's what it comes down to. They tell you they care about you, but they don't. They don't even care if you die or not, except that it makes them look bad when you do. And every time you believe that lie, that they care about you, and you in turn care for them by committing years of your life to them, you're destroying your soul." Diego had a real flair for melodrama. "Piece by piece you're destroying your soul. Your integrity. You're telling the Universe, 'I don't matter. I'm worthless. I'll stay in the Army because that's all that I'm good for.' Don't be that pathetic guy. Don't." Diego let his hands go and stood to rise.

As Diego turned to go he stopped and looked back at Private Damien, who looked as if somebody had just smashed everything he had worked so hard to earn for himself and had been proud of. As a matter of fact, that was exactly what had just happened. Diego immediately realized that he was a terrible son-of-a-bitch bastard.

"Hey, Damien, I was just joking, man. No, that's cool, man. Ten thousand is a lot of money. You should do it. The Army needs good soldiers like you, man." Diego smiled and gave him an exaggerated thumbs-up. He left the room with an image of an extremely impressionable young man who didn't know what to believe anymore.

DON'T KNOW WHEN I'M COMING HOME:
AN E-MAIL TO MOM

Dear Mom:

I've got some bad news. I've been told that I'm going to be stop-lossed when I get back from Afghanistan, which means I don't know when I'll be getting out of the Army. Don't go calling senators or anything; that'll just make things worse for me. Nothing's for certain in the Army until it happens—you know that. The rumor mill around here is worse than a housewife's sewing circle, and plans are devised and then dropped or changed, so I'm trying not to completely freak out until it happens. Besides, there's not much I can do about it anyway.

Suddenly I hate it over here. My entire ability to handle this was all based on the fact that four months after we got back to Hawaii I was getting out. I've just lost all my motivation.

I'm okay on food; the SF guys have a lot of food here, so don't worry about sending some for a while.

Things are pretty quiet, so don't worry. Everywhere they send us they keep saying we're going to see action, and nothing ever happens. We go on patrols, and the most that happens is that we find guys with guns who aren't supposed to have them, and we detain them for a while or something. The SF guys go on these missions where they're airlifted deeper into Oruzgan, and they come back with stories about killing all these people, but that's like in Cougar Base's area or something. I don't know.

The point is, don't worry. Nothing's going on here. I'd be surprised if anything happens this entire deployment.

I'll write soon.

Love,
Johnny

Chapter 25

THE VIRGIN MARY TRADING CARD

And then the road blows up.

Instant migraine.

Instant blood thumping in your ears.

Instant depression.

Instant anger.

Instant hate.

It was neat how swiftly they were packaging emotions these days. This was fast-food rage. Take it and go.

Freemont was slightly aware of the screaming that faded in and out between the shrill ringing in his ears. The god-awful screaming. And when he wiped the blood from his eyes that poured in runny drippy rivulets, he was vaguely aware of the soldiers tossed into nearby ravines from the explosion who were slowly rising to stagger. He was vaguely aware of yelling and confusion and of no one being sure what to do.

What he remembers most is the uniquely sobering smell of burning gasoline on flesh.

Word got back to us at Dizzy from Cougar Base that Freemont said blowing up had been the best experience of his life. Nothing beat blowing up. You hadn't lived until you had been blown up. He felt sorry for all the rest of us who hadn't yet had the opportunity to be blown up. All of us sad, sorry, non-blown-up motherfuckers.

Freemont was the .50 caliber gunner on top of the Humvee when it exploded. Strengthened reinforced metal crinkled like Christmas wrapping paper. He was wired after that, always kinetic and tense, asking to go on patrols, hoping for a repeat of near death so he could choke on his new death habit.

We heard about Freemont and Miller and Adams over the radio while watching a cheerleader movie, lounging in beach chairs that surrounded the small flickering television in our narrow command center. The natural sounds of movement had been muted while everyone sat transfixed in a strict attention posture that bordered on meditation, our smiles anxious and happy that something was occurring. The only sound other than the static garble from the radio was the anxious rustling of fabric that moved with subtle shifts in position. It was as if we were in an earlier era and were listening to the news from the war front while gathered around our radio.

It was one of those miracles of physics that Freemont hadn't been utterly consumed. Like the stories you hear of the skydiver whose chute doesn't open and who hits the ground but lives. Or the freaky transference of accelerated momentum and kinetic energy being released and distributed at randomly perfect angles so that every once in a while someone manages to walk away from an unopened chute breaking only half the bones in their body. Or a .50-caliber gunner escapes death when his Humvee is blown into confetti. Three double-stacked antitank mines have a way of doing that.

Miller wasn't so lucky. Miller had been in the passenger seat. Miracles of physics hadn't helped Miller. Miller's body just popped like a balloon pierced with a needle and had covered Freemont with his bubbling, boiling, gooey, still-sizzling guts. You don't forget hot frying sticky intestines that belonged to your friend splattering you in the face. Miller's body slime had a slightly bitter acidic taste, I'm told. Second platoon had been forced to walk around a one-hundred-meter area picking up little pieces of Miller: an arm over here, a leg over there. Specialist Miller left Afghanistan fitting neatly in a trash bag.

Sergeant Adams went differently. His body parts hadn't been violently coughed out of the dying Humvee in all directions, but instead had melted and dissolved into the passenger seat. Sergeant Adams had been transformed into a thin little layer of gooey gloss that kind of coated the rear of the vehicle like a factory-installed layer of protective sealant.

That's how it was. Sometimes you became chunky pieces of flesh and bone debris littering the landscape; other times you became glue.

This realization requires some adjustments. Some fine-tuning to one's thinking. A realignment forcing you to realize that in the same reality where you are presently alive there are now people you used to know and laugh with and joke with and sometimes drink with who are now a pile of bloody body parts.

It's easier to make this adjustment if you forget. Pretend they never existed at all. Kill the remnants of their spirit so that along with their physical body, nothing at all remains of them. That's the way to approach it.

Over at Cougar Base, Specialist Davis, who was supposed to have taken Miller's place in the passenger seat and by all rights should have been the one who died, felt guilty for being alive. Typical survivor syndrome. Nothing new.

Davis raided Miller's clothes before they were immediately confiscated after word of Miller's death came across the radio. It was strange, Davis would state later, how quickly they tore down his cot and his little area and packed away his things, erasing all evidence of his existence and thereby fully completing his death not thirty minutes after he had been blown up. He wore Miller's boxer shorts for the rest of the deployment. He figured wearing his clothes meant that he couldn't get hit. Lighting doesn't strike twice in the same spot; right? As long as he kept Miller's residual ass molecules close to him, he would be safe.

But a day or so goes by, and you adapt and get back into the *Sopranos* series and the video games that you were watching before you were so rudely interrupted, and you dismiss it as a soldier's fate.

What is there to do but live and die, he was a soldier and so am I . . .

So then you're returning from the showers in flip-flops, whistling a tune that's caught in your brain. You cross past the gym and the Special Forces building that's off limits, and the auto garage and the jail, and you get to the small corner of the base that's assigned to your command center and the next-door cement barracks, and everyone's outside, congregated like flocking birds. There's a palpable, sickly, greasy tension in the air. Some are happy and excited, and others are scared, and others are nervous, and everyone is starry-eyed.

Something shifts in tone. People speak a bit quieter as if it would be improper to speak at normal volumes. Something shifts in attentiveness, because for the first time in a while people are paying attention to what you are actually saying and not just waiting for their turn to speak. Something shifts in their eyes, which open a little wider and don't scan the background as much.

While you were jerking off in the fly- and spider-infested shower ten minutes ago, second platoon hit another improvised explosive device. Four soldiers are seriously injured, status unknown. A medevac would've been there sooner if not for the attack by Taliban that followed the explosion. While you were cumming all over the floor and swatting flies, someone you know was screaming as he crawled from a fiery Humvee that smelled of overcooked flesh and burning gasoline.

After that, people started praying.

But as Specialist Ryan periodically pointed out, there were more of them praying to Allah out here in the wastelands of the world than there were of us praying to Jesus. And personally, I had never believed in God and couldn't imagine a God who would have so little integrity as to let you into Heaven after a lifetime of disinterest. A few times I had wanted to believe in him, but at this point it would've been a sacrifice of ego to believe. I had always been confronted with the "just in case" reason for belief. Why not believe just in case? At least your ass will be covered if you die. But I could never have respected a God who would cover me under his insurance policy for a payment of faith that amounted to little more than me hedging my bets.

But still, there was Freemont and that freaky unanticipated survival. Maybe it was all predestination. Maybe the guys who died had a bad feeling in the back of their gut ever since we'd left Hawaii. I had never had a bad feeling in my gut, so I was safe. The next day, wondering if the guys who got hit had bad feelings in their guts, I started to get a bad feeling in my gut; so, of course, I quickly disregarded this theory. I couldn't believe in theories that might lead to my eventual demise.

We desperately searched for talismans and tested them with an extremely scientific method. Sergeant Kroeger wore a crucifix around his neck and his rosary loosely on his pants like a low-riding pistol. We used to joke that he was a real quick draw with the Holy Jesus Spirit. He said that the ghosts of his family, of his grandfathers and uncles who had all been soldiers, walked beside him on missions to protect him. I made persistent fun of him for that. Really made the guy feel like shit. I didn't want him to be secure or feel confident. He needed to feel antsy and fidgety like all the rest of us. It was no fair not being afraid of dying.

We granted supernatural powers of protection to plastic baubles and various pieces of crap we found that didn't fit into the texture of our environment. They were our toy cereal box protections.

Send in five UPC proofs of purchase and two dollars, and you get to keep your life.

Private Allison had a plastic pink whistle purchased at a bazaar in Ghazni. Private Darrenowsky had a little girl's fake emerald clasp, both hollow and plastic. Private Jerome had an orange shoelace he had found on the side of a mountain.

A pink plastic whistle can be the difference between life and death.

And while I didn't believe in the prohibitive powers of my Virgin Mary bubble-gum trading cards, I loved the absurdity of an atheist going into war surrounded by fake Jesus Fire. I had been running around the firebase wildly yelling that I was invulnerable to all harms and ill wishes because of the wall of Jesus Fire that surrounded me at all times.

That was my supposed protection: the Virgin Mary. My real protection was my sense of absurdity. God wouldn't dare kill a person with a healthy sense of the absurd.

And after we had found our protective charms, we started the mental gymnastics required to create the accompanying arguments to justify why it couldn't be us who died next. We made quiet prayers to God to make it be the guy next to us next time.

We were too young, too old, too needy, too enthusiastic, too intelligent. There were so many reasons why it shouldn't be us but the guy next to us instead.

They say that soldiers in combat form a bond, a bond so tight that they would gladly give their life if only to save their fellow brothers.

That was some serious bullshit. The truth? I would've gladly handed the Grim Reaper a fellow soldier to save my own skin.

But some soldiers *were* that honorable. Sergeant Santiago was one. Sergeant First Class Derrens was another. He kept walking around the firebase saying how he had to protect us; he couldn't let anyone hurt his soldiers. He had to be hard on us so that we'd follow procedure because he was trying to save us, to bring us home in one piece.

And then, after the superstitious protections, the negotiation started. The deals. The back-room trades. Lieutenant Michael had always said that the one thing he feared most was getting shot in the face. He didn't care if he got shot anywhere else, and he would agree to be shot anywhere else, just please Lord don't let him lose his pretty-boy good looks. That was the deal. That was the negotiation. Then we got the call from Cougar Base a week or so after the second IED about Lieutenant Michael taking an RPG through the bottom of his neck and out the side of his face. He lived. But his face was ruined.

Specialist Travis didn't mind getting shot in the face. He didn't mind getting shot in the leg or even losing a limb. All he cared about was living. He just didn't want to die. So a few weeks after Michael got hit, Cougar Base called to say that Specialist Travis got blown up real good, too.

You named your injury, your pain, your harm; that's the way it was working out on this deployment. On other deployments it might be random; on this one you got to choose what happened to you by stating what you didn't want to have happen to you. It was the reverse-injury deployment. Sometimes they were straightforward injury deployments; sometimes they were reverse-injury deployments. It always changed. It was good to figure out which one you were on as soon as possible.

The fear was that you would name your destruction in a moment of weakness, in a moment of silliness when you'd comment slyly about how much it would suck if your balls got blown off. Consequently, I stated loudly to the entire world that the thing I feared most was to get a nonlethal nondebilitating gunshot wound to the arm or leg that was just enough to take me back home and out of the Army, but after a small bit of hassle—not enough to cause any real long-term damage. Please God, if anything happens to me, just please don't make it a small gunshot wound to the leg or the arm that is just enough to take me out of the Army but not cause any permanent damage!

Our newly arrived platoon leader, Lieutenant Mitch, repeatedly told everyone that the thing he feared most was to lose his pinky toe. He could die, get shot in the face, lose his nuts—but Lord, just let him keep that pinky toe. So we made these announcements to the world and then held our breath patiently over the days of boredom and the lulls of activity, and then reaffirmed them to ourselves weeks later in silent moments of the night as if we had to renew our vows every so often.

Lord? Are you listening? Remember the pinky toe agreement, Lord; that's all I ask. Just remember the deal we worked out about the pinky toe. But then, over at Cougar Base, Cusher died. Cusher had carried all types of good-luck charms and had made a very solid agreement about getting a nice safe ass shot injury. The consensus was to treat the Cusher situation like a statistical anomaly, an aberration. And then Steadman went blind in both eyes, and Droper and Kielman got blown up and lost legs, it just seemed that there was nothing to do about it all.

Those Cougar Base soldiers were doomed. God must have hated 2nd Platoon. And we would all be wise to keep our distance from the 2nd Platoon soldiers, who might taint us with their bad luck.

And I kept my Virgin Mary bubble-gum trading cards.

Chapter 26

WHY I NEEDED TO DIE

"**You need to die,**" Sergeant Santiago says.

"I know!" I reply. I look at the ground, somewhat sad that I'm not dead and that if I were, I wouldn't be able to see the eulogy Sergeant Santiago is composing for me.

"It'll be a thing of beauty, Rico. An absolute thing of beauty. I'm going to tell the chaplain to fuck off. Shit, sir, that motherfucker didn't believe in God! You know they're going to have a church service for you. You know they will."

"Yeah," I say, somewhat distracted. "You gotta stop them, Sergeant Santiago. You can't let them do that to me. That'll disgrace everything I've stood for."

I'm bothered that they would give me a proper military tribute. Extremely bothered.

"And what is it that you stand for, Rico?" Sergeant Santiago asks.

"I don't know," I shrug, completely disinterested. "A bunch of stupid shit. Maybe nothing. I don't know. That's not the point."

"So what's the point?"

"The point," I say with growing concern, "is that you have to promise me to tell them that I wasn't a good soldier. I don't want any of that shit about me suddenly being a war hero because I'm dead; I'm this selfless guy who sacrificed for everybody and shit."

"I'm telling you, Rico. Thing of beauty! Thing of beauty! I'll stand up and say, 'Rico actually didn't like most of you. And he didn't like the

Army. And he didn't want to be over here, and he damn sure didn't want to die for his country. In fact, he would have preferred that one of you die instead. But you didn't, and he did. That's his crummy luck.' "

"Oh! That's good! That's good!" I say, excited about the idea of my death. "And don't let them sing 'Amazing Grace' or anything retarded like that!"

"What do you want them to play?" Sergeant Santiago asks.

I think over my response to this for a while and then respond, " 'Karma Chameleon.' I want you to play 'Karma Chameleon' by Culture Club. I want everybody outside in a solemn formation around the chaplain, heads down, hands folded, eyes averted, mumbling, 'Karma karma karma chamellleon . . .' "

"It's done!" Sergeant Santiago says, clapping his hands and relaxing onto his cot. "Now all you need to do is die."

"Yep, sounds like it," I say more to myself than to Sergeant Santiago as I slide my hands in my pockets and lie back against the cement wall of the barracks. "Now all I have to do is die."

A day earlier, an overcast November day, we'd had the funeral service for Cusher, the most recent Cougar soldier to die. The wind blew in fiercely above the mountains, dropping to a mere breeze by the time it hit Firebase Dizzy.

Local Afghans, propped up on trucks, stared in a daze at our base as if it were an entertainment, their bodies whipped by the dust and the wind. Starving dogs limped by on the overbaked desert hardpan.

It was just another day.

The Special Forces soldiers, having no tolerance for the Army, retreated into the shadows and the secret hovels and rooms. The rest of us more unfortunate regular soldiers were gathered in the center of one of the many courtyards surrounded by the dilapidated buildings that sprouted from the base, squinting in the sunlight as we listened to the funeral service. (Sunglasses had been forbidden for the general's visit; he mustn't know that sometimes we wore sunglasses to protect our eyes from the light.)

The brown leather-skinned chaplain was singing "Amazing Grace" in a craggy off-key voice while a barely audible murmur that faintly resembled the melody of "Amazing Grace" issued forth from us men. We were soldiers. We didn't sing. We were embarrassed to be singing.

"Come on, guys, this is bullshit! Cusher's dead. The least you can do is sing! He's dead, and you're all too fucking embarrassed to sing," someone said, although who I could not tell because I had my head down, staring at the ground out of embarrassment from singing.

This resulted in a brief momentary increase in volume and at least a few audible words from a few of the braver, less self-conscious soldiers among us, who, quickly realizing that they were alone in actually attempting to sing the song, reverted to the shared incoherent mumbling.

We finished, and there was a pause that was meant to be solemn and filled with contemplative thoughts about Cusher. However, the truth was that most of us were distracted, wondering how much longer this awkward performance was going to continue before we could return to our PlayStation games and movies. Sergeant Santiago wrinkled his nose and concentrated on wrinkling his nose. Specialist Ryan kicked the dirt around his feet back and forth, making neat little piles with the toe of his boot. I played with the buttons on my belt, half raising my head to see if anyone else was taking this moment of silence seriously.

The general, with his white hair and heavily creased face, was talking about David M. Cusher, who had been killed the previous week at Cougar Base. "David was a great soldier. He is a hero. And he did what each of you is ready to do, which is pay the ultimate price for his country. He's a hero because he was contributing to something bigger than himself. He was fighting for freedom. He was telling the terrorists, 'Never again; not on my watch.' He was fighting for freedom. For freedom he paid the ultimate cost."

Typical general bullshit.

The general kept going on and on about David Cusher. About how he always put his fellow man first. About how he would've died for any of us. About how he loved the Army and was thinking of reenlisting.

All lies.

"We must honor his memory by continuing the fight that he died for!" the general said. He paused, forgetting for a moment his line, his cue. And then I realized that this was a prepared speech. He said this exact same thing each time a soldier died. And then, not a second later, he remembered the next line and continued talking nonsense about love and valor and honor and country—all things that David would've laughed at. He never strived to be honorable. He had laughed at machismo and grandiose notions of duty. He had just wanted to be a decent guy and live a comfortable life. "We must not dishonor his memory by giving into laziness and truancy of discipline!"

I could barely control my anger.

Goddamn, I hated it when someone was turned into a propaganda tool when he died.

Next we were ordered to dress right dress, which was a command given to military formations to make nice neat even rows in a nice neat orderly manner. We stumbled in confusion, swaying as a group back and forth as the individual components within the formation pushed one another back and forth, jostling for positions. Our chain of command looked at us in a manner suggesting appropriate disappointment.

Lieutenant Colonel Marcus took the podium. The sun was still blinding us, and our faces were scrunched into wrinkly squinty-eyed masks. The colonel talked about how our company had seen more firefights and lost more soldiers than any other company in Afghanistan and how we had the most dangerous area of operations, and to reward us for that they were giving all of us medals. They walked up and down the ranks offering firm handshakes and asking how it felt to be pinned with their medals and accolades. Most of us just smiled or said nothing. Somebody in the back row responded that it felt heavy. Someone else responded that it felt good, sir.

After they finished passing out the medals and pinning each medal onto each soldier's pocket, we stood in a line to hand them back in as the colonel and the general beamed proudly about the good deed they had done for us. But we hadn't really won any medals and we weren't allowed to keep them, because we had never been actually awarded the medals. It had all been pretend. It was only supposed to have made us feel good.

Next, the sergeant major took the podium. He said that if we had problems, we needed to utilize our chain of command. Apparently, some soldier's mother had written his congressman about how he had not been fed while in combat. They'll take care of our problems for us. We're not to write directly to those who could solve our problems; instead, we should utilize our chain of command.

This, I'm afraid to report, was another lie. Your chain of command never helped you. They made fun of you for having problems or resented the fact that you were taking up their time, and they would forget that you had asked about a pay problem or legal issue. I kept statistical documentation of all my personal experiences in the Army as a reminder to get the fuck out at the earliest possibility—as if I was otherwise lacking in motivation. A quick look into my Palm Pilot showed that in my two years in the Army I had gone to my chain of command eight different times with problems that I couldn't take care of myself. The problems ranged from a difficulty with my paycheck to my need for a particular day off. Out of eight times, my chain of command had helped me once. An asterisk next to this single event denoted that this had been done only reluctantly.

Then the sergeant major asked if there were any questions.

No hands were raised.

Any questions at all?

You can ask about anything.

A single hand was raised. Someone asked about the Airborne school slot he had been promised when he was fooled into reenlisting when everyone had been told that they would be forcibly extended beyond the normal term of service.

"What the hell did I just talk to you about, son?" the sergeant major berated him, shaking his head in disbelief. Already, we had all forgotten about the whole "utilizing your chain of command" conversation. Private Gibber then quickly asked Sergeant Pauley, who asked Staff Sergeant Riley, who asked Sergeant First Class Derrens, who asked First Sergeant Santiago. All of this happened in an unusually quick and effective manner for the Army. And it was First Sergeant Santiago who asked the sergeant major about the slots for Air Assault school, which wasn't the question that had originally been asked. But that was beside the point, anyway.

And the sergeant major responded in his thick Georgia accent while chomping on a cigar that stained his teeth with tobacco that, well, actually, they had all been duped, and they were "incentatatives," not promises, and it was highly doubtful that they would get the schools they had reenlisted for, after all. The sergeant major stated that the Army didn't owe us anything and furthermore stated that we needed to quit our bellyaching. We were receiving a paycheck and three hot meals a day; what more could we ask for?

And he ended on a final note.

There was a lot of negative press circulating about the Army. And he was sick of it. It was our duty, our solemn responsibility as soldiers to tell our families, our friends, our churches, and our communities about how great the Army was. Together, all of us working together could reverse the stream of negative press about the Army.

I walked back to the command building and relieved Mulbeck at the radio. He was watching *Dirty Dancing* and was upset that I was five minutes late. I sat in my beach chair, fuming. The blood was pounding in my temples.

I wasn't infuriated that Cusher had died. That was the risk every soldier took. That was the risk I took. I knew that and understood that. What infuriated me was the honor that we had pretended to bestow upon him. Indifferent commanding generals and lieutenant colonels and sergeant majors folded his memory neatly into an Army propaganda slogan.

I would reopen "Fatty Ryan and the Sodomizing Taliban." Finally I had a philosophical foundation for my book. This time there would be substance. Before, I had attempted to capture the personalities of soldiers in combat, but it had been against a blank canvas of monotony and boredom.

Now there was death and destruction and suffering.

Suffering always made things more interesting.

And then I began to write.

The words came rapidly.

Chapter 27

SUFFERING MAKES THINGS INTERESTING

Sergeant Stein walks in slow semicircles around me as I do push-ups. He slowly squats his increasingly hefty self on a folding chair in the courtyard while I struggle to move my shirt cuffs up over my palms so that the rocks don't cut into my hands as much.

I'm receiving corrective training because I told Sergeant Stein that in two days' time, when we all get to cast our ballots, mine is going to be for John Kerry.

"I can't hear you. You better start counting them push-ups, girl, or you'll be down there all day," Sergeant Stein says quietly as he reaches for a cigarette he doesn't have. "Shit; I'm out. Let me get a cigarette, girl."

"They're in my pocket," I wheeze. The longer I stay in Afghanistan, the more out of shape I seem to get.

"You can rest while you get me a cigarette; then you get your ass back down."

I stand up, toss him my cigarettes, and then get back down on all fours. I knock out a few more push-ups and rest as I arch my back.

"You can just stay down there until you get your head right, Rico."

"My head is never going to be right, Sergeant. I refuse to vote for Bush, and it doesn't matter how long you keep me down here doing push-ups; I'm still not going to vote for him."

"Kerry threw his goddamn medals away at a protest with that lesbian commie bitch Jane Fonda. If you're in my Army, you going to get some respect for yourself and your country."

"I do respect my country, Sergeant. That's why I can't vote for Bush."

Sergeant Stein is quiet. Then he asks, "You an Afghan sympathizer, Rico? You want to hug them? You an Afghan hugger?"

"No, Sergeant, I want to kill. I'm a motherfucking killer!"

"That's right; say it again."

"I'M A MOTHERFUCKING KILLER!"

"I can't hear you!"

"I'M A MOTHERFUCKING KILLER!"

"Dirty dogs, go!"

At his command I rest on my arms and begin lifting up my leg back and forth like a dog taking a piss on a fire hydrant. Sergeant Stein stands and walks around me, saying, "You need to learn a few things about the way the world works, Rico. The world doesn't operate off of rainbows and sunshine. You kill me; I kill you. That's the way of the world. You get me? Let me hear you, killer!"

"I'M A MOTHERFUCKING KILLER!"

"Bark like a dog when you say it!"

"Woof! Woof! I'm a motherfucking killer! Woof!"

"Mountain climbers, go. If you think I'm being mean to you, go complain about it in your little romance novel you're writing."

"Roger that, Sergeant!"

Sergeant Pauley, Sergeant Riley, Sergeant Stephens, and Sergeant Kibbul sit on lawn chairs in our command center, laughing at me. They tell me that I'm wrong. That if John Kerry is elected president, the military will be decimated. Welfare mothers will make more each year than I do. The borders will open, and the country will be flooded with illegal Mexicans. They give me random undocumented statistics and single-serving anecdotes as evidence. I argue back. I'm the one with the master's degree in political science; you guys are the dumb soldiers. But no one listens.

I lie and manufacture impressive statistics from reputable sources that perpetuate my worldview and state that, in fact, the Democrats haven't eviscerated military spending in the past. And then I reference

192 | JOHNNY RICO

military spending bills during the Clinton administration and fabricate numbers to prove my point. It sounds very impressive, and I'm quite sure that somewhere in the multiverse of the communication networks of Internet, radio, magazines, newspapers, and cable television, someone has said the exact same thing.

"I'm not voting anyone into office that will pull the U.S. Army out of the Middle East until I've had a chance to kill a Haji," Sergeant Pauley states.

"Maybe we should stop killing them," I suggest, trying to play devil's advocate even though I also want to kill at least one Haji before I leave.

"Four of our soldiers have died, Rico," Sergeant Kibbul says. "Four! How does that make you feel? Because I've got to know how a commie liberal feels when four of his fellow soldiers die."

Not knowing how to answer that question, I try that oh-so-witty tactic of asking the same question as a response: "How do *you* feel about it?"

"How does it make me feel? It makes me feel like we should quit dicking around and start killing people like we were sent here to do," Sergeant Pauley yells, jumping out of his chair and moving about the room intensely, undecided where to go.

This is met with laughter and other nonverbal statements of support as a smile grows on his face and his story becomes exaggerated. "I think we need to drop a J-Dam on every Afghan we see. We see an Afghan, call up air support, bam! J-Dam! Fuck their world up!"

I laugh and say, "This is ridiculous. Everyone keeps talking about all the people they're going to kill, but nobody's going to do that! Nobody's going to nuke Kabul, or kill a bunch of innocent Afghans!" Ever since our soldiers died, all everyone talks about is revenge. About killing as many Afghans as possible. It was more male posturing, hollow gestures from soldiers who couldn't face the reality of their own impotence in the face of their comrades' deaths.

I meet a firestorm of dissent: boos and yells.

A small barrage of Styrofoam cups pelts me as I hold my arms over my face in a meager defense.

Attacked by a periodic
malicious sand storm.

Moving throughout the
countryside making promises
we don't intend to keep...

Interior view of Cougar
base in Ghazni province.

An overambitious
driver turns a Humvee
into a boat.

Interior view of Firebase Dizzy in Deh Rawood.

Interior view of the
Humvee after the gun
fight at the Taliban
Corral.

A makeshift IED
composed of an old
mortar round, a few
wires, and maybe
some bubblegum.

At Firebase
Cougar in
Oruzgan
province,
mail arrives
from kind
people from
places with
names like
Ohio.

What occurs when the makeshift IED goes "Boom!"

Another blown-up Humvee at Firebase Cougar in Oruzgan province.

A helicopter swoops in to offer air support during the firefight at Zamburay Valley.

Third Platoon struggles up the side of another mountain on a routine afternoon patrol around Firebase Cougar in Oruzgan province.

Members of 3rd Platoon climb a mountain to get in a secure overwatch position to cover soldiers in the valley below.

Keeping arrested bad guys in the trunk of the Humvee proves an efficient means of transportation.

A soldier takes up an overwatch security position during a mission with a sniper rifle during "Operation: Hamster Saliva." The soldier in this picture has, in fact, never before fired a sniper rifle.

A soldier who should have his helmet on takes up a guard position in preparation for an impending attack that never occurs.

Handing out shovels and farm tools that the Afghans don't want. Oh, yes, and also fake Nike shoes.

Sergeant Kibbul says in his normal sarcastic theatrical tone, waving his arms around wildly, "I don't know what planet you're on, Rico, but on this planet, on the planet that I'm on, you just lost a bunch of your fellow soldiers. Now I would pray to God that if you're going into combat with me, you'd want some motherfucking revenge."

"Yeah, but Rico doesn't go on patrols; he just watches movies," someone from the back adds. I nod my head in sad confirmation.

Sergeant Riley flips back his long out-of-control hair and shakes his head in dismay. "This isn't the Peace Corps, Rico. You joined the wrong fucking service. Go build a fucking well or teach some fucking shithead poor people how to read."

Sergeant Pauley informs me that he very much is going to kill a bunch of Afghans in retaliation and he doesn't care how he does it. "You think I'm fucking joking, Rico?"

"I don't think you're serious. I think you're a little upset right now."

"Maybe I should kill you, too? Huh? You want me to kill you, too?" He starts tickling me, forcing me to lose all my assumed composure and collapse on the ground, laughing and trying desperately to defend my exposed sensitive flanks.

"I think Rico is a Taliban sympathizer," Sergeant Stephens states, not laughing like the others but eyeing me suspiciously.

"He's a liberal!" Private Marciano shouts out gleefully.

"Liberal faggot communist," Sergeant Pauley adds while laughing. "It's not his fault; he was indoctrinated with all those liberal faggot hippie college kids. When I was in Ranger battalion we used to beat up college kids after the bars got out on Friday nights!"

Finally, recovered from my attack of tickles, I sit up and say, "You know, this wanting to respond with violence? It doesn't help the world. All it does is create a perpetual cycle of violence. So you kill four more, then they'll kill four more, then you'll kill four more. When does the madness end? Can't you see that revenge is not the answer?" The smile on my face from my ridiculous response is large and well advertised.

Sergeant Kibbul breaks out laughing and starts singing, "We are the world! We are the children!"

Tower three looks behind Dizzy, and in the distance is the town of Deh-Rawood. Mulbeck is behind his rifle, taking careful, well-aimed imaginary shots as he locks his rifle in on Afghans farming the field behind our base. He's angry that he has been taken away from radio guard for a shift and forced to fill in for a sick soldier on the towers.

"Spot for me," Mulbeck says, hunched up into the butt stock of his weapon.

I scan the field and say, "Your three-thirty: man holding baby."

"Baby! Perfect!" Mulbeck pivots his rifle to his three-thirty and yells out, "BAM, BABY, BAM! Double shot. Double kill."

"Mulbeck, four Cougar soldiers have died; how does this make you feel?"

"It fucking pisses me off!" Mulbeck says, standing up from his marksmanship practice. "I think of those Taliban motherfuckers; oh my God, I get so angry! This shit now is double payback time. Before I leave this fucked-up country, I will take out four of them. They pull a knife; you pull a gun. They take out one of your guys, you take out two of theirs. They take out two of your soldiers, you take out four of theirs. They want to play this game—fine, we'll play their silly little game . . ."

To know Mulbeck, though, is to know that he tends toward operatic displays of anger for even the slightest infraction. This is an imperative construction of his ego, the exterior appearance that he is your friend but that you don't want to piss him off. He feeds off the few poor schmucks who bought into this and give him a wide berth because they are afraid of him. It makes him feel tough.

"So that's it?" I ask. "That's all that you feel about it? Double revenge payback?"

Mulbeck scans the base of the tower to make sure no sergeants are around. He pulls out a cigarette and stands close to the wall so no one will see him smoking and says, "My dad raised me to stand up for myself and my friends. That's all there is fucking to it." He points his cigarette in my face as he talks. He does that every time he thinks he's about to offer a profound thought. "Okay, you want to know some profound fucked-up shit? I think maybe it's a good thing they died, because at least they're getting this shit going. We came here to kill Haji, not to fucking guard towers, and if their death is what it takes to get this shit started, maybe that's a good thing."

I laugh, "You're so full of shit!"

At this Mulbeck looks at me, concerned that I'm not buying his tough-guy image.

"All this talk about getting revenge!" I say. "Getting the action started? You're not going to do anything you're not told to do! Please! You act like you're in charge here instead of some lowly private!"

Mulbeck pauses and then says, "Maybe, but I bet you I kill me one Afghan baby before I leave this fucking hellhole!"

Diego screeches to a halt behind tower two and jumps out, one hand carrying the water from the Humvee to the guard tower, the other perched on the cigarette in his mouth. He offers me one, but I decline. I've quit.

Mulbeck continues his thought. "For some guys, they can go home now, and for the rest of their lives refer to their time during the war when they lost two guys that they will now claim to be very close friends with even though they might have hated them. So these deaths were necessary. They confirmed that we are actually in a combat zone. These guys dying might be the only action they get; they have to vicariously live through them dying. If they hadn't died, we'd have nothing to brag about to our families back home about how dangerous our year here was. We can all go home and pretend to have seen a lot of shit that we don't want to talk about while we defer to the mention of our dead friends."

I scratch my head and grab a case of water from the back of the Humvee. "I don't know about that. I don't want anyone to die."

Diego starts to leave and says, "Of course you do. Let me ask you this. How many people did you excitedly e-mail back home as soon as they died, partly to share the news because you were shocked, but partly because deep down you wanted everyone back home to know you were in danger?"

Twenty-three. I had immediately e-mailed twenty-three people.

———

I walk toward the picnic table with my folded piece of paper in my hand. A large crowd of soldiers has gathered. People laugh and call out "Liberal!" and all eyes are on me. Out of the thirty-three people in my platoon, I'm the third and final known vote for Kerry.

I feel like a black in the American South immediately following the passage of the Civil Rights Act, when I'm for the first time exercising my newly won right of universal suffrage.

I smile to everyone, hold the ballot up for all to see while the crowd hisses and boos, and start to drop it in, when Sergeant Pauley tackles me from the side and drops me to the ground and wrestles with me for my ballot as he screams, "Get him! Don't let him vote! Don't let him vote!"

I struggle, but Sergeant Pauley is stronger than I am, so I stuff my ballot in my mouth and start to chew it as he sits on my chest trying to pry my lips apart. After a few moments with my face buried in his crotch, he laughs, pats me on the stomach, gets up, offers me a hand, and helps raise me to my feet.

Winded, I spit out my ballot and cast one saliva-covered vote for Kerry.

Of course, our ballots will end up being lost, but then so is the election.

Chapter 28

THE FURY OF THE FIRST SERGEANT

The radio call from 2nd Platoon comes over the ASIP radio, and I put down the supply request for the moment. This means they're calling from their Humvees, which are close to our base. The Humvees don't have the nifty satellite radios that connect all over Afghanistan.

I'm about to answer the radio when Devon jumps up from the movie he's watching with me in the command center. He grabs my arm and says, "Tell them we're not here. Tell them to turn around. They can't arrive here."

I laugh, caught off guard. "Why?"

"Second Platoon is cursed," he says.

"That's absurd."

"Listen, as of this moment we've had nothing happen, and 2nd Platoon's getting ass-raped. They're obviously carrying a type of negative energy. They're taking infection everywhere they go, and if they come here, they're going to leave some of that energy behind them, and then we're going to start getting ass-fucked. You can't let those nasty Cougar soldiers come here and infect Dizzy."

"I thought you wanted to get some action?"

"Yeah, but they're getting hurt."

I stare at Devon for a moment, I pick up the hand mike, call to 2nd Platoon, and say, "Roger, we hear you. We'll see you shortly. Over."

Devon, pissed at me, turns his back to me and throws his hands in the air.

We watch from tower one as they pull up at the front gate in their jerry-rigged decrepit Humvees and get out in their filthy grime-covered uniforms, wearily marching toward the entrance of Firebase Dizzy.

"Look at them!" Devon says in disgust. "They're filthy. Why don't they take a shower?"

"They're going to drink all of our soda," says Mulbeck, voicing his primary concern. He's been trying to forewarn us all evening, ever since hearing of their impending arrival.

"You know, if we let them in here they're going to be on e-mail all fucking night," Cox says.

So we're quite happy when the Special Forces soldiers stop them at the front gate and ban them from our base, telling them they can eat MREs and sleep outside the walls.

Hearing that a soldier on the outside has been asking for me, I move through a side exit in the base's walls to our pistol firing range, where the convoy is setting up camp.

Graham, a devout Baptist and the most decent human being I have ever met, waves me down. He's a scout attached to Bravo Company but is temporarily assigned to Cougar Company for the convoy mission, which is tasked with finding out where the hell the Afghan jingle trucks that were loaded down with U.S. equipment and food have disappeared to. The trucks left the Army base at Tarin Kowt, passed Firebase Dizzy as they moved deep into Oruzgan province, and then were never heard from again.

What they didn't yet know was that the convoy trucks have been destroyed, the Army materials taken, and the Afghan drivers killed. It would take the sacrifice of a great many Afghan drivers until the U.S. Army decided that all future resupply would have to be done with Chinook helicopters. This same night, the U.S. Special Forces at Dizzy got the idea to hire a local Afghan driver to pose as a resupply driver and drive them to Camp Cougar, where they would hide in the back and then jump out and kill all the bad guys when they were stopped en route. Their plan would be very successful, and they would return to Firebase Dizzy happy and elated about all the people they got to kill.

Graham, his normally inspiring contagious smile lost behind a tired sleep-deprived grimace, approaches me from the other side of the barbed wire. I feel as if I were visiting a prisoner of war. I'm carrying my kitten, Brian, in my arms.

"What gives, Rico?" Graham asks, frowning. "You guys aren't even letting us into your base?" There is a slight pause. He looks ashamed and says, "We're U.S. soldiers too."

I look down at the ground and avoid his stare as I pet Brian. Graham and I arrived at the unit at the same time, and we went through much together in the early days in Hawaii, scrubbing bathroom toilets as sergeants screamed at us and doing push-ups for small infractions of Army policy. But now a lot separated us.

"Our base isn't big enough to accommodate your group," I state quietly.

"There are only twelve of us," he responds, his eyes scanning the exterior wall of the base, which seems plenty large and stretches on for quite a distance.

"You like my cat?" I ask, raising Brian for his inspection and approval. I shift direction and tone and ask, "How's Cougar Base treating you?"

"How do you fucking think?" he replies. "I can't die, man; I just got married on leave." He is kind of pleading with me, as if I have the ability to save his life. "You guys been shot at yet?"

"Um, yeah, a couple times," I say, lying, thinking back to a few times when we heard distant gunfire.

"Fucking scary as shit, huh?"

"Yeah, it was pretty scary."

"Man, first time I got shot at, I didn't even know how to respond. It was like it wasn't real. I kept thinking, they're firing at me? They're firing at me? It was crazy. I had to remind myself what to do, even though we've practiced it a hundred times. Poking your head around some cover to return fire is the scariest fucking thing in the world, you know?"

"Yeah, yeah, it was the same way with me, man. Same way. Listen, I have to, uh, I have to go," I say, realizing that the e-mail line is now probably at its lowest point.

"Well, you take care, man. Take it easy," says Graham.

"You, too," I reply as he leans into the barbed wire for a light hug and I reluctantly receive it.

I look back to see Graham slink toward a sleeping bag laid down between two Humvees, quietly lower himself into his bag, and squirm and adjust himself to avoid the larger rocks he's sleeping on.

Poor fucking dirty bastard.

Back inside, I walk from the chow hall after a midnight snack to the far corner, which houses 3rd Platoon's command center and barracks. Sergeant Mitchell, from 2nd Platoon, is sitting on the picnic table outside the command building. I look down, pretending I don't see him as I walk by and I sip my soda, but he calls out, "Rico!"

I look up, feigning my best look of surprise. "Sergeant Mitchell!"

"Rico, think you could get me a soda?" he asks, his eyes intensely scanning my soda while his lips quiver.

"It's the last one; we're all out," I lie.

There's an uneasy silence while he accepts this, although it's obvious that he knows I'm lying.

"So how are things here?" he asks.

I laugh. "Oh, fine." I don't want to tell him about the midnight chow, the e-mails, the phones, the round-the-clock movies, the excessive sleep.

He lights a cigarette and inhales deeply and then says, "Things are terrible."

"I didn't think you smoked," I say.

"I didn't," he replies. He asks if I want one, and I decline. I've quit.

"Did you hear about two nights ago?" His cherry-tipped cigarette bobs up and down, and I can barely see his face in the almost absolute darkness of an Afghanistan night.

"Well, we had a big movie festival going on that I was in charge of. I . . . why don't you tell me?"

Cougar Base is quiet. The peaceful respite of two o'clock in the morning. Against the pale faint reflection of moonlight on the ground, the sleeping forms of soldiers snuggled deep into the dirt can be seen as vague silhouettes that barely break from the shadows of the night, and around them are four twelve-foot clay brick walls. It's early October, and the night is cool without being frigid.

And then a rocket-propelled grenade slams into the single existing structure, a small metal container in the corner of the base.

The explosion penetrates outward as a deafening boom that envelops the quiet tranquil sounds of night for miles in all directions like a vacuum sucking in all extraneous sound.

The flash, although brief, instantly peels back the shadows that cover the base.

Everyone is now up, ripped from dreams with a stomach-churning immediacy.

There is a slight break between the RPG and what is to follow. And soldiers use this moment, scurrying in the dark, their asses on their sleeping bags, feeling around their areas desperately for gear, for weapons, for helmets, for body armor, for anything that might protect them.

And then it comes. It sounds a lot like firecrackers.

It's a crackle snap. Crackle snap. Crackle snap.

They're shooting. The enemy is shooting.

The sounds, though, distract from the danger. No one knows where the bullets are hitting. It's not like in the movies, where the dirt is conveniently kicking up next to your feet to mark the route of the rounds. The bullets could be hitting anywhere. The next bullet could be through your head, spraying eyeballs and tongue and teeth on the guy next to you.

Above Cougar Base there is a large enemy force. And now the bullets rain as in a typhoon.

The first sergeant emerges from his tent, screaming and frothing at the mouth. Soldiers who have been sleeping in T-shirts throw on boots and run to the walls to return fire. The first sergeant, suddenly running up a primitive hierarchy of Army standards, starts yelling for people to tuck in their pants. To button up their Army desert camouflage tops.

Before you can return fire on the Taliban, your uniform has to be up to standard.

The RPG rockets slam into the base, sending concussive echoing

202 | JOHNNY RICO

blasts throughout the valley while the first sergeant has people sitting on the ground tightening their bootstraps.

Amid the fire and torrential downpour of bullets and whizzing tracers of light, the first sergeant, finally satisfied with the state of his men's dress, leads a full frontal charge up the hill while screaming, "KILL THEM! KILL THEM!"

The soldiers, led by the fanatical first sergeant, race in the darkness out of the walls of the base and up the side of the hill, where they stumble and fall over rocks and uneven ground, making slow progress in their upward progression. For a moment they take on the form of an antiquated army charging the enemy flank.

But the enemy has retreated, dispersed to the craggy ravines that run on the flip side of the hill that borders Cougar Camp.

The next morning, the soldiers stand in their compound as the morning sun brings first evidence of the damage done the night before. The first sergeant calls together a formation of tired weary soldiers and he addresses them, the tears running freely down his face as he berates his soldiers for their lack of courage, their inability to close with and kill the enemy, their inability to follow even the most basic tenets of the training the Army has offered them.

"Cougar Base is filled with sunshine," Sergeant Mitchell says. He follows this with a long pause that allows me to soak up the dramatic residue of his statements.

And I wonder, just for a moment, about the transitional properties of negative cursed energy. Bad-luck energy can't really attach itself to other places, can it? It stays firmly rooted to the carrier of the bad luck, doesn't it?

Two days later it starts, and I realize that Sergeant Mitchell has indeed infected us after all.

We never should've let 2nd Platoon visit.

Devon was right.

We should've told them we weren't home.

Chapter 29

THE PROTECTION OF A HAYSTACK

I'm outside a compound waiting for the rest of my platoon to finish a search mission. I try to pet a donkey, which looks at me with bashfully cute dreamy eyes. But he's fidgety and won't let me pet him, to my great dismay.

I say to Devon, whom I convinced against orders to move outside with me so I'd have someone to talk to, "The donkey doesn't want me to pet him. Why doesn't he like me?" I hate it when donkeys don't like me. I'm twenty-eight years old, and I'm upset because a donkey doesn't like me.

Devon spits out a bit of chew, sucks in some brown saliva lingering on his lip, and says, "Maybe he doesn't like you, Rico; did you ever consider that? Why do you assume something's wrong with the donkey? Maybe something's just wrong with you. God, your fucking arrogance astounds me, man—really fucking astounds me."

I back away from the donkey and collapse in front of a haystack ten feet away around the corner of the compound at the edge of an open field as the rest of our fellow soldiers exit the compound.

"There ain't shit here today," Sergeant Riley angrily says as he exits the compound.

I pop a Jolly Rancher and lean back on my pack, flicking some hay between my fingers. I open some cherry beverage powder and pour it into my canteen.

This infantry life isn't that bad sometimes. Lots of moments, like this one, are relaxing. Relaxing as the warm beams of sun hit my face, a gentle glow of heat absorbing into my skin. I lightly squint and wish I hadn't lost my sunglasses.

And this is when the machine guns open fire on us. And this is when the rocket-propelled grenades swoosh by overhead.

And this is when I, and the soldiers all about me, make a mad desperate dash for cover, shoving one another and knocking one another over in the process.

And this is when my training takes over and I don't hesitate for one second to perform my duties as the operational expert in radio communications. My face alight with a permanent smile, my hands trembling from happiness, I move swiftly but surely as I raise my antenna to its ten-foot position, where I can get a weak but sustainable signal.

On the radio, my voice is screaming, "Dizzy Base! Dizzy Base! This is Hunter-6 Romeo! We're under heavy enemy attack! Unknown but large number of assailants, heavy arms, and RPG fire! Prepare to copy my grid! Over!"

Sergeant Riley peers around the corner of the building and yells back to the others, "We've got one fucking old Haji with a rifle taking potshots at us from behind a wall about two hundred meters to our twelve o'clock!"

Dizzy Base responds, "Hunter-6 Romeo, you came in broken. Say again. Over."

I pause, taking in Sergeant Riley's report, and then say, more slowly and calmly, "Um, Dizzy Base, we've got shots fired, one enemy assailant with a rifle. Prepare to copy grid. Over."

And then I notice Sergeant Riley and the others staring at me. Have I been shot?! What the hell are they looking at me for? I check my body for bullet wounds. I don't think I've been shot. But then I could have just been so excited at getting shot at that I didn't realize I'd been shot. And then I notice that the cover I'm hiding behind is a haystack.

A bullet rips through the haystack by my face, sending little bits of hay floating gently to the earth.

I make another mental note to myself: next time, hide behind something solid—a building or a rock wall, for example.

I don't want to leave my haystack. I'm so enchanted by the absurdity of the idea of seeking cover from gunfire from behind a haystack that I want to stay where I'm at and laugh crazily as the bullets whiz by. It's more that I love seeing just how far this absurd situation can be taken. Sometimes this requires my temporary cooperation.

But then the shooting stops. Our shooter has run off into the maze of streets and alleys that is the village. But I don't care; I'm happy.

Thank you, Jesus. I know I don't believe in you, but all the same, thanks for not letting me leave Afghanistan without getting shot at. I really appreciate it.

Chapter 30

THE ATTACK OF THE TALIBAN LIGHTNING BUGS

Our Humvee speeds across the open desert under the night sky, bouncing and jostling over small bumps. Occasionally we are launched into the static desert air and held there for entire seconds before slamming back down into the dry cracked desert hardpan.

We are on a routine patrol to the Taliban Corral.

"I didn't fucking sleep with a Mahoo!" Private Marciano squeals like a little girl from the top of the Humvee, where he is manning the .50-caliber machine-gun turret. Inside, Ryan and the rest of the soldiers are pulling on his shoelaces and reminding him of his unfortunate habit of picking up transvestite prostitutes back in Hawaii.

"Do you get a discount for a Mahoo? If it comes with a dick do they knock like, maybe fifty percent off or something?" Specialist Devon asks the rest of us from the driver's seat. He is wearing his token pink star-shaped Barbie sunglasses. Ryan loves it when he wears those sunglasses.

Ryan, laughing in the backseat, says, "Did you ever have that dream in high school that you could snap your fingers and freeze time and walk around and rape all the hot cheerleader chicks?"

"No!" I say, feigning polite civilized outrage. "No, I don't fantasize about raping women!"

"Bitches, Rico; the correct term is bitches. And I'm not saying that you'd ever act on it; but admit it, you've had the frozen-time dream when you were a teenager and you could fuck any bitch you wanted because they were frozen and couldn't move!" Ryan yells, pointing at me. "You're probably also going to tell me you've never had a dream about fucking your mom!"

"I've never had a dream about fucking my mom! Ever!" I say, disgusted, staring outside the window into the darkness.

"Bullshit! Even Freud said that every child has sexual dreams about their gender-opposite parent! That's psychologically some true shit, man! They're just too ashamed to admit it, so they block it out and pretend it didn't happen. What if you were the dad of Pamela Anderson; don't tell me you wouldn't jerk off to a picture of her in one of her naked layouts, or secretly order the video of her getting drilled by Tommy Lee and get a woody."

"Do you have dreams about fucking your mom, Ryan?" I ask.

"Dude, have you seen my mom? My mom's fucking hot!" Ryan exclaims.

"Okay! Okay! That's enough, no more of the fucking family members topic. Pay attention to that little world outside your fucking little windows, you stupid little vaginal blood farts," Sergeant Santiago yells from the front seat, more upset that at this moment he has to play leader and can't join this conversation.

Silence permeates the Humvee and airs out the dirty thoughts. Suddenly Ryan punches Marciano in the leg and says, "Marciano, what would you do if you picked up a Mahoo and it turned out to be your mom but your dick was already up and hard. Would you fuck her? You would, wouldn't you!"

Our Humvee comes to a screeching halt on top of Taliban Ridge behind another American Humvee. It's a small ridgeline that overlooks a series of brick compounds at the bottom of a hill. Sergeant Santiago, Ryan, Devon, and I all exit the Humvee while Marciano pulls security from the top of the vehicle. Sergeant Santiago moves over to the first vehicle to discuss with Sergeant Bryson as he directs Cox and the rest of his own soldiers into position. We pretend to pay attention and pull security from the top of the ridge.

I pull my night vision goggles down from the top of my helmet, click them into place, and turn them on. My world suddenly turns into the green luminesence of infrared. I sigh and settle on my haunches, squinting my eyes at a scratch on the inside of my night vision goggles while Cox walks over from the other Humvee and asks if I want a stick of gum. Juicy Fruit. I like Juicy Fruit. Someone shoots the Humvee door behind us.

Cox and I both slowly turn to look at the door behind us and then back at each other. We look over at Sergeant Santiago for guidance. He pauses in his own conversation to look over at us.

Another shot rings out against the hood near Devon, who jumps back and laughs. He looks over at Sergeant Santiago for guidance too.

Sergeant Santiago calmly says, "Well, shoot back already!"

The other soldiers around us move into their own positions. Devon and Ryan fight over who gets the driver's-side door, shoving each other back and forth.

"Start shooting," I say. "You heard Sergeant Santiago."

"I don't know what I'm shooting at," Cox says. "I'm not shooting until someone else starts shooting. You shoot."

"I'll shoot if you do."

The bullets rip up the outside of the door of the Humvee. The impact sounds like thuds from a sledgehammer. Then Cox opens fire and then Devon and Ryan open fire, and then, satisfied that everyone else is shooting, I open fire.

Suddenly the world is labored breathing and screaming and icy veins flushing adrenaline into my heart and sensory overkill and tight chests gripping silent screams of excitement and fear.

Marciano is on the .50-caliber machine gun on top of the Humvee, unloading into the compounds below with a constant thunderous spit of light from the weapon's muzzle.

Sergeants shout commands, none of which I hear. Everyone is screaming and opening fire. All their mouths are locked open in displays of rage, except for Cox, who loves deployments, calmly chews his gum, a huge smile plastered on his face.

In the compounds below we see single sparks of muzzle flashes that seem to float and change position as our enemy moves back and forth, sideways and forward. Only a few at first; then their numbers are joined by others, and soon it's a constant onslaught of fire headed toward us. A nonstop symphony of blinking Christmas lights flashing bullets in our direction. For a moment I become transfixed by the idea that our enemy is nothing but little lightning bugs—the type that infested Iowa, where I grew up in the summer. That's what the Taliban look like: cute little lightning bugs that give off little flashes from their asses as they gently float and change positions in the courtyard below.

Sergeant Santiago screams to back the trucks up. The other Humvee backs up deeper into the ridgeline so that its .50-caliber gunner can just barely see down the hill and return effective fire, but where, with the hill in front, they would be mostly invisible to the Taliban, who would not be able to shoot up without most of their rounds simply flying into the night sky above or hitting the hillside dirt below.

Private Hugh from the other Humvee is left out in the open as the Humvee squeals backwards. He crouches over his weapon, trying to clear an ammunition jam. Devon runs out from behind the driver's door and grabs Hugh by the back of his body armor and drags him backwards into the steep of the hill. A rocket flies by where they had both been just seconds before.

Everyone pauses after the RPG explodes. The game has suddenly changed. Hiding behind the doors of the Humvee isn't going to work any longer.

Ryan jumps into our own Humvee and revs the engine to a scream. There's a horrible screeching and grinding of the gears before the Humvee stalls in place and then a second later squeals back farther into the ridgeline as another RPG flies by the space where just a second earlier the Humvee had been.

Suddenly RPG rockets swoosh through the air and fly by over our heads. It's like a Fourth of July celebration where you lie out on the grass on a blanket and watch the fireworks explode in the sky above a ball game. We all lie flat against the desert floor, covering our heads and screaming as we ride out the attack.

The enemy has done what we had been told was not possible: the ragtag Taliban militia has more firepower than the professional, technologically advanced, and well-armed U.S. Army.

And then, the volley over, we stand back up on wobbly and shaky knees and begin again to return fire.

We fire, change magazines, and fire again. Sometimes we take careful, well-aimed shots. Sometimes we just pray and spray. Whenever I resolve to stick to one method, I immediately surprise myself by jerking forward from the cover of the Humvee door and doing the opposite of what I just had resolved to do.

"You want some gum!" Cox screams in my ear.

"What?!" I ask, completely confounded.

"GUM! YOU WANT SOME GUM!" Cox screams again.

"Sure!" I scream back in his ear.

Cox hands me another stick of gum and then makes his way around the perimeter of the vehicle to be sure that everyone is adequately stocked up on gum. After that, he dives to the second vehicle to make sure everyone over there has gum.

We seem to be protected by magical bubbles. Thousands of rounds are being fired at us, yet we stand there facing them, facing the repeated and continual stream and chorus of muzzle flashes from the courtyards below. Somewhere between us and them the rounds vanish. Some are likely entering the dirt of the hillside below us. Others are probably flying into the sky over our heads, only to lose their momentum a kilometer out and fall slowly to earth. Only occasionally now do we hear the ping of a bullet striking one of our Humvees.

Through the night vision goggles we see our bullets form a stream of infrared beams that crisscross and move back and forth erratically with every subtle shift of a rifle's position. A slight movement of the wrist sends a beam arcing hundreds of meters into the air in the distance. I'm not even sure if this is real. The world of my night vision goggles seems removed, secondhand, and vicarious. Suddenly I'm quite sure that this is all a big virtual-reality simulation, a massive first-person shooter video game that I'm not particularly enjoying.

How long have we been firing? Hours, it seems. A quick glimpse of my watch reveals it to have only been six or so minutes.

———

I find myself getting restless and bored thirty minutes in. My knees are tired of supporting my weight. I keep sighing and looking down at my watch. My father used to sigh a lot, and it's an annoying habit that I'm afraid I've adopted. I start mentally composing e-mails to my friends, writing out how I would describe my first major firefight.

For moments at a time I don't return fire at all and just stare at the situation around me. I put my weapon down for a moment, resting my arms, which are now tired of holding it.

We don't seem to be killing any of them. I wonder how this can be. I look over at Sergeant Santiago and see him cocking nose to lever, taking careful well-aimed shots. Our infrared night lasers are all carefully calibrated and zeroed to our weapons. How can we be missing so much? How come they're not all dead? I feel as if my bullets are having no effect. That my weapon is shooting blanks. If I put my hand in front of the muzzle of my weapon and pulled the trigger, would I simply feel a blast of compressed air? I'm firing bullets, aren't I? Every time I press the trigger I'm sending a lethal metal projectile downrange, aren't I? And I'm a good shot; I always qualify well on rifle marksmanship tests. What the fuck is going on?

I look at my watch. Fifty minutes and counting. And still it goes on. Where was the quick reaction force that was our backup? I hear somebody yell that they're out of ammunition, and I see a sergeant hand a private one of his own magazines of ammunition. Marciano screams from the top of the .50-caliber machine gun that he's out of ammo. Specialist Ryan, who ran out of ammo a long time ago, is shooting an AK-47 that we took off an enemy soldier we found on a previous patrol.

Everybody is yelling and screaming things that I'm not listening to, because I'm tired of listening.

How long is this going to go on? How long can this continue? Would anyone notice if I just slowly slunk away and walked back to base and pretended later that I had never been on this patrol? Maybe I could just adamantly insist that I had been watching movies all night and that they were all suffering from a form of mass hysteria.

——

Suddenly it's over. It's abrupt. Like the peaceful respite in sound that comes after a long-running lawn mower or wood chipper has suddenly been turned off. For the first time I notice my ears ringing in the silence. The enemy has retreated and left.

Cox taps me on the shoulder and asks if I want a stick of gum.

We stand up on unsure fidgety knees that don't quite properly respond as we want them to and flip our night vision goggles back up to get a sense of the normal world again. We suck in deep ragged breaths and exhale forcibly. Some of us laugh and smile. We make nonsensical comments. Others are quiet.

The Special Forces soldiers finally arrive about five minutes after the shooting has stopped. Their Humvees screech to a halt, and they jump out ready for action. I won't learn until later that one of the two teams garrisoned at Dizzy had been drunk when they received the call that we needed their help.

It takes a lot longer to get your gear on and find a grid coordinate in the desert when you're drunk.

The mood back at base is jubilant. It's cause for celebration. We break out the nonalcoholic beer and the cigarettes, and I decide I haven't quit smoking after all. The stories exaggerate and quickly become fantastical fabrications. To listen to us, you'd think each of us should be awarded the Congressional Medal of Honor. The other squads enviously listen to our stories.

We retire to the barracks for a night of war movies—*Platoon, Full Metal Jacket, Born on the Fourth of July.* We watch them long into the morning while the soldiers laugh and exclaim "Goddamn!" and slap high fives as little Vietnamese villages are burned and the occupants are shot by U.S. soldiers.

Two days later, Sergeant Riley's squad is on a routine patrol. They crest the top of a hill and stumble upon a party of resting Taliban fighters who scramble for their gear and their weapons as Sergeant Riley screams for a full retreat.

The American Humvees struggle for a reverse footing in the

farmer's field, which is cut deep with irrigation ditches, as bullets start to slam into the vehicles. Private Marciano, on top with the .50-caliber machine gun, shrieks as he realizes that his weapon is jammed. He spins himself around with his back facing the enemy as rounds pound into the back of the metal lid that protects him. A rocket-propelled grenade bounces off the ground and, by act of God or luck, just happens to hit a rock on its arc toward the Humvee, causing its arc to skewer over the hood. The RPG explodes just twenty meters farther, sending shrapnel raining into the back of the Humvee.

The Humvee stalls and emits a shrill scream as it struggles to capture a gear. Inside, the soldiers all scream in unison, stretching their lungs as a second rocket-propelled grenade flies by just inches over the top of the hood.

Twenty minutes later, back at base, the same soldiers tell their stories with a child's boundless enthusiasm.

The soldiers of 3rd Platoon have finally met combat. Not a D-Day Normandy Invasion type of combat, and certainly not a battle for Fallujah type of combat. Not a sort of combat that causes heart tremors or difficulty sleeping at night, but the exciting sort that is fun and carefree and makes everyone squeal with delight.

That *type* of combat.

Chapter 31

TALIBAN GREETING CARDS

"**We're cutting off your ammunition.** You'll get no further ammo re-supply from us if you're going to continue to waste it," the battalion supply officer tells Lieutenant Mitch over the satellite phone. Lieutenant Mitch walks back and forth in quick darts out in the gravel motor pool, attempting to retain capture of the ethereal connection that is our only link, apart from e-mail, to our faraway battalion base.

Lieutenant Mitch pauses momentarily before responding. "But, sir, my men were engaged in an hour-long firefight with Al Qaeda. We had to shoot back. They had to live, didn't they? What should they have done—not returned fire?"

Lieutenant Mitch has just learned that to persuade us to stop getting into firefights, the Army is not going to supply us with ammunition any longer. Just an hour before this, he learned we had to release one of the Afghans we arrested in connection with the attack. We hadn't filled out the paperwork correctly. You can stop terrorists only if you have the paperwork right.

Lieutenant Mitch lunges in the air toward a pile of gravel and almost falls on the ground, losing his precarious signal. He stands and steadies himself, sighing. Word around the battalion headquarters is that we lied about the firefight. That we made it up to get some attention. "Are we in a war or not?" Lieutenant Mitch asks. "This is a combat zone, isn't it?"

I laugh from my seat on the hood of a nearby Humvee and wave my pencil and paper in the air, all animated and angry, "Goddamn, he's a saucy bitch, sir! A damn saucy bitch!" Then abruptly I turn my attention to the supply request that I'm filling out on the back of a Superman comic. "I'm going to e-mail them and tell them two pallets of blueberry muffins. Do you think that's enough? Or should I make it three pallets of blueberry muffins? The men are awfully fond of blueberry muffins, sir. Awfully fond, indeed. We can never have enough blueberry muffins. But they probably taught you that at the officer combat course. You don't need me to tell you about the importance of having a well-stocked larder of blueberry muffins and its corresponding effect on morale for the fighting men on the front line."

"Who the fuck does he think he is?" Lieutenant Mitch exclaims as he paces back and forth, his arms flailing angrily.

"I'll make it three pallets of blueberry muffins," I say to myself as I jot the reminder in my notepad.

"You know what we should do, Rico," Lieutenant Mitch states, turning to me with solemn resolve. "We'll expend all our ammo that we have now. We'll tell them we don't have a single bullet left. That if someone attacks the base or wants to come in, all we can do is throw rocks, and then they will have to resupply us!"

I tap my dried-up marker rhythmically against my chin, lost in deep thought. We ordered pens, but they have not yet arrived. "What do you think about a line of ciders? Like a variety of good ciders around this joint? I haven't had a good cider in quite a while. I think a line of good ciders could make a world of difference."

Lieutenant Mitch says, "I'm more of an apple juice man, Rico." The phone rings. He answers it, and his body stiffens. He looks concerned; his face shifts, and his top lip covers his mouth. He makes little reflexive sighing grunts. He keeps trying to speak, saying, "Sir . . . Sir . . . Sir, if I could just explain . . ."

Lieutenant Mitch hangs up the phone and turns to me with a defeated air. "The colonel heard that we were using the beige body armor vests. He says he's going to fire me. He's coming here tomorrow to 'unfuck everything.' " We have determined that the body armor vests offered us by the Army are bulky and inefficient. We purchased new vests from the black market in Kandahar through our company supply sergeant at our own expense. These vests used the same metal plates as our issued body armor, but they offered an increased range of motion and pockets on the outside of the vest, which negated our having to wear a tactical vest. But now the battalion lieutenant colonel is incensed that we took the initiative to improve our gear.

Preparations would have to be made. The beige body armor vests would have to be buried in the desert. Pornography would have to come down off the walls of the soldiers' barracks. Cigarette butts would have to be picked up. Fake PT schedules and training schedules would have to be posted in the operations building. The DVD players and PlayStation that we normally use to pass time would have to be hidden, replaced by striking solemn poses of us studying maps on the walls, the locations they mapped strange and unknown to us. Dirt would have to be smoothed in high-traffic areas, such as outside the operations building and the barracks. All of us should get back in Army uniform and get rid of the bathrobes and baseball caps and sandals we have taken to wearing.

The truth of the matter was that we inadvertently stirred up trouble in an area of Oruzgan province that has been defined as quiet. And the Army wants quiet. Afghanistan is going into a stage-three combat zone, which means that violence is deescalating and things are quieting, and suddenly we are making it difficult for the battalion to paint rosy pictures of quiet subdued happy Afghani peoples in our corner of the world to those in charge of Afghanistan.

"Turn off the television," Lieutenant Mitch says. I flip off the television. The squad leaders sigh, waiting for the latest as they take their seats. Lieutenant Mitch broadcasts a big smile that makes everyone groan. We know we're in trouble when he broadcasts a big smile like that.

"Yeah, here's the thing," Lieutenant Mitch says. "You, um, you can't get into any more trouble. So no more shooting."

Sergeant Wu stares emotionlessly. He does that when he's upset.

Sergeant Riley flips out, as is characteristic for him to do. "Oh, okay!

Okay! Yeah, I wanted to drive up on a bunch of Taliban! Next time, we'll just flip them the bird when they shoot at us!"

"Could you?" Lieutenant Mitch asks, barely suppressing his laughter. "Yeahhh, that'd be great. Thanks. The Army would really appreciate it."

Sergeant Stephens quietly shakes his head. Sergeant Santiago starts laughing and asks, "So, seriously, sir. What do they want us to do?"

Lieutenant Mitch pauses for a moment, trying to contain his outbreak of the giggles, and then says, "Maybe you could hug them? Try some hugs out for size."

Sergeant Stephens shakes his head in quiet dismay, the way he does when he's given bullshit Army orders. Sergeant Riley stumbles about the room, talking angrily to himself. Sergeant Santiago says excitedly, "Sir, maybe we could make them some greeting cards out of construction paper! Get some glitter, some tape, and some glue! That'd be nice!"

Lieutenant Mitch laughs and says, "Yes, that's the type of thinking outside the box that I'm looking for! That's innovative! I like that! Somebody promote this man!"

The next night, Sergeant Wu and a host of 3rd Platoon soldiers are on an overnight watch position in a small nearby town with the Special Forces soldiers. They have been sitting quietly in the dark, hidden in the shadows of the moonless night, trading turns at the helm of the .50-caliber machine gun, where the guard will click on his night vision goggles and scan the outskirts of the town while the others sleep scrunched into the seats below.

A U.S. soldier stationed at Dizzy who listens to area radio traffic breaks the silence of the predawn hours on the radio. This startles Sergeant Wu. A Special Forces soldier in the other Humvee parked fifty meters to their right flank answers the call, but Sergeant Wu listens in.

You've been spotted!

They're coming for you right now!

You've got to get the fuck out of there!

There's anywhere from fifty to one hundred fighters!

Sergeant Wu glances over at the town and adjusts the focus knob on his night vision. The foreground goes blurry, the rear comes into focus, and then he can see them—vehicles on the edge of the town and men running about preparing to attack.

"You don't have long to act!" the voice on the radio says.

"Wake the fuck up! Wake the fuck up!" Sergeant Wu screams, frantically kicking everyone in the vehicle. The sleeping soldiers quickly awake from uneasy sleep.

The two Humvees flee into the night while the Special Forces soldier works the radio, calling out a greeting to their friends in the sky.

The Taliban Toyota trucks start filing out in hot pursuit when the sky rumbles and rips apart.

It's not every day that you get to blow up a town. You only get to do shit like that when you hang out with SF. The regular Army isn't allowed to blow up towns.

The next morning, on their return to Dizzy, Lieutenant Mitch meets Sergeant Wu and the returning 3rd Platoon soldiers as they start unloading their gear.

"Yeahhh," Lieutenant Mitch says, with the big smile that says he's about to start laughing uncontrollably. "I don't know if you remember, but we had a little talk about not shooting anymore? Yeahhh, I guess I didn't specify, but that also included blowing up towns."

Chapter 32

AN AFGHANISTAN CHRISTMAS

This sort of thing required an early three-in-the-morning type of courage. I was not well endowed with that type of courage. My morning mentality was more along the lines of a slow soft dethawing from sleep through many yawns as I slowly shuffled around the house in bunny slippers while the sun christened the day and *Good Morning America* issued forth from the television.

But there I was, peeking under the wood canopy attached to the back of the deserted airplane hangar that housed refugee soldiers in transition who were, thus far, without a permanent home. Dripping icy rainwater rippled from the holes and cracks in the shoddily built wooden canopy, which was soaked through and looked as if it was made of soggy cardboard. The rain had not let up for three days. It reshaped the ground, which swallowed everything the sky could give; the land in Afghanistan was desperately thirsty, its barren earth chapped and parched like blistered lips.

But now the rivers and pools of knee-high water hundreds of meters long were settling in the small contours and imperfections of the base at Kandahar. Moving from one side of the base to the other required careful navigation along wooden pallets and planks and tires that had been placed strategically, allowing one to almost jump from one position to another. I refused to use these makeshift sidewalks and instead marched through the water, swinging my legs in large exaggerated arcs as I tromped and stomped to and fro with splashing steps in soggy boots.

Beyond the hangar that housed me were strings of lonely Christmas lights adorning the 25th Lighting Chapel. A camel borrowed for the occasion to make the nativity scene a bit more authentic grunted in the rain, and a loudspeaker someone forgot to turn off sang Christmas tunes.

Jingle Bell, Jingle Bell, Jingle Bell Rock

That's right, I reminded myself. It was Christmas.

Merry fucking Christmas.

I had almost fallen asleep, my back against the dripping wall, knees to chest, lulled by the rhythmic pulse of the sheets of rain, when a distorted arc of headlights swung through the early morning night and across my face. I could now hear, somewhere out in the rain, the quiet murmur of a settling engine. Footsteps sloshed toward me, and then there was a voice.

"You. What are you doing sleeping in the door?"

"I don't know, seemed as good as any other spot," I replied, looking up to see the E6 sergeant, who always tried to get me to go to church.

"Get your shit on; it's Christmas. We've got a Christmas party for you to attend."

This was the danger of sleeping in the designated sleeping area. They would come and randomly pick people up for details and odd jobs. It was best to fall asleep in the library. No one came looking for you in the library to do odd jobs or attend Christmas parties.

I spend the rest of the day sitting at a desk in a command office, watching people play computer solitaire while I attempt to read a western novel left on the desk as the rain slams into the ground outside.

During lunch, I go to Burger King and I talk to our company supply clerk, an Asian fellow named Tyce, who is in charge of getting supplies forwarded to Dizzy and Cougar base. Tyce has sat at the Burger King all day, laughing about the idea of actually doing his job. I comment on the excellence with which he disregards his job, and then start to leave to wait around the office some more. Tyce introduces me to his friend Bobby, who has ducked out of his entire deployment. He says the Army managed to reassign him from his unit and assign him nowhere else. He has been in limbo. He proudly speaks of the abandoned tent at the end of the flight line where he lives. He will only resurface on the Army's radar once the time comes for him to redeploy home. And, yes, he says, he's still collecting a paycheck.

Finally evening arrives, and I'm told to load up in the back of an open cargo truck with twenty other soldiers who have been drafted just as I have. We're told that we're being driven to Kandahar to attend a Christmas dinner, and they need a representation of regular U.S. soldiers.

I was sent to Kandahar a week earlier to attend a USO show for a job well done. I missed the show entirely and instead was drafted to work the mail detail, despite my protests that I had been sent there as a reward.

So I sorted mail. There was a group of us, all quiet and cranky. Every time someone found a package being mailed to the sergeant major, he would yell out "sergeant major!" Everyone would stop work, and instantly a delicate and complicated "pass the package" game ensued as the package was tossed from one person to another until eventually it was tossed into a container headed for the Pakistan border. Or some small engineering unit off in the middle of nowhere. During that week we shipped a great deal of the sergeant major's Christmas presents to the far corners of Afghanistan.

"I don't have any wet-weather gear," I tell a sergeant, who tells me where to sit as I stand outside the truck completely drenched in the rain, already shivering as the temperature drops abruptly now that the daylight has dispersed.

"Yeah, me either," he says behind a rain poncho and raincoat. "Get in."

I climb aboard and sit in a puddle of water. The rain continues to pound me. The trucks start up, slowly at first as they navigate the traffic obstacles in the road at the exit to the base. Then, released onto open highway, the trucks pick up the pace and cut through the night at top speed. In the back, the wind cuts through us like knives. My body starts to shake uncontrollably for the next hour as we drive through open fields and then finally make our way into the Kandahar city limits.

In the dark and rain I feel as if I'm entering a mythical fantasy world of trolls. Our caravan makes its way through the twists and turns of this strange and peculiar city of blackened slick wet buildings and rubble and trash.

Finally we arrive at a series of metal gates, which open as we proceed up a long driveway with a carefully maintained lawn. We're deposited at a roundabout at the front door of a mansion that looks more like Beverly Hills or Malibu than Afghanistan. Special Operations soldiers stand on the porch in their baseball caps and their sunglasses as security for important dignitaries.

I move inside with the other freezing soldiers, leaving a puddle of water on the plush carpet. We're herded into a waiting room and sit there for three hours, shaking uncontrollably.

A photographer from an Army newspaper moves up and down the aisles and asks me to smile and takes my picture. I grit my teeth and attempt a meager smile, with blue lips. He asks me for a quote.

"Fuck you," I tell him.

"Great—you're happy to be here and are excited at the progress that the U.S. and Afghanistan are making together. Thanks," he says as he writes this down and then moves on to the freezing soldier next to me.

The hallway beyond our waiting room is open. Important Afghans in suits mill about with British and American men in the latest spring business collections.

Finally we're led to a dining room, where massive tables are filled with rows of expensive china and an impressive selection of cuisine. We're each given one Pepsi and a bottle of water and told to take our seats.

The Afghanistan governor and several leaders of international nongovernmental organizations make speeches about cooperation and unity between the United States and Afghanistan. And then the commanding colonel for Afghanistan stands at the front of the room and starts to speak. He tells us all about the long friendship that has existed between our two great nations. As cameras flash he tells us all about how the United States has always been an enemy of the Taliban, and about how the United States will always be an enemy of the Taliban until they are destroyed, and that this destruction can come about only through the cooperation and unity of nations.

Didn't the U.S. used to support the Taliban, though? Hadn't we given them hundreds of millions of dollars in funding in the years before September 11, 2001? Didn't the Taliban visit Bush in Texas as his guests? Or maybe I'm wrong. I can't even remember anymore. Maybe the U.S. has always hated the Taliban. Maybe I'm wrong. Maybe the past doesn't even matter anymore. Once you control the present, the past can be rewritten. Everyone is speaking in Orwellian newspeak.

Next, the brother of Hamid Karzai, the president of Afghanistan, takes the microphone and says to all of us soldiers in the room that we're to be honored because we're fighting and dying for a friend, for something that isn't even our own country. This makes our sacrifice all the more noble.

All the pogues, the noninfantry soldiers in the room who man safe desks back in Kandahar and have never even been in harm's way, give this a thunderous round of applause and whistle in response.

"We don't care about you! We're not here to help you! The only reason we're here is because we want to kill a few of you before we leave so that it validates our job as infantry soldiers!" This is what I want to scream. Instead, I just clap dully, an insipid sour smile on my face.

We leave the palace and board the trucks. The rain slaps me in the face, but this time I don't mind. The soldier next to me, some desk jockey who is outside the wire for the first time, says, "I feel inspired! What he said about us being more noble than Afghan soldiers because we're fighting and dying for a country that's not even ours? That about brought a tear to my eye! What a fun thing to do for Christmas!"

Chapter 33

A SUNDAY MORNING KITTEN MUTILATION

I wake up. It's Sunday morning. I don't know this, of course, because all normal measures of time have ceased to exist. There is no distinction, no separation between days.

Where's Brian? Where's that fucking cat off to now?

I lie in my cot in the darkened closet attached to the operation center's hallway. I've taken to living in a closet now. It started getting too cold for the roof. I'm happy to have a closet all to myself.

I lived in a closet once before when I was seven or eight years old. I decided the closet in my bedroom was cozier than my actual bedroom and moved into it, to the befuddlement of my mother. I dragged my blankets and my comic books and my hamster all into the closet with me. Twenty years later, and I'm back in a closet. At least it's a big walk-in closet.

It takes all my mental ability to calculate backwards to the last time I recalled anyone naming what day of the week it was.

It's Sunday.

I hate Sundays.

I've always hated Sundays.

Sunday was the end of the weekend. It was when you had to make amends and restitution for your Saturday nights by nursing a hangover and trying to recall exactly how much money you took out of the ATM.

This is my last Sunday at Firebase Dizzy. Just last night, word came down on the satellite radio system, and quick arrangements were negotiated over the satellite phone. The 3rd Platoon is to turn Dizzy over to

2nd Platoon, who would be replacing us. We, in turn, are to take their place at Firebase Cougar.

I sigh. Life's so comfortable here, and I'm reluctant to go. Cougar doesn't even have tents to house the soldiers in.

I look at my watch. It's noon. I've missed breakfast.

Fuck.

I haven't eaten breakfast all week.

I sit up and fumble in my green army duffel bag, which is presently holding all the snacks my dear mother mails me. I find a pudding and I eat it with my finger for lack of a spoon.

I move to the front gate of the base, where a local vendor brings his wares for the soldiers to purchase. Today he has sawed-off shotguns, which several soldiers have purchased, anxiously wanting "throw-down" weapons that they can claim the enemy owned if they end up shooting someone just for the fuck of it.

I scan the black-market DVDs packaged five and seven films to a DVD. We have developed a new type of film criticism and critique. Instead of simply judging a film on its screenplay and direction, we now judge films based on the black marketers who produce them. "Look at this guy," I say as I slouch in my chair during one of our frequent midnight film festivals while I'm on radio guard. "Look at the way he takes great pains to keep the camcorder even and steady on the screen. He doesn't cut off the credits on either side of the screen. You can tell he's slouched down in his seat, but he makes sure to hold the camera up during the movie so that you don't see the heads of the people in the audience. That's gotta be awkward to hold steady like that for two hours. That's good cinematography there."

And then I notice a rare gem in the normal selection of films available to us. A quadruple feature of *Chinatown*, *Casablanca*, *GoodFellas*, and, strangely, the Kirsten Dunst cheerleader feature *Bring It On*. I excitedly make my purchase, adding some ribbons for Brian the cat to play with and a pack of cheap Korean cigarettes.

In the command center hallway, Lieutenant Mitch is putting all his Christianity-based military leadership books in the footlocker.

"Sir, you won't believe the DVD I found at the front gate," I say, kneeling down next to him and grabbing his books from the locker for inspection. "I didn't know you were practicing a Christian style of leadership."

Lieutenant Mitch takes the books from me and puts them back. He laughs and says, "It's the same as normal leadership, except I'm supposed to pray for you all more, I think."

After a pause I say, more out of playful boredom than any serious impulse, "I can't go to Cougar Base. You gotta let them leave me here."

"Why?" he asks with another short laugh. Lieutenant Mitch laughs a lot.

"I'm not going to be on the radio at Cougar Base. They have all these other people for that. I'm going to be back out on the patrols with you. In the vehicles. Everyone keeps dying over there. Listen, I've done some statistical analysis. We all left Tarin Kowt together four months ago. So Cougar Base has been operational for four months. In that time they've had four U.S. soldiers die and four Afghan soldiers die. That's one soldier dying every two weeks. We have six months left of this deployment. Now, if I'm your right-hand man, which means I have to be point on patrols every fucking day, and your average patrol consists of nine guys, that means that every two weeks I have a one-in-nine chance of dying. Which means, I think"—I pause, pulling out my notebook— trying to make sense of my own math—"Well, it means, I'll probably die by the end of the deployment."

"Yeah, I know," Lieutenant Mitch says. "That's kinda the risk of being over here."

"The thing is, sir. The thing is. I don't want to go."

"Why?"

"Because they're trying to kill me!"

"Who is?"

"The Taliban!"

"They're not trying to kill you; they're trying to kill everyone!"

"Exactly my point! They're trying to kill me!"

Lieutenant Mitch pauses for a moment. Then he stops packing his books and says, "Did you just get done reading *Catch-22*?"

I pause before replying, "Maybe."

Lieutenant Mitch smiles, "Go pack."

We both laugh at my little performance.

"You seen Brian?" I ask, scanning under the command hallway desk and around the room.

"That's the cat, yeah?"

"Yeah."

"I heard some soldiers outside laughing about a cat in the barracks."

I pause.

My heart speeds up a bit.

Just a bit.

Something feels wrong.

Certainly there's nothing wrong with Brian heading over to the barracks.

Lots of soldiers here like animals.

Some soldiers are probably just playing with him.

But maybe I should check on him, just in case.

In the barracks, Cyndi Lauper is belting her heart out while *The Goonies* plays on television in an empty foyer. Nonalcoholic beer cans are randomly knocked over amid empty bags of chips. I don't see anyone, but I can hear a dull roar and muffled squeals of laughter coming from a room at the end of the hall. I move slowly down to the room and enter in a fake action-man pose, hoping to elicit a laugh, but nobody notices my arrival.

"Is it dead yet?" Jerome asks, in his typical faux voice of manufactured gruffness. I make my way through a few people to see what he's talking about.

Brian, my adopted kitten, is dead on the floor.

My heart goes icy.

His little kitten head is attached only by skin and lolls loosely, inverted on the rest of his body.

Blood stains his whiskers and mats his fur.

I look up at the wall to see the bloody stain where he bounced after being projectile-shot at the wall like a fastball.

"You guys are fucking sick!" Cox yells before leaving the room, disgusted. Devon and Ryan follow, both shaking their heads in wonder. The room is divided. Half the guys are watching with a residual morbid curiosity and are still laughing, while the other half are repelled but are unable to look away. Everybody starts to stumble out, looking a bit queasy, leaving only two soldiers standing triumphantly over their kill with stupid smiles on their faces: Jerome and Allison, the same two soldiers who the previous summer at West Point squashed chipmunks with their Army boots and bit the heads off frogs when they were left alone in the woods awaiting some monotonous detail.

"Well, he shouldn't have tried to rub up against me, stupid fucking cat," Jerome says, as if arguing his position and trying to win back his audience.

Allison, a giant of a man with a child's face, has a goofy grin that exposes his crooked teeth. He asks, "Should we burn it or bury it?"

"Don't fucking touch it!" I yell as I move in and shove past the both of them.

"Ahh, Rico, are you going to nurse him back to health? Are you going to take care of him now?" Allison coos into my ear in a whisper. "I can give you some glue if you want to glue his head back on." Allison laughs.

I don't say anything. I just pick Brian up and carry him outside.

"Don't be mad, Rico; it's just a fucking cat," Jerome calls out after me, confused by my agitation and anger, for some reason bothered that he's upset me.

I'm at the edge of the burn pit, where all our trash and feces get burned, sitting on my haunches and balanced precariously on a tire. Burned blackened piles of toilet paper and shit are all about my feet.

I wonder how people can be so cruel as to kill a kitten, of all things. How were they able to find amusement in that?

I shake my head in disgust and set Brian's gas-soaked corpse on fire, saying to no one in particular, "Well, that's great. Now I don't have a fucking cat."

Chapter 34

I ARRIVE AT COUGAR BASE AND
LEARN THE PURPOSE OF SANDBAGS

It's a textbook case of low-intensity conflict, Captain Nigel tells me as I
fill sandbags and he stands off to the side, looking casually dapper in
the blowing wind. He should've been a model for the new spring catalog of soldier wear, what with his scarf oh-so-casually tucked around
his desert camouflage top, and his black beanie cap. Captain Nigel is a
civil affairs officer. Or psyops or something. He deals with the indigenous folks and fools them, he tells me. Today he's here to hand out lots
of money. He's got almost half a million dollars in U.S. greenbacks to
hand out to the local warlords-in-waiting, and all they have to do is
pledge their allegiance to the U.S. flag, and to the Republic for which it
stands, with indivisibility and liberty and justice for all.

These sandbags I'm filling?

He tells me that even they have a purpose.

I'm winning the war with every sandbag I fill.

He's one of those asshole officers who try to inspire the men with
meaningless drivel about every action being important. If you take a
good bowel movement, you're helping win the war. Captain Nigel became attached to me on a previous trip to Dizzy when he found out
how much I've traveled.

Today our exchange of travel stories has turned into a lecture on
how it—all of it, the whole big mess, Afghanistan and the rest of the
world—is working wonderfully, and I should keep my chin up. Eventually the U.S. would have everybody straightened out.

He describes for me the processes I am intricately involved with but apparently have no understanding of.

You looked at the terrain and the locations of anticoalition forces activity, and you threw a firebase of infantry soldiers up smack dab in the middle of the hot zone, he said. There would be some attacks and fired rockets at first, but eventually the enemy would disperse to areas farther away and less infiltrated with U.S. forces. The U.S. firebases, small remote camps housing only a hundred or so soldiers, would act as bubbles of security for the region, creating "safe zones" in small radii that ran congruently around the firebase in all directions. Daily patrols would leave the wire and patrol the area, always at different times of the day and the night, and always to different locations around the firebase. Sometimes the patrols would be mounted and head out in armored Humvees, and other times the patrols would be on foot so the soldiers could quietly wait it out in heavily trafficked ravines or ridgelines that were inaccessible to Humvees. The soldiers often felt that they weren't doing anything helpful by conducting these patrols, which were almost always boring and without incident, but there was an underlying purpose, Captain Nigel said. I grunted my approval.

The purpose was to further extend the bubble of security provided by the firebase. Now the security extended not just to the area immediately around the firebase, but to a farther radius, to anywhere that a security patrol could potentially end up driving through. This was the day-to-day operation of the firebase, he said, as if I were not aware of our own daily activities. Patrols and force protection. Two squads would pull security around the base serving force protection. The other squad was the patrol squad. And then every few days, or every week, they would rotate and switch duties.

While the business of the firebase was being conducted, the CERP officer would start the area reconstruction projects. They would engage the local structure of government, whatever it was—sometimes a highly visible district chief or city mayor, at other times a vaguely agreed-upon village elder—and work with them to bring in local contractors to bid on projects. Hundreds of thousands of dollars were funneled into each area of operations. Locals were paid to build wells and schools and renovate government facilities. And, of course, at every level locally there was corruption, and contractors were forced to divert funds to the government officials who had recommended them. But this was understood, and was tolerated, as it made the local government officials dependent upon the United States for their income and power and authority within the community. This was, after all, the second poorest nation on earth, with the average Afghan making less than two hundred U.S. dollars per year. And slowly, word would get out that the United States is not like the Russians; they're not here to kill us; they're here to rebuild us. And surely but slowly, the collective consensus of Afghan public opinion would turn toward the United States.

Simultaneously, as the reconstruction projects were started and implemented, an S2 officer attached to the base would gather intelligence. Intelligence would come from all different types of sources: from monitored radio and phone communications, from locals eager to gain favor with the United States in hopes of a contact, from local officials hoping to continue their funding supply with the United States, from the tactical questioning (interrogation) of arrested locals, from the Pakistan intelligence community.

From these intelligence reports, the movements and activities of a hierarchy of wanted Taliban and Al Qaeda would be plotted and collated. Every few weeks, either the remaining squad, or a platoon, or the Special Forces guys at base would launch air assault operations, where they would fly by helicopter to remote locations in the rural areas beyond their immediate bubble of security to raid compounds and search for wanted individuals. Many times they would be successful in capturing desired targets. Oftentimes they were not. But even when they were not, it would feed the intensifying sense of claustrophobia felt by Taliban targets perpetually displaced by American movement.

One by one, the Taliban's most wanted would start to turn themselves in. A program had been started in Kandahar where former Taliban could turn themselves in without fear of arrest or detainment, and after a small and short rehabilitation program where they would learn that the U.S. was good and that the Taliban was bad, they would be allowed to swear allegiance to the new government, and all past crimes would be forgiven.

A critical threshold would be reached where the remaining targets would one day wake up, look around them, and realize that they were the last of an outlaw group that no longer had much momentum or hope for success. And then, on this day, the threshold of sustainability would be reached, and overnight the Taliban movement would be dead, its final members dispersed into quiet hiding or into new lives, where they'd be hesitant to speak of their past.

Of course, he says, turning away, offering a slight suggestion toward the possible failure of his theory, there seems to be new Taliban all the time. He doesn't even know if the force we're fighting now can even properly be called Taliban anymore, what with there being so much turnover in the rank and file of the group that originally offered refuge to bin Laden. Those guys are long since gone, dissipated, or captured. The guys we're fighting now—these are new folks we just call Taliban because it's easier when you have an easily identifiable label for the enemy.

That is the way it's supposed to work, anyway, Captain Nigel says, dismissing his own suggestion of the failure of his theory. I shovel another bag of dirt into a sandbag.

He asks me how my book is coming along, and I say I haven't actually started to write it yet. Well, I've written some of it, but I erased it all. I don't know what to write about. Occasionally I interview the soldiers I work with about their feelings. Stupid shit like that. He laughs and says that's what I'm doing wrong. Fuck the masses, he says. They're sheep. They're interchangeable units to be utilized and controlled on the battlefield by their superiors. You can write their story easy, he tells me. Write about Ford pickup trucks, and how much they miss Georgia, and finger-banging little Mary Jane, and six-packs of beer. Fuck them.

I want to write about something interesting. I should keep my eyes open this next mission. I'm part of the instrument of force that determines global political authority that determines the rise and fall of nations. Have I ever read any Heinlein? Any *Starship Troopers*? Yeah, I changed my name because of that guy, I think to myself. No, I've never read Heinlein. I've never heard of him. Heinlein who? Violence, naked force, has settled more issues in history than has any other factor, and the contrary opinion is wishful thinking at its worst. That's Heinlein, he tells me. Force is brutish, ugly, and raw. That's Hobbes—he thinks; he's not sure. Point being, I'm looking in the wrong direction for my inspiration.

Captain Nigel smiles and tells me to remember that I'm doing my part, that I'm destroying the Taliban one shovelful of dirt at a time. Every contribution of action is helping to perpetuate the momentum of larger systems of force I can't begin to fathom.

He turns to go and then pauses, turns back with an expression of slight worry, his scarf blowing in the wind, and tells me to be careful during this big offensive.

Things sometimes get messy.

Chapter 35

THINGS SOMETIMES GET MESSY

know I shouldn't drink anything, but I'm thirsty. And I shouldn't drink, of course, because lately it seems that every time I start to mix a flavored beverage for myself, someone shoots at us. There is some type of cosmic correlation between cherry-flavored beverage powder and bullets starting to fly in Afghanistan.

I'm in a field in the middle of a narrow valley, with large steep peaks that almost pass for sheer cliffs only five hundred meters on either side of me. The middle strip of the valley is composed of farmers' fields that plateau off one another and border a dried-up riverbed. On either side of the valley are strings of compounds that hug the respective bases of the steep vertical inclines behind them.

My satellite antenna is all folded out just so, and I have just established communications with the battalion base after adjusting the antenna ever so slightly to be on the correct azimuth and heading. Actually, the azimuth and heading that were given to me resulted in nothing but static, but using my intuitive Army sense, I pointed the antenna in the opposite direction and was immediately able to hear people talking over the radio.

I sit down Indian style in the grass and start preparing my meal as I watch my platoon a few hundred meters east on the north side of the valley kicking in compound doors and clearing buildings from one side of the valley to the other. The helicopter that inserted us just flew away, and the sound of its rotor blades fades as it passes out of sight behind a distant mountain. We're looking for a high-profile Taliban leader. We're the searching element, and a sniper team sits positioned on top of the ridge on the valley's north end, watching the east end of the valley which collapses in on itself into a narrow mountain pass. The west end, which broadens into a series of fields and rolling hills, is secured several kilometers away by Sergeant Derrens and his element.

Devon sits behind the machine gun, resting on its tripod, pulling security on the south side of the valley, covering our platoon's rear as it searches the north side.

"I'm thinking I want to either be a nuclear physicist or a porn star," Devon says as he picks aimlessly at a piece of grass.

"Well, those are both good options," I reply.

"Or maybe a child psychiatrist," says Devon. "I could go to a community college and get my associates in probably only a few months, huh? What's a psychiatrist—a couple years of college?"

"Yep, that's it," I respond through clenched teeth as I tear open my cherry beverage powder and start to mix it in my canteen.

And that's when it happens.

At the moment that the cherry beverage powder hits the water.

That's the catalyst.

Suddenly, on the south side of the valley, on the side that Devon is supposedly pulling security on, gunfire rips toward us.

Once again, in a matter of seconds, quiet sludgy calm has turned into hyperkinetic intensity.

Devon's training takes over. He opens fire with the machine gun and starts to lay waste to the south side of the valley.

I sigh, gently set my cherry beverage powder aside, and lie down on the ground, lifting up my helmet, which has dropped low across my face and into my line of sight. "Hey, what are you firing at? Where are they?"

Devon lets up on the trigger, his shoulder all hunched up into the buttstock of the machine gun, and says to me over his shoulder, "I don't know. But it's a chance to shoot my weapon." Devon starts firing again. Massive, earsplitting bursts. And then he pauses again and turns back to me once more and says a bit guiltily, "I just, well, it's just that I don't want to carry all these rounds. They're really heavy." He pauses, looking at me for approval.

I shrug and ready my weapon, scanning the opposite side of the valley.

Where are they, the little buggers?

Fuck it. This is a chance to shoot my weapon, right? I open up with my M4 and start firing randomly at rocks.

I look to my left to see Lieutenant Mitch and the rest of 3rd Platoon a few hundred meters away, now even with me and Devon, using the riverbed for cover as they string themselves out along its length and return fire. I don't think my platoon knows what they were firing at, either.

"Hey, Devon!" I yell over the gunfire. Devon pauses in his return fire and turns around. "Do you think we should get behind some cover?" I ask, motioning to the open field around us. "I mean, we're just sitting out here in the open."

Devon looks around. Finally, after a moment, with our platoon engaged in a pitched gun battle a few hundred meters farther down, he says, "Yeah, good point. Help me move the gun, will you?"

Devon picks up the machine gun and sprints with waddling steps, weighed down by his machine gun and ammunition, to the next adjacent field, which offers the protection of a rock retaining wall and an adjacent berm. I follow him with his tripod. I run back to our old position to grab the satellite radio. I can hear the rounds getting closer. Whizzing by my head, actually. I grab the radio and my cherry beverage in my canteen and run to the berm near the retaining wall.

Now protected, I set up my little area, stir my cherry beverage powder a bit more, neaten my mess, and then call up on the satellite radio system in a manner later described to me by a friend who is listening to the very same net at Firebase Dizzy as "indifferent" and "casual." So, all indifferently and casually, I say into the satellite net for all of Afghanistan to hear, "Bobcat 2-6, this is Hunter-6 Romeo. Yeah, um, we have, uh troops in contact. Over."

The panicked radio operator on the other end tells me to hold while the radio changes hands a few times. I imagine elevator music as I'm placed on hold, and I hum along to a song that isn't playing until finally the battalion colonel speaks to me: "Hunter-6 Romeo, this is Bobcat 2-6. What's the situation? Over." In the span of mere seconds I have superseded more than half the Army's rank structure and am now talking with the number one American commander in this portion of Afghanistan.

"We're taking contact from the south side of Zamburay Valley from an unknown number of assailants who have small arms and machine guns. Over."

"Roger; we need to speak to the Hunter-6 element, over."

"Yeah, the thing about that is," I say, pausing and momentarily depressing the hand mike as I think about my next choice of words before continuing. "The thing about that is I'm not colocated with the Hunter-6 element, over."

"Hunter-6 Romeo, this is Bobcat-6. You need to put on Hunter-6 now or move to his position, but I need to speak with Hunter-6 immediately. Over."

"Yeah, that's the thing, he's um," I stammer looking for the proper words as I look down the valley to see Hunter-6, Lieutenant Mitch, pinned down under heavy fire. "Well, he's preoccupied at the moment. He can't come to the phone."

"YOU GET HIM ON THE DAMN NET IMMEDIATELY!" the colonel screams.

I pause for a second and then meekly reply, "Roger; wait one . . ."

I hear more traffic for me, but I drop the hand microphone into the grass so as to not have to listen. I pull out my internal platoon radio and say, "Hunter-6, Hunter-6, this is Hunter-6 Romeo."

"You know what would be cool?" Devon tells me, letting up from the trigger for a moment. "A zombie movie set in Afghanistan. Wouldn't that be some crazy shit? And it could have all this subtext of racism and third world versus first world as U.S. soldiers fucked up the Haji zombies."

"That does sound like a good idea," I reply. And then again into my internal platoon radio, "Hunter-6, this is your Romeo radio fellow. Respond please."

"This is Hunter-6!" comes my lieutenant's breathless reply.

"Yeah, Hunter-6? Yeah, um, you're needed on the radio here. Battalion commander wants to talk to you. He sounds kinda pissed."

There is a long pause of consideration. "Right at this moment? I'm kind of in the middle of a firefight."

"I know, sir! I tell him, but he says he needs to talk to you. I would move down to your position, but, well, there's people shooting all around you, and I've got this big bulky satellite dish and . . ."

"Hold on, I'm en route!"

A few moments later Lieutenant Mitch comes bounding around the corner of the stone wall that borders the farmer's field, flushed and out of breath. He collapses to his knees and gasps for air as I hand him the hand microphone.

"This is Hunter-6," he says through long strenuous gasps.

"Hunter-6, this is Bobcat-6. I need a situation report," says the colonel.

"We're taking contact from the south side of Zamburay Valley from an unknown number of assailants who have small arms and machine guns. Over."

"This is absurd! Devon, do you even see who we're firing at?" I ask.

Devon turns to me and shakes his head. He does not know who we are firing at. "Aren't we firing at that compound? I see a guy on the top of that compound."

I squint at his enemy and reply, "That's a bag of wheat, Devon."

"Oh," Devon says, shrugging his shoulders. "I don't know who we're shooting at, then." He returns to firing at the wheat.

Lieutenant Mitch hands the hand microphone back to me. I ask him, "Sir, do you see the enemy?"

"Yeah, there's uh, there's uh," he keeps saying, trying to regain his breath before finally admitting, "No. I have no idea. Some bad guys over there." He waves southward, indicating that side of the valley.

"Sorry to call you over here, sir. I told him the exact same thing you did."

"Try and get in touch with our sniper element, will you? Can you move the radio any closer?" he asks.

I take in a sharp breath as I scan the steep mountains on either side of us. "Gee, I don't know, sir. I just don't know. This is a pretty narrow valley. I've got a good signal here. I'm hesitant to give up a good spot where I know I have a signal." Saying this, I know that I could probably move the radio and still maintain a signal. Still, I don't want to risk moving the finicky system under enemy fire and not be able to get communications set up again. The radio takes a couple of minutes to set up, and the likelihood they will move to another position as soon as I set back up is highly probable. It's best to stay. Besides, I have my cherry beverage powder here, and I'm already set up in my little space.

Lieutenant Mitch nods at my explanation and runs back off for the riverbed, all hunched over. I watch Lieutenant Mitch arrive back at the platoon and consult with Sergeant Santiago and Sergeant Riley. After a moment, Sergeant Santiago's squad rushes out of the riverbed to the closest compound on the south side of the valley, hiding behind its protective walls, while Sergeant Riley's squad lays down suppressive fire. They know the enemy fire is coming from the west end of the south side of the valley, so Sergeant Santiago's men move from compound to compound from east to west while Sergeant Riley's men move down the center of the valley, protected by the riverbed toward the valley's west end.

This goes on for twenty minutes or so, during which time I decide that the sensible thing to do is finish my lunch while I scan the battle with binoculars and try in vain to contact the sniper section somewhere on one of the mountains behind us. (We will later learn that they were extracted earlier and we never actually had any sniper protection.)

Suddenly I think I see something behind the compound Sergeant Santiago has just moved to. I call him over the radio, "Sergeant Santiago, you've got someone behind your compound!"

I watch through the binoculars as Sergeant Santiago peeks around a corner and throws a grenade. The grenade explodes. He peeks back around the corner at what he's hit. Then he turns and looks across the valley at me and gives me the finger as he calls over the radio saying, "Thanks, I just blew up a rock."

"You're welcome," I reply, laughing.

And then the Apache comes on station and begins firing hellfire missiles.

I call up Lieutenant Mitch and ask if he knows where the enemy fire is coming from. He replies that they're firing from somewhere on the top of the cliff that forms the southern half of the valley, but he's unsure of their exact location.

"Hunter-6 Romeo, this is Bobcat-6; I need a situation report. Over."

"Bobcat-6, this is Hunter-6 Romeo. We've got Apaches on station, which is firing on the compounds. Third Platoon is clearing the compounds. We're still unsure where it is we're taking fire from, but we think it's from the top of the ridgeline.

"Hunter-6 Romeo, Bobcat-6. Listen carefully; you need to get yourself colocated with Hunter-6 immediately, and he needs to be a lot more aggressive. He needs to be chasing them up the mountain and killing them. Close with and kill the enemy—do you understand?"

"Sir, I really can't get to their location right now because there's all these helicopters that are blowing up the middle of the valley," I say, imagining myself running down the center of the valley dodging hellfire missiles as I drag my tangled antenna behind me. And then I pick up the internal platoon radio and say, "Hunter-6, this is your Romeo. Listen, Bobcat-6 says you have to be aggressive. Show a little spirit out there. A little chutzpah."

Lieutenant Mitch, who has been under fire for about thirty minutes now, starts screaming obscenities back at me over the radio.

"Hunter-6 Romeo, this is Bobcat-6. I need to speak with Hunter-6 Actual. Over!"

I click the walkie-talkie back on, "Sir, he needs to speak with you again." And then into the satellite radio I state to the colonel, "Sir, there's helicopters shooting up the middle of the valley. I really don't think it's a good idea for him to . . ."

"I DON'T CARE WHAT YOU THINK IS A GOOD IDEA; GET HUNTER-6 ON IMMEDIATELY!"

A few moments later, dripping with sweat, Lieutenant Mitch falls onto his knees and crawls to the radio, knocking his helmet off into a pile of rocks. The sweat slides off his bald head as he collapses against the stone wall.

"Hunter-6, I need a situation report," comes the incessant whine of our battalion colonel, who just can't seem to shut up.

"We've got Apaches on station, which are firing on the compounds on the southern side of the valley which we took fire from. Third Platoon is bounding forward from the east, clearing the compounds one by one. We're still unsure where it is we're taking fire from, but they seem to be at the top of the ridgeline."

"Why haven't you killed them yet, Hunter-6? It's very simple—close with and kill the enemy, just flank them . . ."

Lieutenant Mitch eyes the sheer ninety-degree vertical cliff that is the flank of the enemy and says, "Sir, they're on higher ground."

"Lieutenant, you're an infantry platoon leader. Now start leading your men and get after them! Bobcat-6, out."

"Jesus Christ!" Lieutenant Mitch screams. "We're so fucking tired!"

"I know! Me too!" I say as I sit Indian style on the ground, munching on my cookies and sucking cherry water through a hose.

And then just like that, the firing stops.

We move to the riverbed that borders the southern side of the valley and start moving through the last of the compounds. There are a thousand things to do. The local Afghans who need to be questioned, photos to be taken of the damage to the compounds, sketches to be drawn that illustrate series of movements, grids to be taken at each intersection where there was an intense pause by the moving platoon. It's already late afternoon. And to make matters worse, no one has eaten lunch or breakfast.

Oh yes, and they found several wounded locals and one dead who were hit by stray bullets. I'm on the radio in my new position (where the radio works just fine), calling in a medevac request to battalion to get choppers in to extract the wounded. Not much gets done in the way of collecting the necessary information for an investigatory follow-up as we sit smoking cigarettes. We start to move the shot-up locals to the landing zone when high up above us, our foes open fire on us again.

The wounded Afghans are dropped to the ground and left out in the open as everybody runs for cover. One by one the soldiers fall over the side of the berm and pop back up occasionally to return fire. The berm is eaten up by machine-gun fire as we hunker low and wait for a break.

This lasts for another hour. Or maybe only twenty minutes. To tell the truth, no one knows.

And then, just like that, it's over again. And we sigh with relief.

It's late at night, and Lieutenant Mitch is certain he'll be fired for returning fire or for getting the innocent bystanders shot up.

Battalion calls throughout the night, wanting particular pieces of information. At 11:54 p.m. they call, wanting to know exactly where Third Squad had been standing when the Apache opened fire.

At 12:12 a.m. they call, wanting to know what building we found an AK-47 in.

At 1:06 a.m. they call, wanting to know the second detainee's father's name. At 2:33 a.m. they call, wanting to know what our grid was the third time we took fire.

Had we taken fire a third time? Some of us were quite certain of it. Others weren't so sure. It sounds absurd to say that you don't remember a thirty-minute gun battle, but that's the truth—sometimes you don't. The further truth was that we didn't know any of the information battalion wants.

So we sit up on the hill and, like authors constructing a screenplay, lay out index cards that list our "facts" and our lies. We have to keep notes of the things that we've already told battalion, because already they've called up asking for the same information twice. It's as if they're testing us, searching for holes and weaknesses in our story.

The next morning when we wake up there is more gunfire, but to be honest, I can't remember any of the details. Besides, we have more important things to think about.

Chapter 36

OPERATION HAMSTER SALIVA

Before we left for the mission, I had been alone with Lieutenant Mitch late at night in the command building while he appeared to be studying satellite imagery in preparation for the offensive. Instead he asked, "Did you borrow my *Smallville* DVD? Someone has my *Smallville* DVD. I have to find out what happens to Superman, and it's very frustrating to be left hanging like this."

"What are we calling the big operation, sir?" I asked.

"I think we're going to call it Someone Better Give Me Back My *Smallville* DVD." He looked over to see me staring at him with no response and then offered, "No, it's, uh, Lightning Thrust, or Desert Shadow, or some macho military thing."

"Why are all military operations always all tough-sounding? I despise tough-sounding military operation names. I think it's time for some originality. Something totally absurd. How about we call it Operation Hamster Saliva. Something really stupid?"

"That's perfect!" Lieutenant Mitch stated excitedly. He wrote it on the marker board above the mission seating plans for the helicopter in big block letters and underlined it a few times. "Operation Hamster Saliva—I like that! Tell you what, though," he said, putting his arm around me. "That'll be the real name of the whole operation, but let's keep it a secret name just between you and me. That way it'll be more special, okay? So when Captain Grimes and everyone refer to it as Operation Lightning Thrust, you and I can secretly laugh because we'll be the only two who know its real name. Okay?"

"Fine by me, sir!" I said, laughing.

I stand there, my face buried in my hands. I've got an oncoming case of the giggles.

All of us Army soldiers stand on top of the small hill, with the loudspeaker behind us. The electronic voice tells the people of the village, in Pashtu, that the Taliban are cowards and that the people disgrace their families if they join the Taliban. The local Afghans of the village, whom we have arrested and released multiple times this morning while searching for the owner of an obscure radio transmission describing a planned attack, stand there blinking in the sun, appropriately confused and bewildered. We had forgotten who we had already arrested and just kept rearresting the villagers as soon as we searched them and released them. After a while, the villagers, after being released, had just gotten back in line to be arrested again. And then the electronic voice says, "The U.S. Army is good; the Taliban is bad."

The U.S. soldiers look on proudly. You're able to look on proudly when you can forcibly detain other human beings and make them listen to you.

All I can think of, behind a huge smile that's spread from ear to ear and is about to collapse under its own weight into laughter, is Operation Hamster Saliva!

Our new company commander, Captain Grimes, all clean-shaven and muscular and all-American, looks on proudly, hands firmly on his hips, and says, "Well, guess we showed them, huh?"

I can't understand him at all. He believes adamantly in America and the U.S. Army and the criminal justice system and the legal system and has never tried drugs and was a Boy Scout before the Army and is ardently religious. He's one of those individuals who make it a point to pray when the president offers some hollow "Prayer Day" gesture after a national tragedy. Who is this person who believes in everything when I can find nothing to believe in? It seems the only thing he's leery of is jaded cynical individuals such as me, who complain all the time and offer nothing positive in place of their criticism.

And he definitely believes in Operation Lightning Thrust.

I want dreadfully to believe in Operation Lightning Thrust, too. After all, I'm at the tip of the spear, as Captain Nigel would say. I'm part of the instrument of force that determines the global political authority that determines the rise and fall of nations.

But as I sit on the tip of the spear of geopolitical international relations and look out at all the bewildered Afghans holding their Army tote bags and coffee mugs and cans of Play-Doh, I'm just not feeling it. I didn't know the tip of the spear handed out Army tote bags.

And then the dam collapses, and I break out into loud obnoxious laughing in the silence just before Captain Grimes resumes his speech.

He pauses and looks over at me.

The Afghans look over at me.

I turn around and cover my face in my hands as tears stream down my face.

It isn't so much that this is funny as much as that sometimes I love seeing just how far absurd situations can be taken. Sometimes this requires my temporary cooperation. Other times, like now, it does not.

The helicopters land in a small narrow valley next to a river and a series of lonely compounds. We race off the helicopters when Lieutenant Mitch trips and does a nosedive into the ground. This makes us lose some of our intensity as everyone busts out laughing. First Squad moves into a cordon position around the perimeter of one of the compounds to stop anybody from escaping as Second Squad enters, kicking in doors and waving their rifles at the screaming women inside. A few local Afghans in the area, stand in fields and against a fencepost, watch us silently.

One of the privates in Second Squad asks if someone should stop the old man who has been sitting down quietly watching us and is now casually walking away. The old man has already walked past several soldiers who ignore him because of his easygoing manner when Sergeant

Stephens, almost as an afterthought, says, "Yeah, might as well bring him over here."

We ask him his name and he tells us. We're shocked to discover that we've just captured one of America's Most Wanted. And for this, Cougar Company makes international news. Sometimes that's how it happens. You don't catch the guy in some dramatic gunfight. Sometimes you arrest one of the most valuable players, as an afterthought.

After being arrested, the old man walks gingerly on leathery, calloused, bare feet over the piles of excrement and crumpled soda cans that litter his compound to a small stool. He is sat down and guarded by U.S. soldiers, who seem massive in comparison with the old man's thin frame and slight build and who also have to constantly be reminded to stop talking and watch him. To add to the ambiance of destruction, I kick a water pitcher into a pile of feces. There are feces everywhere in Afghanistan. It seems there are more feces per square mile than anywhere else on earth.

After Captain Grimes and Lieutenant Mitch finish questioning a few men found inside the compound, they turn them over to us privates, who continue the interrogation. The men's hands are still bound by plastic ties.

"Who holds the record for touchdowns in a single season in the NFL?"

"What's the number one grossing movie of all time?"

"Which actor has appeared in more *Star Wars* movies than any other?"

We circle them angrily, demanding answers to our questions. They stare up at us, scared and confused.

The mission over for the day, we take over the compound and kill the rest of the afternoon with laughter and play.

For dinner I have a chicken tetrazzini main meal from an MRE, along with crackers and jelly and a bottle of water.

Devon is next to me, talking about his plans after the Army, "I want to be either a pediatrician or a fireworks pyro engineer."

Private Ryan is laughing over his photo of Corporal Billy's shit, squealing with delight that it looks like Dairy Queen swirl.

A few meters away, Private Sorbil is laughing as the dog that's supposed to sniff out weapons for us humps his leg and starts to cum. The game is to get the dog excited, have him hump your leg, and then try to pull away before the dog can finish. Sorbil's losing.

A few meters away, Corporal Billy is playing the absurd question game. At this particular moment the question is this: You come home from a business trip to find a line of men at your house. You enter the house to find that they're gangbanging your daughter. What do you do?

Corporal Billy has encountered an interesting sociological response. Although responses are split, with about half kicking everybody out and trying to talk to their daughter and the other half going on a murdering rampage and killing everybody including the daughter, whenever he throws in the follow-up question of the clown that comes to the door to participate, without exception everyone knocks the clown the fuck out.

"Rico!" Corporal Billy shouts from his small distance away. "Same question. You open the door, and there's a clown. He has a balloon in his hand. You ask if you can help him, and he says he's there for the gang bang. What do you do?"

"Knock him the fuck out," I respond through bites of cracker. "You have to."

Billy laughs, explaining to the soldiers around him that everyone always knocks out the clown.

Outside the compound, the Afghan National Army soldiers who accompanied us on our mission are tossing bombs that they have found in the dirt back and forth in a game of catch.

One ANA soldier finds a rusted bicycle with a flower basket and rides around in circles in front of the compound, waving at everybody with a flower in his mouth. He looks like a figure out of a foreign black-and-white art film that has never been made: *The Afghan Bicycle Thief.*

Next to him some soldiers start singing, "Video Killed the Radio Star." Aileen, our strange, mysterious, indigenous ally, dressed in a turban wrap covering his entire head except for a pair of Ray-Ban sunglasses to conceal his identity, is a self-styled Taliban hunter. His identity is unknown, and for the present circumstances he finds it convenient to work with U.S. forces. And although Aileen has not said much the entire helicopter ride to the objective, suddenly he starts tapping his foot and smiling to the beat of the song. This makes me smile, too.

Nothing brings my spirits up like Taliban hunters who tap their feet to "Video Killed the Radio Star."

I don't know why I've started petting the top-ranked Taliban in Afghanistan the way one would pet a little puppy, but I feel compelled to do so. There I am by the fire, its flames sending creepy cavernous shadows around the walls of the compound, the wicked sharp cold of winter blowing on us miserably, and it just seems the appropriate thing to do. I'm on the night shift charged with watching the prisoner we arrested, and I just start stroking the guy's head lightly and affectionately. I feel bad for him.

Staring at the frail old man, I sense a disconnect that someone seemingly so powerless could be the enemy of the big bad United States. This is one of those rare moments of clarity when I see him for what he is: a scared ignorant man who for much of his life has endured things that most Americans could never imagine, like warfare, virtual starvation, and a lifetime of cold winters with no socks. If I had gone all my life without warm socks, maybe I would've been a Taliban too. You never knew.

He awakens to my gentle strokes on his head and motions to his mouth indicating that he is hungry. He sits up and nestles close to the fire. My mom has mailed me Scooby-Doo graham cracker snacks that are labeled "Scooby Snacks." So I feed the Taliban fighter Scooby Snacks and water. He munches them through an open mouth, and crumbs fall into his lap as he stares at me and I back at him. He smiles and I return the smile. He lies back down, and I tuck in the outer edges of the blanket that he can't reach.

I'm a good person, acting all humane and shit toward our enemy. Who else would be so kind? No one. That's who. Just me. Damn, I'm a good person.

Buoyed by my feelings of goodness, I stare up at the night sky and suddenly feel overwhelmed by how much beauty is in the world sometimes. Fuck paying attention to the point of the spear.

For the rest of the mission, I'm going to forgo my normal negativity and only pay attention to the things that make me smile. I'm too negative. No wonder I haven't found anything in life to be passionate about. How can you be passionate about something when you criticize everything?

So this is my Afghanistan travelogue. See the sights, kill a few folks, spend a few nights at the Cougar Base youth hostel in beautiful Oruzgan province, and smile at the warm hospitality and experiences that Afghanistan has to offer.

The next morning, a Chinook picks us up and flies us to our next objective. As we fly in our helicopter, the ammunition-sniffing dog we have with us runs up to an open window, tongue hanging out his mouth. He sticks his head out, taking in every second of the ride.

There is something reassuring and right with the world when you know that dogs are the same everywhere, and that they care little if the window is in a ten-year-old Honda on a city street or in a Chinook helicopter skirting the caps of lonely mountains.

We enter the compound expecting to find bad guys. Instead, all we find is a stoned seventeen-year-old kid and a compound full of hashish and opium. The seventeen-year-old boy stares at us, quite amused, through glazed eyes and a slack mouth that hangs open.

"God, this pisses me off," my lieutenant says. "Fucking drugs." He scans the compound and says the words that you can tell he has practiced in his own head and has been waiting the entire deployment to say: "Burn it. Burn it all."

At this same moment, Diego calls me on the radio to ask for a situation report. He's with the commander. I inform him that we have searched the compound and found nothing but drugs, which we're preparing to burn.

"Uh-huh. Yes, I understand," I say into the radio before turning to Lieutenant Mitch. "Sir, we're not allowed to burn it."

"What? What do you mean we're not allowed to burn it?" The two soldiers who have lit a pile of hay and are approaching the stacks of hashish in hopes of having a residual high pause and stare at us.

"I don't know, sir. He just said don't burn it. He's not sure if we're allowed to do that or not."

"The opium or the pot?"

"Hold on; I'll ask. Cougar-6, Hunter-6. Are we not allowed to burn the opium, the pot, or is it both?" I look up from my radio. "He's checking, sir."

We all scan the compound as we wait for an answer. Most take seats on the ground. The soldiers with the fire take turns trying to burn one another, and Lieutenant Mitch sits in the corner, angry that his orders have been put on hold.

After several moments I finally hear back. "Yes, yes, I understand. Roger." I turn to Lieutenant Mitch and say, "Sir, we're allowed to burn opium, but not the pot."

Lieutenant Mitch walks around the piles of hashish, all sad and frustrated, like a little kid who has been told by his mother that he doesn't get anything from the store. "But I wanted to burn the hash!" He pauses for a moment, drumming his fingers on a bundle of pot, thinking. "Okay, well, if we can't burn it, we can't burn it. Burn the opium though. Where's that opium at?"

Private Mulbeck brings the bag forward and sets it on the ground. The two soldiers with the fire light the small bag of opium, and all watch as it hisses and melts and becomes a black glob on the floor, looking not unlike congealed wax from a burning candle.

Lieutenant Mitch approaches the stoned-out occupant of the compound and says to him, "You see, that's what happens when you grow opium. It gets burned, buddy. It gets burned. I'll bet you'll think twice before you grow any opium again, won't you? Come on guys, let's go." The stoned-out Afghan smiles and lolls his head.

Suddenly, Lieutenant Mitch does a double take and walks back into the compound, with all of us following him, and says, "Because drugs are bad, okay?" The interpreter interprets, trying not to smile. "And because this road, this whole drug thing, it leads you down a road that frankly, my friend, you don't want to go down. You know, there's lots of good, um, crops out there; there's lots of good crops out there besides hashish and opium. You could grow wheat, or um, barley, or, uh, what else could he grow?" he asks the rest of us.

"Um, corn?" I offer.

"Well, point is," Lieutenant Mitch continues, "he could grow something besides drugs, which just lead to negativity and doing bad in school and a nonproductive life. He could grow wheat or barley or some other things which we're not sure what they are, but we're sure there are other things that he could grow." Lieutenant Mitch looks around the compound one final time to see if he has missed anything. Then, satisfied, he turns to leave. We follow him out of the compound.

A second later, we all turn right back around as Lieutenant Mitch reenters the compound, apparently not done saying what he feels needs to be said: "Because drugs are like—no good. The mind, tell him, the mind is a terrible thing to waste." The interpreter translates. "And tell him that there's peer pressure, but he just needs to say no sometimes. Just say no to drugs!" After the interpreter finishes, Lieutenant Mitch again walks us all out of the compound.

We leave the Afghan local laughing in his drug-addled haze.

The thirty of us are marching toward our target, a house on the far side of a village that is suspected of being a relay point for Taliban weapons and supplies. As we walk toward the edge of the village, the local radios start to chatter. We pick up voices that talk about us to one another. They're tracking our position as we move.

They're behind those compounds; they're moving across the river; they're in that field.

We scan the fields for someone who could be following us, but we don't see anyone. The locals all appear to be minding their own business and ducking inside as we pass.

And then the reports turn malicious.

As soon as they cross that bend in the road, open fire!

252 | JOHNNY RICO

We reach the bend in the road, and nothing happens.

Pull back to the alley on the far side of town, and when they hit the alley, open fire!

We hit the alley, and nothing happens.

Pull back to the compound! We're gathering here! We'll make our final stand here!

When we see the compound come into view, we pause and lie low in the grass at the rear of a compound at the edge of the village, and try to scan it with binoculars. There are people everywhere. Not people, Taliban. A hundred or so are next to the compound. Congregating. Preparing for something.

It seems this time they are being true to their word and aren't pulling back any farther.

They're in the field watching us with binoculars! Get ready to open fire!

We crane our necks around. How the hell are they getting these reports?

Decisions have to be made. Will we go straight in and see what happens? I'm scared to death of going straight in, but I'm also exhilarated by this option. Or will we send scouts out ahead to try and get a better perspective?

And that's when the Air Force sergeant whose name I always forgot raises his hand and says that he has a surprise for us.

He tells us to sit down. We'll want to be sitting for this.

We lie down in the grass and wait.

And then, the air gets sucked backwards.

Like in a fire's backdraft.

We hear a rumble in the distance that sounds like an earthquake.

The small bits of rock under our palms rattle and slide off the uneven earth.

And then what looks like a stealth bomber thunders by overhead, only a couple hundred meters over our heads, flying hundreds of miles an hour!

Windows shatter, water vibrates in still puddles, and eardrums crack and bleed.

It's as if the hand of God himself has been waved over the face of the earth.

Displays of U.S. military superiority of this magnitude and grandeur give me a hard-on for death and destruction. We can't all help but smile and laugh in delight over the engine's diminishing scream as it quickly vanishes into the horizon.

Yeah, you want to fuck with us now!

Our show of force is enough. The radio chatter stops, and the town empties into the adjoining mountain range. By the time we arrive at the house, it's empty.

I'm supposed to be on radio guard, but I've fallen asleep.

I should feel bad for sleeping on guard, but we have been running around the mountains for weeks now, and I'm too tired to feel guilty. I deserve my sleep. I'm owed my sleep.

And then I hear the voice that awakens me over the hand mike.

That distant voice with the sound of a lulling jet engine in the background. I didn't even know we had a B1 bomber on station. No one fucking tells me about this shit. Goddamn, this is some ridiculous shit. It would have been nice if someone had even bothered to tell me that I was going to have a B1 on station. But then I wonder if someone had told me about it and I simply hadn't paid attention.

That was also a very distinct possibility.

"Last calling station, this is Hunter-6 Romeo," I state sleepily.

"Hunter-6 Romeo, this is Bandit 7-1, I need you to put out an IR to mark your position. Over."

"Roger," I say. I put the hand mike down and fumble through my backpack with numb fingers, but I can't find my infrared strobe. I dump the contents of my rucksack and quickly find what I'm looking for under a *Penthouse* magazine. I attach my nine-volt battery to the tip of it and set it on my assault pack, which is acting as my pillow. I snuggle in warm and deep in my sleeping bag and get back on the net.

"Bandit 7-1, this is Hunter-6 Romeo. Our position is marked by IR, over."

"Roger, I see you now. What can I do for you tonight? Over?"

"Well, if you could just scan the ridgeline on either side. We had some problems with the Taliban taking potshots at us earlier this afternoon. We certainly would appreciate it something proper," I say in my most earnest Texan accent. I always adopt a Texas accent when I talk to B1 bomber pilots.

For some reason, the voice of the B1 bomber pilot soothes and relaxes me. He has a deep voice, and I feel a tough resonance even miles below him on the ground. With his rough but soothing voice, he seems to me like the Marlboro Man or Johnny Cash. I decide his voice sounds exactly like Johnny Cash. I'm talking to Johnny Cash, who is piloting a B1 bomber.

Johnny Cash chuckles warmly and says in a friendly yet masculine tone, "Yes, sir, them Taliban can be real rascals sometimes!"

THE SPACE FLIGHT PARADOX:
AN E-MAIL HOME TO EVERYONE

Hello All:

Well, I'm returned from the big mission. So don't worry; I'm alive and in one piece. I'll spare you some of the more obscene details for now (although I'm sure you'll eventually hear them).

It's strange to return to a firebase and think it the most luxurious accommodations that one could ever desire or hope for, but that's exactly how I felt on our helicopter flight in. Just complete and utter joy at being able to sleep in a cot instead of the dirt and being able to eat horrible food instead of MREs.

So everyone has e-mailed me and asked me when are we going to get Osama? Osama, Osama, Osama—that's all anyone cares about. Isn't he in the mountains between Afghanistan and Pakistan? Can't we just send you guys in there to get him?

The answer is definitely no.

The answer has to do with an extended metaphor involving flight into outer space. The problem with space flight is that a ratio has to be achieved between thrust and weight. For example, why can't we simply launch a huge spaceship into orbit that has all the parts that will be needed for a satellite or a space station at one time? As the weight of the payload increases, however, so does the amount of fuel needed to send that payload into orbit. Having more fuel, which can add more thrust, then requires an even bigger spaceship to hold the additional fuel needed to burn to put the additional cargo into orbit. Adding this additional fuel, though, means that the ship needs to be bigger, but in turn, that increases the fuel for thrust requirements even more. As size increases, there is a never-ending cycle of need.

The Army operates on the same policy. Infantry soldiers are mobile elements for very small periods of time and space. For every day an infantry soldier is in the field, he needs approximately five to six bottles of water, at minimum—more for particularly strenuous hikes or climbs—and at least two MREs (Meals Ready to Eat). This is in addition to his sleeping bag, which is needed at night if he is to protect himself from the cold weather and stay at all combat ready, and in addition to his weapons, night vision goggles, grenades, extra ammunition, rain gear, maps, binoculars, global positioning systems, radios, and for all of these electronic devices, extra batteries. A rucksack weighs between fifty and eighty pounds, which means that at best, a soldier can be gone for three days. Beyond that, the weight of additional water and MREs makes his movement so slow and plodding, weighed down by a rucksack that he can barely carry, that he starts to use up the same food and water resources covering a much smaller amount of distance.

Where once he might be able to cover ten kilometers a day, he now spends all day traveling a mere five kilometers. In the end, for all the extra food and water he only ends up adding a mere five or so kilometers to his distance. And this is traveling over semiflat ground.

Against mountains, things really get tough. And then there's the issue of injury. Helicopters are not as mobile as people think. Contrary to popular opinion, which seems to have been incorrectly recommended by Hollywood, they are actually somewhat limited in where they can land. The fear is that a soldier will be injured while hiking up the side of rocky mountains, twisting an ankle or falling and dislocating a knee, and then have to be carried out. And then you look up and see that between the more traveled valley artery that you're currently in and the next frequently traveled valley artery are about thirty kilometers of the roughest most barren craggy mountains that are without trails or roads of any type. The mountains that Al Qaeda travels in are the mountains that you see on the horizon, about ten mountains back.

Which we'll never get to. To be honest, it's just too hard. Even when those are the bastards that have attacked your country, it's just too hard.

The counterargument, I suppose, is that Al Qaeda operatives are able to move through these mountains, so how come we can't?

And the traditional counterargument to the counterargument is "Yes! Yes! But these guys have been living here their entire lives. They know of small goat trails and have spent a lifetime being conditioned to these elements and this altitude."

And the counterargument to the counterargument of the counterargument is "Sure, it's hard, but you're soldiers. That's what you're supposed to do. We don't care how hard it is; just get out there and get them!"

To which the counterargument is "Fuck you! *You* do it!"

Which, ultimately, is what it seems to come down to. I suppose in the end we could be air-inserted somewhere in those mountains that nobody ever visits, and we could hike our way out. But could thirty soldiers huffing and puffing and making slow tedious progress over the mountains do it stealthily? Not at all. And could these soldiers find the terrorists in the three days that their food is going to hold out? No.

So, again, the only sane response seems to be to shrug and say, "Well, guess Osama will get away."

My point being, since I just got done doing it: It's really hard to search those mountains. And I really don't care where he is. I'm going to sleep.

Take care,
Rico Dico

Chapter 37

**HOW WATCHING *THE JOY LUCK CLUB*
ALMOST GOT ME KILLED**

"**I**NCOMING!"

It's a practiced and well-rehearsed ritual. Movies are left in midplay, PlayStation games are advanced just a bit further to a Save point, and started e-mails are quickly saved as drafts, which are then immediately followed by the requisite number of double mouse clicks to sign out user names and passwords.

Soldiers run to their bunks and quickly don body armor and helmets and sling rifles around their backs. And then, as if orchestrated in a perfect symmetry of timing, the front doors open to the wooden barracks tents, and the soldiers squeeze out, racing to their respective positions around the base.

Ladders are climbed, walls are mounted, and the guard towers double in occupancy as the residents of Firebase Cougar move to the perimeter preparing for the theory of attack, the idea of attack, the possibility of attack.

Cigarettes are lit and wisecracks are offered as soldiers begin the long wait for the order to stand down.

And in the operations building, Lieutenant Mitch and Lieutenant Collins point their fingers at each other, each squealing the lyrics to the next line in their favorite song as they do-si-do, arm in arm, swinging each other around: *"Where they play the right music, getting into the swing!!"*

Moments earlier, when the first missile hit, they both raced into the operations building, laptops under arms, slamming each other sideways in the doorway, each attempting to leverage a moment of advantage from the other. Each lieutenant hunched over his respective computer, whispering words of encouragement to power up and move through the initial start-up windows just a little bit faster than the other as they sat on the central table facing each other.

Behind Lieutenant Mitch, I attempted to be his cheerleader offering lame messages of inspiration, "Go, sir! You can do it, sir! Get 'em, sir!"

Lieutenant Collins's computer, being a slightly newer model, moved through the requisite start-up windows a bit earlier. Lieutenant Collins quickly performed a series of double taps, entering iTunes and activating the song. He immediately jumped back from his computer and sang in a disjointed uneven unison with his laptop.

And pretty soon, everybody in the operations building was either dancing to ABBA's "Dancing Queen," singing at the top of their lungs, or else looking on with goofy self-conscious smiles at all the silliness.

I was on the satellite radio. I called up to battalion to let them know our base was taking fire and to formally request permission to return fire. I waited for a few moments as Lieutenant Mitch danced next to me, coaxing me to dance with him. I smiled and held up a serious finger as I listened with one ear cocked toward the hand microphone.

Permission denied.

You are not allowed to return fire on the Taliban.

"We can't fire! No firing!" I yelled as if everybody weren't in the same room as me.

At the expected news that we couldn't return fire, Lieutenant Mitch and Lieutenant Collins both doubled the intensity with which they belted out the lyrics—a small but important rebellion to what they saw as a slightly insane "No Taliban Killing" policy: "You are the Dancing Queen . . ."

And, having nothing left to do, I threw the hand microphone to the ground and started doing pelvic thrusts back and forth across the operations building.

There was nothing left to do but sing.

My hands are over my head, and I'm on the floor of our tent staring under my bunk. Peripherally I can hear people screaming "INCOMING!" as I hear the trail of rockets fly by somewhere outside the base. And then there's a split second, which stretches itself into more time than I need, to cohesively think all the thoughts that go through my head.

I think about the movie that's on pause and if it'll rewind correctly if I have to restart it, since the disc is scratched. I think about whether or not our getting attacked tonight means I'll still be able to get on e-mail. I think about a lot of things.

But the predominant thought is, where is it going to land?

It all seems like one giant game of Battleship, with the enemy blindly lobbing rockets hoping for a hit.

You've sunk my Army base!

I imagine the roof of the tent with its meager two wooden beams exploding inward as a fireball surges forward, engulfing me in debris and shrapnel. I wonder if there's any possibility that instead of my being consumed by the fireball, the fireball will instead only propel me toward the back of the tent, as in the movies. I think I might not mind being propelled by a fireball to the back of the tent. That would at least be an interesting experience.

In this same moment, I look under my bed and am pleasantly surprised to find a Butterfinger candy bar. Damn, I was really hungry for a candy bar all last month. How long has that been under here? And then a few inches beyond the candy bar is a grenade, and I think to myself, *Yeah, grenade, I should probably pick that up.*

I will never remember to do so.

And then there's the boom. They usually come in groups of three or four.

Immediately I feel bored. After all, this is getting pretty typical. It's almost every night now. It's their retaliation for our big offensive. We're planning some retaliation of our own for the rocket attacks. Everybody's always retaliating against everyone else.

So that's the next sensation: boredom.

Boredom because I now have to put on all my gear and run around all night chasing phantom bad guys who are long gone.

My night has just been ruined.

I jump up and move through the tent and smack into someone in the darkness. I mutter my apology, grab my gear, and make my way through the back and around the back edge of the tents to the command and operations building. Inside, I sit against a wall at the back of the room on a little wooden bench, staring at a map in a dull quiet, my radio beside me, ready to go on a patrol.

In the front of the room there are people everywhere, milling about, arguing important details: Air Force personnel who bring in jets for air support; mortar personnel who fire mortars; fire observers who direct the fire of the mortar personnel; the fire observer sergeant, who directs the fire observers; and the company commander and first sergeant, who direct the fire observer sergeant. And there is the RTO on duty and all the lieutenants in charge of each platoon, and everybody is yelling at everybody else, seemingly unsure of who is in charge despite being in such an intensely hierarchical system. As usual, there are radio problems, and nobody can hear the soldiers in the mortar pit, who are waiting for word on the radio to return fire, even though they are only a few feet out the front door of the operations building.

Why do they keep trying to pick them up on the radio? Why don't they just peek out the window and talk to them?

A call is made to all the perimeter security towers. Who saw what, and where did the attack come from? Tower two immediately calls up, saying it came from the west. Tower three calls up and says that it came from the north. There are more arguments and discussion as a course of action is devised. Forty minutes pass before it is decided that a patrol will go out in a northwesterly direction to see what they can see.

I run outside with the quick reaction force. We run to the Humvees in almost complete darkness. The sky is overcast and cloudy, blocking the residual light of stars. Without the ambient glow of streetlights and distant cities, the night sky looks more like the outer reaches of space turned in a starless direction. Complete utter darkness. We might as well have blindfolds on.

Sergeant Santiago tries to open the first Humvee, and it's locked. Someone has put a padlock and chain around the door. A second later, Ryan cries out the same thing on a second Humvee. It's locked, too. Someone has locked all the Humvees.

Moments after everyone else is already aware of the situation, Mulbeck cries out the obvious. "It's locked!" he states firmly for all to hear, trying to gain some authority over the situation.

We find out that the Humvees are locked because people keep stealing from them, and we have to plead our case that we need the Humvees for a mission. It takes ten minutes before we have the keys. No one can ever remember where the Humvee keys are. We can't see our way around the vehicles and are forced to feel our way around, our arms outstretched in front of us, feeling for familiar shapes and surfaces. Even our night vision goggles are useless without any peripheral light.

Sergeant Santiago yells out the names of who are going to be in which vehicle, but so many voices are asking for where things are that nobody gets in the right vehicle. "Rico? Is that you?" says Sergeant Santiago.

"Yes!" I reply.

"You're in the wrong vehicle, Rico. You're in Charlie five!"

"Oh!" I say. "Which way is Charlie five? Is that to my left or my right?"

"It's to your left!"

I move with outstretched arms through the darkness, expecting to bump into another Humvee at any moment, when I hear voices.

"Goddamn, this fucking handle . . . can someone pull this fucker back? The charging handle's stuck. I can't get it to slide back!"

"Where's my fucking night vision goggles? I can't fucking see shit. Do you have my fucking night vision?"

"Does anyone have my weapon? I sat my fucking weapon down right here, then went to go help Davis unlock the vehicles, and now it's gone. Has anyone seen my fucking weapon?"

"I can't get this goddamn charging handle. Can you help me with my charging handle? Who is that? Who the fuck is that in the passenger seat? Can you help me with my charging handle?"

"I can't find my night vision . . ."

"Do you have my weapon? Okay, this shit's getting old. Who has my fucking weapon?!"

It takes us twenty minutes from the time we hit the motor pool to roll out.

I close my eyes and go to sleep as the vehicles move through the night desert in total darkness, forgoing the use of headlights. My body bounces back and forth as our vehicle hits rocks and moves over embankments and drops into a riverbed. I'm a very deep sleeper. From some distant place I hear someone talking about a flashlight up on a mountain in the distance.

I wake up, and we're where the flat desert ends in a semicircle of mountains that rise up in front of us, both steep and sharp. We exit the vehicles and leave a small security force with them. We start to climb the mountain after this supposed flashlight. We'll get that goddamn flashlight! No one shines a flashlight in our neighborhood in Afghanistan! A flashlight that nobody can agree on. Sergeant Pauley saw it on the mountain to our left. Sergeant Stein, Sergeant Bryson, and Private Hugh saw it on the mountain to our right. Sergeant Pauley, however, being in charge of the mission, decides that it was, after all, the mountain on our left.

We climb for hours. First it's up the slope of a steep hill. Then the steep slope turns increasingly vertical until we are left with sheer vertical walls. Maybe this is a good time to turn back?

Keep climbing; we've got to get the enemy; keep climbing. The enemy climbed this way; we'll climb this way too. We know the enemy climbed this way because they had a flashlight.

We start climbing hand over hand, searching for crevices and footholds in the darkness. In the distance we can see the lights of Cougar Base, now looking like an airport at night as seen through the windows of a plane.

Why do they have all the lights on?

Are they trying to get attacked or something?

But still we climb.

Rocks tumble underfoot, echoing as they fall down the side of the mountain. More than once I almost fall off perilous drops, unable to see what is mountain and what is air in the darkness.

Halfway up I hear Mulbeck's voice in the darkness. "This is bullshit, Rico. I didn't sign up for this shit. Fucking hate this shit. Fuck the Army. I hope the Taliban kills us. I hope the Taliban kills every one of us motherfuckers. I hope we lose every war we go into. God, I cannot wait to get out of this shit. Only place I'm going to after this is Fort Fucking Living Room. That's my new duty station."

"Yeah," is all I can say through labored short breaths as my freezing hands reach in the darkness for another cold firm granite handhold. My hands are bleeding. But if your hands don't tear when you grab on to rock, you can't be sure it won't be too slippery. You need grips that will support you. It's best if you can find one that will tear your hands.

After reaching the top, several hours later, we all stop to catch our breath. We look around in the darkness at the view from the top of the world that we can't see. Sergeant Pauley concludes that nobody was up here, and perhaps the flashlight had been on the other mountain after all.

We hang out for another thirty minutes to make it worth our troubles.

"Did I ever tell you that I think the two most brilliant minds in the world are definitely Che Guevara and Einstein?" Sorbil styles himself as a pot-smoking philosopher. He strums some chords from a Nirvana song on his guitar, pauses, and says, "Educated sadness. Isn't that a great phrase. Put that in your book, will you? God, I come up with some great shit. I'm a writer too, you know. I keep a diary of my life. I'm going to try and get it published when we get back."

"Okay, I wanted to interview you, ask you about your perceptions regarding war, about combat, now that you're an official combat veteran. This is most definitively a distinct turn as a soldier. So what do you think?"

"This is tower three; we've got gunfire outside the base," the radio in my lap crackles.

"Tower three, are they shooting at you?"

"Not yet," tower three responds.

"Well, call me back if they do," I say rolling my eyes. "I'm sorry, Sorbil, forgive the interruption. Please continue."

"Well, when the bullets were like . . ." He starts laughing. "Like about to go through my face and I could hear them hitting like a foot from my face, I thought, man, I could've died. That shit makes you think, man."

"Any conclusions you want to draw from this?"

"Cougar operations, this is tower three," the radio bristles again. "They're shooting at us now."

"Shoot back," I say, again rolling my eyes. "I'm sorry, please continue. Your conclusions?"

"Yeah, my conclusion was that it would've been bad if I died. I don't know, it's like, it's kinda fun in one way, and I kinda like it, but then in like another way, I kinda like don't like it? War is bad, maybe?"

War is bad.

Pay attention; these are important lessons, and there will be a test later on.

Back in Hawaii, Sorbil had barely managed to keep control of a life-long dream to put his life into danger and transform himself into a full-blooded killer for the country he so adamantly believed in, because it would give him something he was lacking in himself. Apparently, in Sorbil's world, he couldn't become a full human being until he had killed someone else.

But now, he has decided that war is bad.

We're drowning in dry, baked desert epiphanies.

The rocket slams into the desert outside our base.

Sergeant Santiago sticks his head inside the door and screams, "Get your shit on! We've got rockets and Taliban attacking the observation posts on top of the hill! We're under attack!"

The few people in the tent groan and moan and slowly slide sideways off bunks and start putting their gear on in slow dreary movements that belong to a lazy Sunday morning. I sigh and put on my socks and then notice Cox asleep underneath his Army poncho. I walk over and nudge him with my toe.

"Whaddaya want?" he mumbles.

"You should probably wake up. We're getting rocketed, and I guess some bad guys are shooting up the OPs."

"Let me know when they get to the motor pool," Cox mumbles incoherently as he turns over and covers his head with his laundry bag, which acts as his pillow.

"Come on, man, I'm serious. Get up," I say, and nudge him again with my toe.

"Quit fucking kicking me."

"I'm not kicking you; I'm just nudging you with my toe."

"Quit fucking nudging me with your toe."

"You could die under your blanket."

"You could die outside my blanket." And then, after a pause, "Besides, this is a magic blanket. Nothing can get through its magical properties."

"Incoming!" the soldier on tower two yells.

Moments later, after the explosion sounds just a few feet outside the base walls, the soldiers scurry about, throwing on body armor and helmets and clicking night vision goggles into place.

Completely typical.

I run to tower two, which seems to have the best view on what has just happened. In the dark I run past Ryan, who stops me. "Rico! Hey, did you return my movie?"

"Um." I try to think. "Yeah, I put it back in your DVD case. I know I did. I'm positive that I did."

"All right, man. I'll check again."

"Yeah, check again," I say before continuing up the ladder. Guard tower two is about ten feet off the ground and sits atop a metal connex just inside the mud wall that houses our motor pool.

"What's up, Mulbeck?" I ask.

"Not much," he says, yawning. "Have I ever mentioned that I hate the Army?"

"Once or twice."

Suddenly we see a burst of rockets fired again from a ridge on the other side of the valley.

"Should I fire back?" Mulbeck asks me as the rockets slam into the ground in front of our base.

"Hell yes! Fire back!" I scream. "They're fucking shooting rockets at us!"

"I don't know if I should," Mulbeck says quietly. He peers down to the other side of the base to look at tower three. "They're not firing back. I don't want to get in trouble. I'm not firing back if tower three isn't firing."

I grab the walkie-talkie and call up tower three. "Tower three, tower two, over." Tower three responds, "Disco!" I ask, "Hey, tower three, are you guys going to fire back?"

Tower three pauses and says, "Nobody else is firing."

Mulbeck has firmed up his resolve. "I'm not firing if tower three is not firing. I'm not going to be the only one to fire."

"This is the most retardest, stupidest thing I've ever heard of. We're getting attacked by rockets, and you're afraid to shoot a gun back at them."

"I don't want to get in trouble!" Mulbeck yells.

"Actually, this is good. This is a perfect scene for my book. The absurdity of modern warfare and all when you're in a semi-police action and there's ambiguity about the rules of warfare and what's allowed and what's not allowed."

"Hey, if you want to open fire, be my fucking guest," Mulbeck continues.

"Okay, I will," I say. Then I pause, wondering if I'll get into trouble.

At this moment the sergeant of the guard climbs up the ladder, breathing heavily, and asks where the rockets are being fired from. Mulbeck points to the distant ridgeline and asks, "Do you want us to return fire?"

"Hell no!" the sergeant of the guard says. "Don't return fire! You don't know who or what you're going to hit out there."

Mulbeck smiles and sticks his tongue out at me. I just frown and start down the ladder.

"Where are you going?" the sergeant of the guard asks me.

"I'm going to sleep," I reply, feeling carefully for the ladder rungs in the darkness as another rocket explodes outside our base.

Army Ranger Sergeant Pauley is staring off into space, leaning against a pile of sandbags, and smoking a cigarette. He has waited with a desperate anxiety all his life for a war. Sergeant Pauley says, "That guy we shot? I was thinking, you know, maybe he had friends that were upset that we killed him. Just like we were upset that they killed Miller? You know?"

The rocket slams into the desert outside our base.

Sergeant Santiago sticks his head inside the door and screams, "Get your shit on! We've got rockets and Taliban attacking the observation posts on top of the hill! We're under attack!"

The few people in the tent groan and moan and slowly slide sideways off bunks and start putting on their gear in slow dreary movements that belong to a lazy Sunday morning.

I get the strange and curious sensation of déjà vu. A feeling that this has all been done before. It's difficult to realize déjà vu in Afghanistan, what with every day being almost identical to the day before and the day after, but I'm quite sure I've been in this exact situation before.

I sigh and pull my socks on and walk over to Cox's cot, where Devon and Cox have pulled an Army poncho tight from a nail on the wall to the floor, where two cots are overturned.

"Hey, guys, we're getting attacked," I say.

"Shut up, Rico; we're in our magical fortress," Devon says. "I don't know what you're talking about. What do you mean—attacked?"

"Rockets. There's more rocket attacks."

"Rockets? Girl, we're in Hawaii. Where are you?"

Magical fortress? I want to be in a magical fortress. A magical fortress where the dim light from a screen leads me to suspect they are playing video games.

"What are you guys playing?"

"Grand Theft Auto: San Andreas, baby!" Cox replies.

I pause for a moment, debating whether or not to get my gear on, and finally say, "How many people does your magical fortress hold? Do you have room for me in your magical fortress?"

The side flap of the Army poncho folds up as an open invitation into the magical fortress.

Private Marciano, who said before he deployed that he had wanted to be in the infantry all his life, admits in the back of a patrol Humvee one night, "You know, Rico, if I stay in the Army, I think I'm getting out of the infantry." He hangs his head in quiet contemplation as if he is about to say something profound and filled with wisdom. "Almost dying all the time is not as fun as I thought it would be, you know?"

After our experiences in combat, it was the rockets that finally got to us. The confidence of an infantryman builds an armor about him. It's composed of a small piece of training, a slightly larger piece of experience, and large elements of bravado. Slowly the rockets wore us down until we had nothing left but frayed nerves.

Lieutenant Mitch tells me that he's convinced he's going to die. He gives me a letter that I am to deliver to his wife. I've already lost it. Sergeant Santiago whines about that stupid baby of his that he has yet to see. Everyone thinks that with four months left in the deployment, they're going to die and wish they had died earlier so that, if they were dead, they at least could've missed out on most of the Afghanistan deployment.

"The very fact that they haven't yet gotten one inside the wire worries me," Diego says as he jumps up on a sandbag. He takes a drag from his cigarette and offers me one.

I shake my head no.

Diego continues, "I don't believe in shit like fate, but statistically speaking, by this point they should have been more likely to get one inside the base—at least one—than have the situation as it is, which is that they're all hitting right outside the base. I mean, they've got to be adjusting their aim. They've got to be spotting where they're hitting. And you know these fucking Haji are reporting back to them the next day."

He points at one of the many local Afghans at our base, this one smiling as he's pointed at and pushes his wheelbarrow of cement to the other side of the base.

"So what are you saying?" I ask.

"I'm saying, either our luck is going to run out soon and we're going to get one inside and a bunch of us are going to get hurt, or you and I are wrong to be atheists because shit like this doesn't just happen. I mean, I'm the last person who wants to believe in God. I hope to hell he doesn't exist, but either way the supported conclusions are scary to think about."

Three days later, a rocket lands in the center of the firebase.

This rocket's kill radius is fifty meters.

The diameter of Cougar Base is roughly one hundred meters.

This rocket's a dud.

I sit outside our tent with Sergeant Santiago watching all the soldiers scurrying about, taking measurements and photographs. Sergeant Stephens walks his squad past us with Mulbeck in tow to head out to try and find the bastards.

They won't. Of course.

"Sergeant Santiago, we should all be dead."

Sergeant Santiago stares at the rocket and only says, "I haven't seen my baby yet."

"Maybe we've all just been given a second lease on life. You know, we're all supposed to do something with our lives now. All of us." Sergeant Santiago shoots me a look to quit being so fucking stupid.

I think back about my grandfather. In World War II, he was loaded on a boat that was shipping off for a fight. A random impulse generated from an unknown place hit him, and he playfully shoved his buddy. Sometimes it helps to ease the pre–boat-loading tensions with some playful shoves. His buddy shoved him back. My grandfather fell back and twisted his ankle and was ordered out of the boat.

The boat shipped off to its fight, and everyone died.

Sometimes a random impulse generated from an unknown place saves your life. Sometimes a random impulse generated from an unknown place gives life to sons and grandchildren who otherwise never would have existed. Sometimes a random impulse generated from an unknown place is the genesis of lives otherwise unlived and future histories not yet realized.

Sometimes rockets with a fifty-meter kill radius don't detonate.

Sometimes. But not very often.

I'm under my poncho liner on my cot watching *The Joy Luck Club*. I'm not overly impressed with the movie, but it's got all those manufactured emotions with mothers and daughters crying and forgiving one another and so forth that I feel my eyes well up at the super-duper happiness of it all. I can't believe I'm about to cry watching *The Joy Luck Club*. I'm such a fucking pussy sometimes.

And there it is. Boom. The distant thud of a rocket.

Five minutes later, and I'm attached to Sergeant Stephens's squad outside the base, heading out the wire and up the hill past the observation posts. Every other time we've been fired at, the shots have come from areas where, within the vicinity, there were locals who lived. The Army didn't want to take a chance killing locals. Which was a fair enough consideration, I figured. But tonight the attack has come from a mountain that perpetually towered above Cougar Base far behind the observation posts and a few smaller mountains that seem like foothills in its shadow. And tonight we're fighting back.

We move to the next large hill behind the observation posts. Once at the top, thirty minutes later, I briefly glance at my handheld GPS and call up our grid as we all find comfortable rocks to wait on. We look out at the next mountain over, a tall foreboding granite husk that in the movies is the mountain that the castle of the evil Goblin King is perched on. Whoever was at the top is going to have a hell of a time getting down, and we're in position, and they're not.

"Too bad we don't have silencers on our weapons," Sergeant Pauley says, never able to appreciate a comfortable silence.

Sergeant Kibbul laughs. "There'd be a lot of dead people. Shit, I don't know how it happened, another dead guy, what can I say. It looks like .556 ammo, but you can never tell."

"I had a buddy over here during OEF 1, the first one, and he said they used to just light motherfuckers up."

"That was a different conflict back then. You could do your fucking job back then. It was all about waxing motherfuckers."

"Yeah," Sergeant Pauley says wistfully. "They'd sit over watch positions and just call in air support on towns and just blow the fuck out of whatever they wanted. Then they'd go down and cut the fingers off all the guys who had burned up to give to some ID specialist, who would try to figure out who they were."

Sergeant Kibbul is jealous. You can hear it in his voice in the slow way that he answers. "Yeah? No shit?" And then there is a long pause. "I wish we had gone to Iraq, man. I have a buddy there, and they'd get a call on the radio to blow the fuck out of every orange car that came down the road. Well, I guess all the fucking cars over there are orange or whatever fucking color they called up, so they'd just go to fucking town and kill thirty or forty people a night."

"Yeah, that'd be pretty sweet, man," Sergeant Pauley says. "Aken said the same thing. Said when he was in Iraq they just killed whoever the fuck they wanted. Nobody fucking cared as long as you were killing people."

"Too bad we don't have silencers over here."

"Yeah."

"Why don't you think they don't trust us with silencers?"

"I don't know, man."

"Sixty seconds until impact," the voice on the other end of the hand mike says.

"Sixty seconds!" I yell. Everyone quiets down.

That voice also happens to belong to my good friend Diego, who, although neither he nor I knows it yet, has also just started the countdown to my death.

And then we all feel it.

Sergeant Stephens asks, mildly apprehensive and suddenly feeling that he's about to die, "Does anyone else feel like they're going to bomb us instead of them?"

Sergeant Kibbul looks off at "them," at the mountain opposite our own, and says, "Yeah, I feel fucking sick to my stomach. Sergeant, we need to get off this mountain."

Private Darrenowsky and Gibber and Marciano look up at the sky with their own worried looks and start to wedge themselves in under small rock outcroppings. They want to say something, but privates aren't allowed to speak in Sergeant Stephens's squad.

"Yeah, I feel it too," Sergeant Stephens says. "But we're staying here. Our orders were to come up here, and this is where we're staying."

Typical. I hate Sergeant Stephens.

Sergeant Pauley says, "Well, nice knowing you all."

Sergeant Kibbul looks up nervously at the sky, trying to track the sound of the B1 bomber that's twenty thousand feet overhead, a dull rolling thunder of an imminent storm. Sergeant Stephens sits Indian style, grimly staring up at God and the sky, his weapon at his side, waiting for it all to end. Sergeant Stephens—he's taking it like a man.

"Forty seconds," Diego's voice tells me.

"Forty seconds!" I scream.

I don't believe in intuition. I don't believe in intuition, I don't believe in God, I don't believe in spirits or fate or past lives or psychics. I believe in science, rationality, and logic, and I'll be goddamned if I can't find a good place to hide from the bomb that's about to drop on my fucking head.

This is my cold panic. My complete unadulterated fear and desperate plea that I don't want to die and that I want to live. It's not rational. It's not logical. In fact, it's more like the whimpering of a dog that's been badly beaten.

I've been shot at, but you never quite believe that you'll actually be shot. There's too much empty space for the bullets to fly through. There's too much to go wrong with angles and vectors and trajectories for it to hit you. But this? This is the absolute certainty of your impending death.

And I can't get my mind wrapped around it. I try to force myself to think critically, to think through the fog of fear. But my head keeps coming back to the big bold letters that scream "DEATH!"

The idea hits me that I should run off the mountain. I stare down the length of the mountain and think that I could make good time in thirty seconds. Sprint as fast as my long fucking legs will take me, and then just launch myself off a rock and fall the rest of the way? Maybe if the bomb is a little off, with a bit of luck I may only get third-degree burns over fifty percent of my body.

Yet, I just sit here. Am I so afraid of not following orders that I'm going to die of following orders? I know now, without hesitation, that I'm going to die. Why not offer myself a shot at life? Go out fighting instead of just sitting here like a good little soldier?

Sergeant Pauley says, "No, no, oh fuck no, there's something fucking wrong here. This shit just don't feel right! Rico, did you fucking give 'em our grid, right?"

"Of course," I say, shaking my head in disgust at his immediate assumption regarding my competence.

Had I given them the correct coordinates?

All I did was glance at my little handheld GPS real quick.

Lots of room for error in the span of a small glance.

Why didn't I take a longer look?

Was it because I'm all put out having to be up here on this cold windy fucking mountain?

Am I about to die and kill seven other soldiers because I'm upset about being interrupted while watching *The Joy Luck Club*?

I frantically turn on the GPS to verify the grid. My hands are shaking so much I drop it twice. I press the power button. But now it's going through its slow start-up cycle.

"Twenty seconds," Diego tells me in my ear.

We've got the little company logo graphic, and the little cute satellite graphic, and now we're searching for satellites in the area. One satellite, two satellite—come on, all I need is one more fucking satellite.

I definitely don't want to die because of *The Joy Luck Club*. If I'm gonna die over a movie, I want it to be a four-star movie, and I'm only giving *The Joy Luck Club* three stars.

Ten seconds.

FUCK YOU, *JOY LUCK CLUB*! FUCK ALL YOU ASIAN MOTHER-AND-DAUGHTER MOVIES EVER FUCKING FILMED! GIVE ME MY FUCKING SATELLITES AND MY GRID!

There's no blood left in my body. Only ice is coursing through my veins now.

My third satellite registers, and the grid comes up.

The grid is accurate.

Oh, thank you, God; the grid is accurate!

Nothing changes, though. I'm still about to die. I can feel it. You can feel it when you're still about to die.

"Five seconds," Diego says through the radio. He's a good friend, but goddamn him, he doesn't have to be so snotty as he announces the last five seconds of my life.

Thanks for playing, and come again soon.

Four.

I want to cry. I want to waste my final seconds crying like a goddamn sissy.

Three.

I bend over at the waist and cover my head. Yeah, this will offer me *real good* protection when five hundred pounds of exploding metal turns this grid square into a fiery hell.

Two.

This would've been an interesting e-mail to send out to my friends. But I guess that's not going to happen.

One.

Good-bye, Afghanistan, and thanks for all the sand.

I sit on the mountain for a second with my eyes closed before I realize that I'm not dead.

Have you ever wanted a snapshot of yourself moments before you thought you were going to die? Want to peruse this snapshot to see just how dignified you are when you go out and punch that final ticket?

In my final moment of dignity I'm in a semifetal position with my hands over my head.

I call up on the radio, winded with exasperation and ask what the fuck is going on. Diego tells me to hold on. A few minutes later he says we're trying it all again.

There's another countdown, but this time everything feels right. Sometimes when you're dropping bombs on mountains it feels right; sometimes it doesn't. And then the top of the mountain opposite us evaporates in a cloud of dust and dirt. Seconds later a rolling boom knocks us off our feet.

We all clap and say "Goddamn!" and make our way back down the mountain, where Diego is waiting for me behind my tent.

I shed my gear and say, "Dude, that was fucking freaky up there. We all had this weird premonition that we were going to die!" I laugh. Now it's funny. Thirty minutes ago it was scary as shit, but now it's funny.

"Sticky notes," he says.

"What?" I ask, pausing in my shedding of gear.

"Sticky notes," he says. "The Special Forces guys wrote the grids down all wrong on the sticky notes."

He holds up two small fingers close together. "You were this close, man. Sergeant what's-his-name from the Air Force caught it at the last second and called abort."

I don't remember yellow office sticky notes playing prominently in the movies I've seen with Special Forces soldiers deep behind enemy lines.

Diego laughs his ass off and leaves me contemplating the continued existence of my life and yellow office sticky notes.

I bum a cigarette off a passing soldier and lean against the sandbags and light up. So much for quitting.

All of this is supposed to mean something. The rocket that lands inside Cougar Base but doesn't detonate. My accurate premonitions and last-minute pardon from death row by the Air Force sergeant whose name I always forget. I'm supposed to learn something from this. I'm supposed to feel empowered by life, more optimistic, or some shit.

I don't feel optimistic or empowered.

I just want to finish watching *The Joy Luck Club*.

Chapter 38

FIREBASE FEVER

We circle around **Sergeant Santiago** on his cot. He slumps to the ground with slow crawling movements as he spits on us and makes cooing noises. A purposeful string of drool extends inches out of his mouth.

"He's lost it," Ryan says. "My God, he's completely lost it."

"Poo on you! Poo on you!" Sergeant Santiago says, now completely on the floor as he imitates the movements that would be required for him to reach into his pants and toss poo on us.

"It's uh, uh, cabin, cabin, uh, cabin, you know island fever. Cabin fever. He's got cabin fever," Cox says, smiling. "That's cool; the dude's got cabin fever. Sweet."

Devon's head twitches as he imitates a nervous psychological tic before he breaks into a cha-cha-cha dance while singing, "I've got firebase fever! I've got firebase fever!" And then Devon collapses on his cot, laughing hysterically and murmuring to himself.

"What the fuck is wrong with everyone?" I scream. "God, you're all so fucking weird!"

"What the fuck do you expect," Cox responds. "We're stuck twenty-four / seven in this place while rockets are fired at us every night, and we can't do anything but take it up the ass. People are going to go nuts, a little looony, girl!"

And then the missions started back up. It was retaliation for the missile attacks, which were retaliation for the last big mission, which was retaliation for the beating 2nd Platoon took, all of which somehow was retaliation for September 11. Searching for stinger missiles, midnight raids in night vision goggles on top Taliban targets, raiding compounds suspected of harboring Taliban. I never knew how exactly the Army knew so much, but they had lists of hundreds of men that the U.S. wanted. Every small low-level asshole that ever helped the Taliban was on our list, and we were going to get every damn one of them.

But at the same time, the soldiers *were* going loony. It was all around us. It exhibited itself in different forms, but after almost a year, the sharp edges of discipline were slowly being replaced with the dull rot of quiet insanity.

Specialist Diego writes letters to exhibit his insanity.

Specialist Diego writes to a great many people while he's in Afghanistan. He figures that if people are kind enough to send us random anonymous care packages, then he can be kind enough to send a return letter. It's only the polite thing to do. He wants to send an unending stream of correspondence flooding forth from south-central Asia to cover and infiltrate the world.

He finds a peculiar romanticism in the idea of a mind being a dirty contagion let out into a clean sterile world.

To the kindergartners in Spokane, Washington, who mailed him stick drawings of himself wearing an orange hat and holding a gun underneath a purple sun, he writes long deep conversations of political discourse about the situation in Afghanistan relating to the United States' establishment of a puppet government in Hamid Karzai, who, he states, is nothing but a spokesman for Unocoal in that company's bid to construct a cross-country natural gas pipeline. The election in Afghanistan is a sham, he tells them. Don't believe the propaganda, kiddos! Viva la revolution!

To Ms. Beth Karrack's second-grade class in Davenport, Iowa, he mails a letter describing how Afghanistan is being promoted prematurely as a success story as a matter of political necessity for the Bush administration to balance out the ever-growing fiasco of the war in Iraq, and, furthermore, how this erroneous label of "success story" is unfortunately pushing Afghanistan toward an inappropriate agenda and nonrealistic time lines.

To most adults he writes very simple, poorly constructed letters composed in bad grammar, in which he gives his name and his favorite color, and states that his dog's name is Michael and that he licks his balls.

Sometimes, purely out of a growing claustrophobic reaction to the Army's rigidity and discipline, which seems to add to his overall increasing thinness and physical deterioration like a virus gnawing at his insides, he thanks those who write him about protecting freedom with a thank-you for your thank-you note that then quickly degenerates into sarcastic theatrics about the United States' more despicable foreign policy deeds throughout the last century. "It is essential that we protect the way of life in the United States so that we can continue to economically subjugate the rest of the world through globalization and that we maintain a strong military so that we can continue to support dictators and fascist deathmongers. Again, I thank you for your support. Sincerely, James Diego, U.S. Army."

Sometimes, when he has no more generous donors of packages to mail letters to, he chooses random addresses that he is confident exist. He has a large envelope of items gathered during raids of Taliban homes, which various officers and sergeants have asked him to hold on to but have never remembered to ask for back. (The Army was very disorganized in its collection and maintenance of evidence and intelligence information; it wasn't uncommon to find junk drawers in the base command tent with a fake ID from some head Taliban leader that had been collected on a mission six months back, mixed in with a notebook found on a different raid three months later that somebody had forgotten to translate.) So to the good, decent, hardworking anonymous folks of America, he mails Taliban phone lists and diaries and anti-U.S. propaganda. (Always with the return address of Captain John Gault of the fictitious 23rd Fighting Panda Bears, his quiet homage to Ayn Rand's *Atlas Shrugged,* which he lost to me in a game of poker.)

He didn't want to treat the Taliban unfairly, though, so as he gives their things away to the people back in the States he gives the Taliban, in turn, the drawings and pictures sent to him by America's children.

Ghul Mohammed, the purported ringleader of a small but feisty Taliban ring in the Charchina district, receives a crayon-drawn self-portrait of little seven-year-old Eric Matthews of Pensacola, Florida, standing outside his house with his dog, Pepper.

Atkar Mashad, an inauspicious member of a particularly zesty ring of Taliban based near Sakhar, gets a picture of Sarah Gollack's cat inserted into his underwear drawer, to be found at a future date.

And so it goes. The people back home send us packages, which we can't use and don't want. The Taliban inadvertently give their personal items to the people of America. In return, the Americans inadvertently give back to the Taliban. It is a beautiful example of sharing and giving: the soldiers, the Taliban, and America's schoolchildren.

Sergeant Mitchell exhibits his insanity via the one-man reenactments he does of *The Odyssey* for me late at night, back again on radio guard in the cement company command center that's tucked into the corner.

I sit for six-hour shifts reading or playing games on my Palm Pilot, and he enters the room, an Army poncho tied around his neck like a superhero cape, and starts calling everything absurd. Not just the Army and strange situations, but the coffeemaker. The coffeemaker is absurd. My Palm Pilot is absurd. I'm absurd. Then he goes into one of his productions. Although it's entertaining at first, after forty-five minutes my laughter slowly devolves into polite giggles and then complete indifference as I turn away from him to play my game. Behind me, without an audience, Sergeant Mitchell continues his performance: "Hark thee, foul knight! Thou shall not take thy fair maiden until thee has wrestled with the hide of the Cyclops!"

Marciano exhibits his insanity by moving into the shitters. He comes out only to recharge his laptop and to eat. He spends hours in there with the feces, sleeping, jerking off, playing first-person shooter war video games about Afghanistan on his computer.

How strange and curious is it to be both simultaneously fighting the real war, and then for entertainment playing a digital simulation of the same war?

Devon pounds on the door to the shitter, calling out, "Hey, I need to get in there. I need to take a shit!"

Only after this continues for a few moments will Marciano call back, "Use another one."

Devon replies, "But I want to use this one. I want to take a shit with you!" Devon erupts in laughter.

"I know to you this is strange," Marciano calls out from the other side of the door. "But this is the only place that I can get privacy. Tell Sergeant Riley that when he finds out what time our patrol is heading out, have someone come tell me. This is where I'll be."

Schultz exhibits his growing insanity by pretending to be insane.

"Dear Jesus! That fucking cheeky monkey!" exclaims Specialist Ryan, throwing his helmet to the ground and tearing off his clothes in anger.

Ryan starts screeching and hollering that he's going to kill Schultz if it's the last thing he ever does. And before we know it, we're all jumping up and down in a strange furious anger, throwing rocks and kicking dirt and shaking ourselves into a tizzy.

Schultz was back in Kandahar, diagnosed with post-traumatic stress disorder, and it made us all seethe with rage. You didn't get post-traumatic stress disorder in a combat zone! If you did, you were a pussy—that was for sure.

We sit around our tent the rest of the night, conjuring up ways to make him miserable and punish him for his mental deficiencies. We decide, after tearing apart his bunk and personal area and finding an envelope with his family's home address, that we will all take turns writing his mother and father, telling them stories about how Schultz cried when shot at, how he crumbled at the moment when courage was required—although the reality was that he had bravely returned fire.

He was a tourist; that was the thing. He didn't really have post-traumatic stress disorder. You didn't get post-traumatic stress disorder from being in a handful of firefights and from having your base attacked with rockets twenty or so times and from having your buddies die in roadside explosions.

Of course, in our anger, we were being tourists as well. We didn't really care that he had post-traumatic stress disorder, only that he was back in Kandahar eating Burger King burgers and getting massages at the day spa while we were forward deployed. He was getting over; that was the thing that infuriated all of us.

I didn't bother to add to their anger by sharing the secret knowledge I'd gained when I ripped my eyeball open after walking into a satellite dish late at night. I had been sent to Kandahar for some eyeball repair and had run into Schultz. I almost missed him entirely, what with the big patch over my eye, and my staring at the ground and fake limping, and my otherwise total concentration on a battery of fake injuries that I hoped would elicit enough sympathy from passing sergeants to obscure my overall state of unauthorization. I was very much unauthorized; I really was. I had left for Kandahar in a hurry and didn't have my hat, which was unauthorized, and I had a uniform top with the wrong pockets, which was unauthorized, and one sergeant had even stated that my eye patch was unauthorized—as if I had chosen to wear it only as a fashion statement. So I had been playing up the image of a seriously wounded war victim walking past the busy Army trucks and vehicles, intent on moving to and fro, when Schultz slowed his walk past me. This caused me to look up for a moment and notice him.

Schultz followed me around Kandahar as I ate a Burger King burger and limped toward the day spa to book a massage. He told me that he had been deemed "crazy" by the powers that be because he had fantasies about killing his tent mates. He sat up at nights contemplating tossing grenades into our tent and then running out into the Afghanistan desert to hide.

I was at the chow hall chomping on a piece of hard beefsteak as I nodded and yawned at his admissions. "Really? You don't say? You were going to kill us? All of us?"

"Well," Schultz explained, "I don't want to kill everyone, you know.

There are a few guys such as yourself that I didn't want to kill. If you guys had died as collateral damage I would've felt bad."

"As long as you would've felt bad," I said through gulps of chocolate milk.

"Although I was always thinking about tossing a grenade under Sergeant Santiago's bed," he told me, his face slack and staring, waiting for my response.

"Well," I replied, "considering that Sergeant Santiago is on the cot next to mine, that probably would have been bad."

"Yes," Schultz said, his eyes squinting, his voice rising in pitch as he got excited. "You would have all died!"

"Where did you get that ice cream?" I asked, eyeing his ice cream bar suspiciously. I looked around the chow hall to see if anyone else had ice cream. "Did they have it in the freezer? I didn't see any earlier."

Schultz started crying. For some reason he felt he could confide in me. It touched me that he felt comfortable with me. That he could cry with me. I patted the shoulder of my would-be murderer while I scanned the chow hall for signs of ice cream. "I can't handle the Army, Rico. I got to get out. I don't care what I got to do—attempt suicide, do drugs, whatever—I gotta get out, man. I can't take this shit."

"Yeah, man, yeah. It's okay, buddy. It's okay," I said soothingly. I moved next to him and rubbed his shoulder. "Are you going to finish that?" I asked, pointing at his ice cream.

Taking his lack of response as a go-ahead, I started finishing his ice cream. Schultz said, "I just can't handle being screamed at. Like when we left the trash in tower two and they took us outside and screamed at us. I thought I was going to kill Sergeant Santiago. I vowed in that moment to kill Sergeant Santiago. I didn't think it was possible to hate this much."

"Nothing wrong with a little hate," I said between bites of ice cream. "Hate keeps things spicy. It's motivating to have a good arch-nemesis around. Hell, I wish I was fortunate enough to have an arch-nemesis. All my life I've wanted an arch-nemesis, but I haven't been that lucky."

———

But that was back in Kandahar. Now, here at Cougar, the soldiers are planning his death. Which seems fair because Schultz was planning theirs, although they do not know this.

After Schultz is in Kandahar, the Army sends a psychiatrist out to our base. He talks with us and tells us it's natural to feel uncomfortable and anxious when people are trying to kill you.

This makes me feel a lot better.

The rank-and-file leaders exhibit their insanity by ceasing their patrols. Our daily patrols are led by squad leaders who walk their patrols thirty minutes outside the base twice a day and then hunker down behind a curve in a ravine or rock wall. Then, confident that they are out of sight of Cougar Base, they call up phantom patrols on the radio. The appearance of a patrol, the illusion of a patrol venturing great distances while the squad itself sits and laughs and smokes cigarettes. Then the rest of the day is spent playing games, watching movies, or sitting outside the tents on the wall of sandbags we constructed around each tent to blunt the blow of another attack. Outside on the sandbags, soldiers place their bets on who will be killed in next evening's rocket attack.

Someone in command exhibits his insanity by disabling the vehicles.

"This whole map, Rico, is the Cougar area of operations," Diego says as he sees me approach. He grandly indicates the entire map, which extends from ceiling to floor. Cougar Base is a small dot in the center. "Now, unfortunately, we can't go north anymore, because that's where they hit like a million IEDs and lost soldiers, so everything north of the wishbone is out. And we really can't go south anymore, because, well, there's just too many Taliban down there, and we always get attacked. We can't go west because of the mountains; they're very big, and that's just not going to happen. So, look at that map and tell me what that leaves us with?"

I study the map intently and then suggest, "East?"

Diego slaps me and says, "Fuck east, man. Fuck east. What I'm saying is that our area of operations is supposed to be forty kilometers in each direction, but in reality we only effectively patrol approximately two kilometers in each direction. And we aim to keep it that way. I've just manufactured fictional ailments for each vehicle on orders from someone within the company—I'm not going to say who, but someone. Battalion wants us to go on a mounted patrol outside our safe two-kilometer area, where we most certainly will die and get blown up? Oh damn, too bad. Vehicle 112 has a blown radiator. Vehicle 114? Its transmission is fucked up. Ask me about vehicle 115."

"What about vehicle 115?"

"Vehicle 115 has a twisted axle frame. What the fuck are you even thinking, trying to take out vehicle 115? Are you insane? You're not getting anywhere in vehicle 115."

I consider this and say, "I'm very pleased. I'm very pleased, indeed."

"Fucking A," Diego agrees.

And we all exhibit our growing insanity by not caring anymore.

"Make room for the little naked guy! Make room for the little naked dude!" Lieutenant Mitch yells, waving us all away. The small half-naked little Afghan child, wearing one purple galosh, his other foot bare, and wearing one long dress shirt in the dead of winter, cautiously moves forward into the ranks of U.S. Army soldiers, his filth-encrusted face filled with wonder and awe. He soon leaves with his small limbs loaded with clothes and candy.

As soon as he leaves our protective ranks, he is mauled by grown adult men, who fight over the clothes and candy.

Cox, pulling security around our stockpile of clothing and farm tools, bursts out laughing. "Yeah, these Arabs, they're something special. Tell you what: this Islam, there's something to this. There's something special here. I'm gonna fucking convert. This religion's got it all figured out."

The next man up is a father, who escorts his child. Waiting patiently in line, he graciously accepts the black-market Nike imitation running shoes, the orange pair of socks, and the pink girl's dress for his son, and bows courteously. Holding his child's hand, he promptly leaves the line and returns home.

"I like that man," Devon says between drags of his cigarette, a few meters away from Cox. "That man had style. He's civilized. No fuss, no muss, just patience and gratitude." After a few more seconds of consideration, Devon adds, "I think I wouldn't mind perhaps having sexual relations with a man like that."

Soon, our supply of children's clothes and candy exhausted, we are left with pink and orange and blue painted shovels and pickaxes.

"Take the shovel. It's a free shovel," I tell the wrinkled old Afghan in front of me as I hand it to him.

The wrinkled old Afghan spits at the ground and walks off, throwing his hands in the air in a gesture of defeat. He, like much of the rest of the crowd, is angry that we have given away all the clothes to the children, and he doesn't want to be bothered with our pitiful gift of farming tools.

"All right, wrap it up, wrap it up," Lieutenant Mitch yells, whirling his fingers around in the air, as he likes to do. This is the sign that we are to wrap it up.

We abandon the rest of the unwanted items to the dirt and form a long single-file line. We march up and down the hills that will lead us back to the rear of Cougar Base in silence. It's late evening, and it has been a long day. This evening there are movies to watch and poker games to attend to.

Mostly, we're going home soon, so we just don't care anymore.

The 82nd Airborne has orders to replace us. More than one soldier comments on memories of our initial arrival when we were laughed at by dirty and tired 10th Mountain Division soldiers. Now the positions are reversed. We can't wait to laugh at the bewildered 82nd Airborne soldiers.

We sigh and wheeze, slowly marking time toward the peak of our second hill, when shots ring out from the river valley to our left. Everyone sighs and pauses and then after a moment's thought slowly sinks to the ground as soldiers examine their nails or rub their weary knees.

I sit next to Lieutenant Mitch. He pops a bubble with his chewing gum while I suck air rapidly in and out of my cheeks as a way to pass the time. Lieutenant Mitch pauses for a moment, lost in thought, and then whirls his fingers around for us to move out.

We stand up slowly and continue our incline.

When we're halfway down the next hill, shots ring out again.

As we continue our trek, someone keeps shooting at us.

But we wouldn't mind if they didn't.

Finally, as we top the hill that overlooks Cougar Base where we have our over watch positions set up, the soldiers on guard move the rolls of barbed wire to the side as we march down the hill.

In the distance, a giant explosion echoes throughout the valley.

We just keep walking.

Cougar Base calls in over the radio, "Hunter-6, this is Cougar Base. We just got a report from the towers that there was a large explosion somewhere to your south. Are you going to go investigate? Over?"

Without even looking at Lieutenant Mitch, I respond into the radio, "No."

Lieutenant Mitch laughs as we make our final descent of the hill above Cougar Base.

There is a slight pause before Cougar Base responds, a bit confused. "Okay. Um, do you have any idea what that was? Over."

I pick up the radio, all exasperated that they keep talking to me, and respond, "I don't know; sometimes things explode."

There is another slight pause before Cougar Base responds, "Roger, Cougar Base, out."

And then, before we know it, we're counting our time left in Afghanistan in terms of weeks, not months. The patrols and missions grind to a halt, and instead we spend our days packing up our gear.

Chapter 39

PACKING GREEN SOCKS FOR AMERICA

There had to be two pairs of green socks in the "A" duffel bag and three pairs of black socks in the "B" duffel bag and two pairs of green socks and one pair of black socks in the "C" duffel bag. That's the way it was. It had to be that way because you'd need your socks divided that way once you got back to Hawaii. If you returned to Hawaii without your socks divided just so—well, who knows what could follow? Catastrophe? Very possibly.

One brown T-shirt went in the rucksack and one brown T-shirt in the assault pack. One brown towel went in both the rucksack and the assault pack, but in the assault pack it was the small brown towel, as opposed to the big brown towel, which went into the rucksack.

"Everybody hold up your green liner gloves," Sergeant Wu says, walking back and forth on the gravel courtyard, pacing slowly, studiously examining us for deficiencies in mental and moral character. I sort through my half shelter and my insect net, looking for my green liner gloves, which I vaguely recollect packing in Hawaii before we left for Afghanistan.

Devon waves his gloves in the air, all dainty as hell, and says, "I got my gloves, Sergeant! I got my gloves!"

I frown at Devon and stick my tongue out at him while I sort through my underwear with the toe of my boot. Where the fuck are my green liner gloves?

Suddenly, to my right, Ryan, who just moments ago has been looking lost and bewildered in his own search for his green liner gloves, pulls them from a canteen pouch and says, "Yeah, bitch! Look who's going home now! I am going home!"

I drop to my knees and start frantically scouring through my gear, shredding my large pile of clothes and gear into several little piles. Socks and shoes and boots and canteens go flying over my shoulder as I become increasingly desperate to find my green liner gloves. Soon, however, the pile in front of me dissipates, and I turn my anxious search to the discard piles I've just sorted. I spin around and around in little circles while perched on my heels, scanning the ground in front of me. I stand, face Sergeant Wu, and sadly proclaim, "But Sergeant Wu, I can't find my gloves."

"You better find 'em. That's all I got to say. You want to go home, don't you?"

"Yes!" I reply, sulky as all hell. I put my hand to my chin and stare at my equipment angrily for not giving me my green liner gloves.

"Keep looking," Sergeant Wu says, shaking his head at me in disgust. "I'm not holding everyone else back so that we can wait on your dumb ass. Okay, everybody—including you, Rico—hold up your balaclava."

After a few brief seconds of scanning their piles, Devon and Ryan both hold up their balaclava head scarves. Everyone stares at me as I frantically search for my balaclava.

"Okay, everyone hold up your fleece bottoms."

"Maybe I don't want to go back to Hawaii! Maybe I want to stay here!" I say, not having either my fleece bottoms or my balaclava.

"Good," Sergeant Wu says calmly, his dull eyes scanning me with disinterest. "Because this is the packing list, and you ain't going back if you ain't got it right."

"Good! Because that's what I want! I don't want to go back to the States," I say, crossing my arms defiantly.

"Good, because you ain't going," Sergeant Wu says, stopping his pacing just long enough to stare at me.

"Fine," I say as I begin to pack up my bags, throwing things in without care or reason. "Guess I'll just go reorganize my tent. Didn't really want to go home anyway, so it's probably for the best that I stay."

Sergeant Wu shrugs and says, "I don't care if you stay or go, to be honest."

I really want to go home.

I'm in the operations building using my creative writing skills to imagine heroic deeds that our various leaders have accomplished while in Afghanistan. I fabricate events and randomly place soldiers in operations our company has conducted, caring little whether or not they were actually there.

Our company commander has tried to give us all awards. He figures we've been through a lot and should be rewarded. These awards have been turned in and turned back eight or nine times at this point. Apparently there are staffers in the Army whose only job it is to mark award write-ups with red pencil. They also apparently don't do anything most of the time, so when they do have to work they seem to feel obligated to make up for all the times they don't work by excessively marking up the write-ups. It's past the point of simply checking to see if thoughts and narrative summaries have been properly conveyed that illustrate the situation and the reason for the nomination.

It has degenerated into all-out absurdity. An entire team of college graduates, including the West Point–educated company commander, three platoon leaders, and two privates—all of whom have graduated from college—scour and go over the reams of award write-ups, using their most delicate and precise phrasing. We scan intensely for small errors in grammar and punctuation. The write-ups are turned in and then are to be returned to the company level, the pages smeared in red pencil marks that make suggestions that have already been tried, or grammatical errors that do not exist are creatively invented.

Apparently, the Army doesn't want us to receive any awards.

A soldier I don't know comes in and tells me that Lieutenant Mitch wants to talk to me.

I walk down to the leadership tent and go inside. Lieutenant Mitch smiles real big. I always know I'm in trouble when he smiles real big.

"Rico, have a seat! Graham cracker?" I wave away the graham

cracker, and he says, "Right. Straight to business. I like that about you. So, listen, this is the radio plan for this next mission."

"Next mission? We go home in three weeks."

"Yeahhh, about that," he says in his typical playful sarcastic tone, with a big smile. "Well, we've got a little mission to do first. We're going on a little—let's call it a little field trip for the kids. We're going to make a few stops, grab some bad guys, and then go back to Zamburay."

Zamburay Valley. The location of our company's biggest firefight, where the Apache helicopters shot up the center of the valley, where we shot up the innocent bystanders.

"Yeah," he continues. "The Army's got like this report that says there's all these bad guys there and that we get to take them out!" He breaks out laughing at my stunned expression. "Aren't we lucky! Aren't we lucky!" He pinches my cheek. "You're so damn lucky, Rico!"

Chapter 40

ONE FINAL MISSION

'm the first to arrive at the side of the fifteen-year-old. I kneel down on the grass, which is slick with deep crimson blood. The kid's blood is shiny. I sit immobile on my knees, staring at my own filthy reflection from the pools of blood that collect around the kid's head.

I'm afraid to touch him. I'm screaming for a medic as I burn off the moments before the medic arrives, hoping that by then the kid will be dead. I'm certainly not performing first-aid medical treatment. I'm certainly not going to try and stop the bleeding. I'm certainly not going to try and save his life. I tell myself that I would try to help him, but I've lost my little bottle of hand sanitizer that I take on every mission. You can't patch someone up without hand sanitizer nearby. It's unfortunate he has to die, but I don't have my hand sanitizer with me. Besides, it's not like I'm not doing anything; I'm screaming for a medic.

We had just dismounted the helicopters and rushed into a series of compounds. Someone called over the radio that we had squirters out back, Haji making a run for it before they can be detained. I and a few others ran behind the compound, and then warning shots were fired, and then Jerome raised his rifle and dropped the boy who was running away from us.

The little boy jerks and jumps, and I sit there under my breath, telling him to die already. Where the fuck is that medic? I start reciting a culling song in my head and sing it over and over:

*Die little Afghan, just you die . . . Die little Afghan, please please
die . . . Die little Afghan what can I say, I just want you to die today . . .*

I reach down to touch him. To make contact. Okay, maybe I'll try to
save his life. Try to pretend that I remember even the remedial first aid
the Army tried to teach me. I gently take off his cap, and his brains
ooze out the back of his head like sausage entrails through a grinder.
He looks up at me and then looks around desperately for what I can
only imagine is his mother. He's deathly afraid and is seeking some bitter solace in this final moment. His eyes dart back and forth frantically
and passionately, scanning my face for some sign of compassion. But all
I have to offer him is disgust.

*Die little Afghan, just you die . . . Die little Afghan, please please
die . . . Die little Afghan what can I say, I just want you to die today . . .*

The medic arrives and kneels down next to me. I try to keep from
vomiting as I stand up and move away, my head dizzy with that iron-
rich doctor's-office stench of blood.

"He's dead," the medic says, laughing. "Oh, he's dead."

The reach of the fire crafts the boundaries of my world, the blackness of
a vacuum broken by the soothing touch of warm searing flames that
die and then erupt again. I keep my legs in the fire until the wet mud
piled on it in generous volumes begins to harden and crack, until my
legs are searing in pain. It's a comfort that brings me back to childhood.

I feel five years old again, cuddling a cat under a beach blanket, huddled
close against the heat register, hot air rising from the monstrous beast
of a furnace in the basement. I lost two different hamsters down that
same heat register. Both of them died. Dead hamster memories make
me happy and secure.

After our first objective, when the kid got shot, the helicopters dropped
us back in the valley where we had made contact on our first mission.

We entered the valley for a little two-day gallop, looking to stir up a bit of a fight. We had been shot at in this valley before, but the enemy hadn't taken the bait. Then, after the helicopters dropped us off, the snow fell, lightly at first and then more intensely. And then the storm front came in, and the helicopters couldn't retrieve us. We took over the temporarily empty compound of a local Afghan who was away in Kandahar on business and thoroughly destroyed his home, breaking off doors and using all other wood to keep our fire going. Before we knew it, one day had turned into two, and two into four, and four into a week.

Now the compound has been transformed into a large pool of mud, and soldiers have dug deep into the mud like burrowing insects. They have carved out holes underneath trees and sit there day after day, staring blankly in numb exasperation as moist roots slowly drip water on them. They have stuffed themselves tightly into small barns littered with animal feces and wet hay that smells of mold. They nest in a miserable world of rot painted with a mute palette of grays and browns. All wait for the sounds of helicopters overhead.

A goat's head on a stake guards the exterior wall of the compound, a signal to all that this residence is under new ownership.

Goat entrails hang from a tree branch, and splatters of crimson red decorate the top of the snow.

Another dead goat sits outside the door of the compound.

We had to eat, after all.

The Afghans knew we were hungry and without food, and the goats had suddenly appeared with vastly inflated prices. We snapped our fingers, and all the Afghans of the valley started piling wood outside the doors of our new compounds for some extra spending cash. Now, from the perch of our compound, slightly elevated on one side of the valley, we can look over the valley and survey our kingdom and see the Afghans who aren't working huddled together in brown, soggy, mud-filled doorways, immersed in muted conversation as they watch us. Children have set up booths outside our new home and sell us cookies for whatever price we offer to pay.

On my knees, I climb the slick mud incline that leads to the small adobe brick room. I feel like a hobbit, bending my tall lanky awkward six-foot frame down at the waist to enter the small three-foot door. I make my way through the darkness, stepping over pitiful shivering forms huddled tight in sleeping bags. The small room has the locker-room stink of sweat and bad breath. There's a constant rustling as all the occupants of the room perpetually adjust themselves in their sleeping bags. No one is comfortable, and everyone's hold on sleep is precarious. I move to a corner and slide into my own sleeping bag.

Throughout the night I hear Diego talking on the radio to the Special Forces soldiers who are driving a convoy of trucks to our location from our base to resupply us with food. There aren't enough trucks to drive everyone out at once, and we can't break apart the unit, or our numbers will be too weak to ward off an attack that such a separation will likely invite.

The Special Forces soldiers are lost in the fog that covers the valley at this late hour, and they refuse to give Diego their location so that he can look at a map and talk them in. For hours, as a pool of mud grows around my neck and water drips onto my face from the thatched roof, I see the soft glow of the lantern and hear Diego's voice pleading with the Special Forces soldiers to look at their global positioning system and let him know their grid coordinates.

I sink deep into my soft mud bed and put my fingers in my crotch to warm their freezing tingling tips. I curl into a fetal position to try and conserve what little warmth I have. Time shifts as I come in and out of sleep to the gentle whisper of voices in the corner talking on the radio. Our company commander is on the radio now.

He's talking to the battalion commander, complaining about their failure to extract us. "Didn't you know about the weather conditions before you sent us up here? Didn't you know there was a good chance we'd get stuck? Do you realize that my men have eaten hardly anything for several days and that we have no water left?"

The battalion commander says that he's aware of these things but that we now have new orders. We're to walk out at first light in the snowstorm with our one-hundred-pound packs and hike the thirty-kilometer distance back to Cougar Base. We're to be bait. That's the thing. Our year in Afghanistan is almost up, and they need another victory to let the people in the Pentagon know that we weren't lazy bums. Surely, if we walked out, some poor Afghan would see the line of strung-out miserable soldiers and take a shot at us.

I move up out of my sleeping bag and catch the eye of Captain Grimes as I crouch down to exit the room. His face tells me that this is a private moment. This is one of those moments of quiet command secrets. This is not to be shared with the rest of the company. I make a mental note to include it in my book.

Outside, I move to the fire around which the privates and low-ranking sergeants are laughing away the predawn hours. The soldiers giggle like little girls and whisper dirty secrets in one another's ears and rejoice in the sound of their voices.

Jerome gives a smug crooked-tooth smile as he rounds the fire, riding a hobbyhorse made from a stick capped with a bloody goat's head. I pull out my notepad and scribble fiercely, making a note of this. Jerome is enjoying the notoriety he's received for his confirmed kill on this very mission, before we became snowed in and stuck in the mountains. He's rewarding himself with a celebratory gallop around the campfire while he is cheered on for his confirmed kill, to which the conversation repeatedly returns.

The campfire is now raging as it is fed one of the last wooden doors from the compound, spitting and hissing and cracking and dancing vibrantly against the night, tossing shadows around the compound where the soldiers sit closely huddled in pools of thick mud.

They argue over who precisely should get to claim the Afghans we shot up in Zamburay Valley the last time we were here. They argue over vantage point and how the hell it was exactly that Sorbil could have been the one when he was still down in the trench. Sorbil counters that he had a line of sight from his trench.

Mulbeck jumps up from the campfire and kicks a burning branch, causing sparks to fly, to the consternation of the restless soldiers who can't sleep in the mud and wet and snow. "Goddamnit, I want to kill somebody! I don't care if it's a little boy or what, I just want to fucking kill something!" Mulbeck has had the misfortune of not being present every time we've had enemy contact. Now the deployment is almost over, and he hasn't gotten to kill anybody, and there is just no fucking justice in the world.

"You should have seen him go down! Pop! Bam!" Jerome says, holding his rifle to his shoulder. "Lesson learned," he continues. "Don't run from us, or I'll kill you." There is general agreement and laughter all around the fire.

I just listen quietly, writing in my notebook. I scribble frantic notes as I study faces and struggle to keep up with quotations.

"What are you doing?" Mulbeck asks, for the first time noticing my busy hand and silence. "You're taking notes for your book or something? That's okay; you can write about me. I should've been written about a long time ago!"

"Put me in there!" Jerome states with not a little enthusiasm, momentarily losing interest in his goat head on a stick.

I smile warmly at him and quietly say, "Yes, I think that I'll put all of you in it."

"Awesome!" Jerome says, continuing to ride his goat-head "horsey" around the fire. "I'm going to be a war hero, and everyone's going to read about me and realize how brave I am!" There is more laughter from the crowd.

"Yes, they will," I say. "They will all see."

Our company commander holds firm with the battalion commander and tells him he's not sending his troops on the long trail to Cougar Base. He doesn't mind working us hard, he doesn't mind us enduring hard conditions, but he also cares about us.

Eventually the snow stops, the skies brighten, and the choppers come to airlift us out.

On the helicopter ride back, I sit near the rear, watching the peaks of snowcapped mountains fly by underneath us, and I say good-bye to Afghanistan.

Chapter 41

PROUD

I'm on my last shift of late-night radio guard in the command center. Everyone is asleep, and the command center is largely empty. Bags and footlockers sit outside the front door waiting to be loaded into helicopters tomorrow.

As I flip through the pages of incoherent notes and scribbles that purport to capture quotes and attitudes and descriptions, I start to panic. A year in the sandbox, and I have nothing to write about. No intense combat experiences, no interesting characters, and no epiphanies or insights about the nature of war or my own life. I have no fucking book.

"What's war without an epiphany?" I ask Ryan, who is sitting on the cot in the back of the main command room, humping a pillow while I sit at the radio desk on the verge of a nervous breakdown, staring at my laptop and my messy random shuffle of chaotic meaningless notes.

"You know, when I get home, some woman is going to get it!" Ryan says. He jumps up and starts humping the cot with a furious angry kinetic energy. "Oh, she's fucking going to get it. I don't care if she's blind, crippled, or crazy—someone's getting it when I get home."

"You would think that the intensity of the situations combined with the sudden and dramatic environmental shifts would together create a texture worthy of an epiphany," I say more to myself than to Ryan, who has now moved back to humping a pillow in simulation of mock sexual rage. "There's no book here; there's nothing. I've been over here a year, and all I've discovered is crap. Fucking crap."

"Some of the sheep over here have some nice-looking asses, kind of bounce when they walk. I'd fuck a sheep," Ryan says as he grunts in coital release and collapses on the cot, exhausted.

"What lessons can be learned? What's the meaning of it all?" I ask.

Ryan looks over and offers an explanation: "It's to kill terrorist scum, right?"

"Sure, supposedly this is about terrorism, but the guys who were harboring terrorists are long dead or gone. We're not stabilizing the country, that's for damn sure. Why are we still here getting shot at? What's this say about the challenge to our generation? Where's the moral struggle? Where's the goddamn impetus for change? Where's my fucking epiphany?"

"I love watching porn—it's like watching a fight, just uhhh, bam! Take it, bitch, take it!" Ryan exclaims with a type of giddy excitement, which he accompanies with some pelvic thrusts into the air. "Oh take that, bitch! Fucking take it!"

"There's really no lesson to take from Afghanistan. World War I showed us the horrors of emerging technology. World War II showed us that sometimes we have to be interventionists. Vietnam showed us the limits of interventionism. With Iraq you have a lesson on the dangers of unilateralism. Afghanistan's just . . . Afghanistan."

"Hey, if nothing else, we always have masturbation," Ryan says.

"Masturbation's not doing it for me right now, Ryan."

Ryan responds, "Hey, man, maybe that just says that you're comfortable with who you are? That you're a relatively healthy person? You're able to put it easily into perspective and not let it bother you?"

I wave my arms around the room in an animated and excitable manner. "I want it to bother me, though! I'm not a healthy person! I'm very very sick! There's so much wrong with me! I have all these obsessive disorders! I perpetually make lists, and I plan things years out, and I'm filled with angst."

"You don't seem filled with angst to me. You're too nice," Ryan states firmly.

I can feel my face fall. "You don't think I'm filled with angst?"

"You want to be filled with angst?"

"God, yes," is all I can say.

"You're making it more complicated than it is. Afghanistan is a struggling nation that we're able to help while simultaneously making it difficult to use as an area of operations for the fucking crazies of the world." Ryan shrugs, not understanding what it is that I don't get.

And slowly my long-awaited epiphany is born. It's as you imagine epiphanies occur: a slow and studied dawning of realization until enlightenment is achieved.

We were in Afghanistan to make it difficult for international terrorists to do business, and while we were here, we were trying to make it a better place!

Sure, mistakes were to be made, but that was to be expected in any operation of this size. Soldiers would die, operations would fail, policies would become convoluted, and people would disagree on how best to run things. The point was, all concerned were trying their best!

The soldiers who laughed at killing innocent people? There was nothing wrong with them; they were posing as tough in a culture of soldiers that demanded they be tough for the sake of survival. The soldiers who had been angry and wanted to kill Afghans when their fellow soldiers died were just being human, acting out momentarily felt frustrations. The leaders were leading as best they knew how. The soldiers were soldiering as best they knew how. The Afghans were surviving as best they knew how. Everyone was coping as well as possible.

Suddenly a synchronistic sense of order fills me. Everything was exactly as it should be!

And then it occurs to me: I am surrounded by heroes. By young men who, even if they didn't know exactly what they were getting into, or joined without pure motives, nonetheless are enduring it. Despite the occasional misstep, in the larger picture, everyone is here to try and make the world a better place.

And then a second thought occurs to me. The rest of these guys are here because they believe in something. They believe in America and Democracy and apple pie and Nike and 7-Eleven and milky white suburban subdivisions that look all the same and Jesus Christ and Kmart and corporate cheeseburgers.

I don't believe in any of that shit. I am only here out of some absurd sociological curiosity. The desire to make my own personal life résumé look more like Hemingway's so I could then become an expatriate in a small third-world country like Nicaragua, where I'd run a dive shop on the beach and drink beer all day in my hammock, reading pseudophilosophical literature.

So if they all have at least an ideological reason to be here, that makes me the sole idiot. I've been risking my life for something I don't really even believe in.

But I do believe in America.

In fact, I love America.

Of all the places where I have traveled, so anxious to get away from America, I have always been just as anxious to return.

And I believe in stopping terrorists. In killing terrorists. And I believe in helping the country of Afghanistan.

The Army didn't lie to me!

I've assumed from a lifetime of liberal ideology that everything the military says is a lie. That all purportedly altruistic endeavors are cover for a more devious subterfuge.

"Hang your head and be proud, soldier," Ryan states. "You're Johnny fucking Rico. You've served in Afghanistan. Not always well, but you were there, goddamnit. You may not have saved anyone's life, or rushed under enemy fire to drag a buddy to safety. You may have complained and whined, but you did fall asleep occasionally on radio guard, and you did masturbate a thousand times in a combat zone, and that's something that none of those other pussy faggots back home who haven't served can say." Ryan pats me on the ass and then adds, "I'm going to go take a shit."

I smile as I think proudly to myself, *Yeah, I did masturbate a thousand times in Afghanistan . . .*

It's the morning.

Today I leave Afghanistan.

No one's up yet. It's just me and the six-million-dollar radar system that beeps as birds fly by thinking they're rockets. The sun is starting its slow march to the position of attention. It's the early-morning crawl as things awaken.

I've traveled a lot, and everywhere I've gone I've always taken a travel book. A *Frommer's* guide, a *Lonely Planet* guide, some book that explains the country to me so I can navigate it a bit more easily than others who have come before me without it.

So, for those who will follow, I type *A Travelogue.*

I stare at a blank screen, start to write the first sentence, and then quickly obliterate the sentence I just wrote. It's difficult to write the first sentence. The first sentence leads you down a path that you're forced to commit to. I decide I'll hold off on the first sentence. I don't know where this story will lead me, and I don't want to be forced to commit to some path I'm not yet sure of. I'll write the first sentence last. One of those cute little habits that writers have. Finish, and then go back and add the first sentence. Some sort of life-and-death rebirth circle-of-life type of crap.

I was somewhere in the desert at the edge of civilization when the psychosis began to take hold . . .

"**B**uddhism."

"I'm sorry . . . what?" Jenson asks, leaning forward, his hands ruffling his wild, crazy hair. He wasn't quite sure he had heard his therapist correctly.

This is the way it works.

You tell your therapist that you're suicidal and possibly homicidal, that you've been fantasizing about killing U.S. soldiers, and then the therapist says to you . . .

"Buddhism," the balding Army therapist intones, his fingers crossed like a fucking little dandy, looking all smug with his pretentious circular glasses in his cheap Kmart polo and blue slacks, which come up short at the ankles exposing green paisley socks. "Perhaps all you need is a different outlook on life. Yes, the world is a messed-up place, but if you change your perception of it . . ."

Jenson sits back to contemplate this and squints as sunlight pours through venetian blinds that hang crookedly over the window. The more his therapist talks, the more the pain at the center of his head intensifies.

"Take this room, for instance," the therapist continues. "Is there anything wrong with this room at this very moment in time?"

"Yes," Jenson says, sitting forward abruptly. "I'm wrong. That's what I've been trying to tell you. I'm all wrong! I'm wrong in the head!"

The therapist collapses in his seat and throws his hands up in defeat. "I don't even really know why you're here."

"I'm telling you! Right now, I'm telling you! I'm wrong in the head! I'm sick! That's why I'm here!"

"I think you're telling me this because you want to get out of the Army."

"Of course I want to get out of the Army! The Army is what is driving me insane! I don't hate Taliban! I don't hate Iraqis! I hate Americans! I hate U.S. soldiers! These are the people I want to kill!"

His therapist offers an uncomfortable pause in return before he sits forward, pops the end of his pen with a quick thumb click, grabs a pad of paper, and says, "I'll tell you what I'm going to do. I'm going to give you a suggested reading list of books about Buddhism that I think you might enjoy."

Although the Army tells all the soldiers who return from Afghanistan to call the mental health hotline if they have problems, they aren't serious.

Not really.

First of all, if you call the mental health hotline and made an appointment, you then have to tell your front-line supervisor, some twenty-one-year-old sergeant, that you have an appointment with a therapist. It's because you have an appointment with a therapist that you can't sit in the hallway with all the other soldiers and clean weapons that aren't dirty. You have somewhere else to be, so you can't lounge in the grimy hallways of a dilapidated barracks where the roof leaks and the doors don't work and the toilets are always overflowing with shit, where rats the size of small cats live in the walls, and you're harassed and tortured by sergeants and other Army personnel until a slow psychosis develops within you.

And if you tell your sergeant this—that you're going to be gone for a few hours visiting a therapist—you're ridiculed. Your pussy is hurting you. What's that wet spot on the ground behind you, Jenson? Oh, that's right—that's your pussy; it's leaking pussy juice all over. You should go buy some tampons so you quit leaking. Plug your little pussy hole up. Maybe your therapist can help you with that.

The second reason the Army isn't serious about the mental health hotline is that when you do show up for said appointment, all the therapist does is suggest some breathing techniques and to try Buddhism.

Sometimes he suggests trying yoga.

Whatever it takes to relax you.

Different things work for different people.

For one person it might be yoga; for another person it might be Buddhism.

So, if you're like Jenson, and every night you go to bed thinking about putting a .45 in your mouth and blowing your itching nonsensical twitch of a brain all over the back of the toilet in the latrines because you're having a hard time getting the screaming of your best friend out of your head and because your father is dying, and because the life of a garrison Army infantry soldier is so maddening that you envision killing your fellow soldiers, perhaps you should try some good breathing techniques.

Sometimes a good breathing technique can be the difference between life and death.

Try some stretching.

Read some books on Buddhism.

Different things work for different people.

When we left Cougar Base, we weren't replaced by the 82nd Airborne, as had been planned. There weren't enough soldiers to go around anymore, what with Iraq and all. So someone in the Army, after a year of slow and steady progress in the region, after Cougar soldiers died trying to secure the area, decided that Oruzgan province was going to be written off. It was too difficult to pacify. They would send the 82nd Airborne soldiers to locations more amenable to U.S. control. It's a point of lost irony to note that in the latter part of 2005, after we left, the violence in Afghanistan between U.S. forces and the network of resistance still loosely being defined as Taliban soared to previously unrecognized levels throughout the country.

We left the one-hundred-man base in the hands of a seven-man Special Forces team. The Taliban, hearing through the covert communication network of local villagers and workers that we were leaving, waited until our departure to get nasty.

Only days after our exfil, while we were still flying back home, an all-out frontal assault was made on Cougar Base.

And the Special Forces, freed of our battalion's traditional Army chain of command, unleashed hell.

They started by destroying the valley our base was located in. E-mails and phone calls back to the soldiers in our platoon described it as a series of B-1 bombers backed up in a holding pattern, each waiting to drop bomb after bomb on the valley.

Good riddance, everyone said.

But still, as we returned home to families and all the difficulties and errands and tasks associated with returning to the world after a year away, I couldn't help but think back about Afghanistan and harbor a slight regret. What was the point in shedding blood, sweat, sperm, and tears to secure a place and make it safer if you were just going to blow it all up?

But there wasn't time to think about Afghanistan. That was now the past. And in the future we had Iraq to look forward to, and in the present there were barracks rooms to be reassigned, apartments to find, household goods to be delivered, vehicles to pick up and register, and cell phones to be turned on.

As expected, there was a mass exodus to the downtown bar district in Honolulu the first weeks back as soldiers immersed themselves in alcohol and at least attempted to reacquaint themselves with the taste of women. And the expected number of soldiers were arrested for drunken and disorderly conduct.

As promised during deployment, many new cars appeared in the parking lot in the immediate weeks following the return to Hawaii. And new televisions and electronic devices appeared in the various barracks. Just a few months later, the company command started getting phone calls from creditors regarding soldiers who were already behind on their payments, and more than a few soldiers, already having spent their deployment windfall, were back to their old ways of bouncing checks and being in perpetual poverty.

Most of the deployment promises quickly became vaporous memories. The soldiers who had promised to talk to girls more often and not be afraid anymore were still quiet and shy. The soldiers who had promised to be faithful to their girlfriends and stop banging the teenaged daughters of vacationing families kept up their philandering. The soldiers who had promised to spend more time with their families and children and to value the important things in life still kept on drinking with the guys, perhaps now a little harder and more frequently than before. The soldiers who had promised to get out more often and to see the sights of the island stayed in their barracks rooms getting drunk and watching movies.

A lot of soldiers left the Army eager to give a crack at being a civilian, and a great many stayed in and transferred to new duty stations, where they would likely be sent to Iraq or back to Afghanistan within the year. And always there were the promises to keep in touch and the exchanges of e-mail addresses and phone numbers, and, as with most things, these too were sincere but hollow gestures.

And there were a great many new soldiers to replace them. Fresh-faced dewy-eyed soldiers who wanted to be infantry combat killers and joked about the people they would kill in combat, and about how fearless they would be.

The Cougar Company bureaucracy rolled forward, allowing for a brief, indulgent, two-week period when everyone was allowed to remember that they had just returned from a combat zone, before everyone was refocused on the new mission at hand: Iraq. Within the year, Cougar Company would be in Iraq.

Resigned to spending two more years in the Army, during the early summer I got drunk every evening on the backyard patio at my house in a Navy subdivision at Pearl Harbor, rarely going out and too depressed to care. I waited for the imminent disbanding of the battalion and the subsequent piece of paper that would announce what new Army post I was to report to. I cancelled my trip to Kenya with my friends and didn't bother applying to any schools.

I walked around that summer with one eye toward the sky, wondering when it would drop. My date with freedom was drawing closer; it was only three months away, and I still didn't know whether I was going to be living in the Army for a few more years, going through it all again in Iraq, or whether after three months I was going to be let go with my initial contract up and able to return to my life.

The soldiers in the class loll lazily in their chairs as they flick pens back and forth in restless hands. They roll back and forth, focusing on the soft muted sound of chair wheels over the carpet. They practice slowly, letting their jaws drop while they stare vacantly at the instructor and then slamming their jaws shut, snapping their teeth with a loud click.

The instructor, a fat middle-aged woman who normally teaches fifth-grade math, instructs us about the difficulties of adjusting to normal life after we've been in combat.

No one knows better about the physical toll that constant anxiety from perpetual rocket and mortar attacks can take on the human body than fat middle-aged fifth-grade math teachers.

"So, what do you not want to do?" she asks with a big pretentious smile. "You do not want to beat people up, and you especially don't want to kill people now that you're home."

From the back of the class, I take prodigious notes. *Do not beat people up. Do not kill people.*

You could never be sure when there would be a pop quiz.

It was always good to be prepared and to take good notes.

"Now in Afghanistan it was okay to use violence to solve your problems. Over here, in America, it's not okay," our teacher tells us.

"Why not?" asks one soldier in the back, who up until a moment ago has just been sleeping with his legs up on the desk in front of him. "I mean, uh, if someone gives me a problem, I should just kill them, right?" The soldier looks around to his buddies in a sarcastic theatric display.

"Well," laughs our teacher, who rolls her eyes and laughs a little too hard and a little too obviously, "if you do that, you'll go to jail!"

"So?" the soldier asks, getting suddenly intensely serious. "I'll just kill them, too."

The teacher, who doesn't quite realize that she's being toyed with, nervously responds, "Oh come on now, you know you can't just . . ."

"Sure I can," the soldier intones calmly. "Kill everyone."

One soldier at the front of the class stands up and starts to walk out. All eyes are on him to see if he'll get away with it.

The math teacher recognizes a flaw in his plan, though, and offers a forced smile, "Oh, you can't leave yet! I didn't stamp your blue card!" She says this while waving the magical stamper in her hand, illustrating for all her control over us.

There is nothing he can do. She does have the magic stamper, after all.

The soldier who is about to leave walks over to her as she moves back a step, gently grabs her arm, and removes the stamper from her hand. She is quiet as he stamps his own card, offers her a big smile, and then leaves.

And then the tide is turned.

Everyone leaves.

She offers a few parting words of wisdom, trying to speak over the rising shuffle of soldiers moving to the front of the class to stamp their blue cards before leaving. "And remember, think before you act. This isn't a combat zone anymore."

The class is finally empty except for me and her. She scrunches her face up and is seemingly asking for a sympathetic or understanding smile.

I smile sympathetically, stand up, stamp my card, and leave.

Specialist North sits at home waiting for someone to take him to his appointment. He would've gone himself, but he can't drive because he was blown up back in Afghanistan, and his leg looks like rotting cheese, and he has this damn wheelchair to consider.

Back in Afghanistan, after he was blown up and he had been pulled out of the vehicle screaming and crying like a little sissy, everyone made promises to him. Whatever he needed. Whatever he needed, they'd help him with. He just needed to concentrate on getting better, and his buddies—Cougar company—would take care of the rest. He was in good hands, they told him.

So Specialist North waits quietly at the front door of his house, wondering if someone is going to pick him up to go to his doctor's appointment. He has to have some pins removed from his leg. Sometimes somebody comes; sometimes they don't come. They can't always come. They're a bunch of busy guys, they have things to do, and besides, when they made those promises they didn't know that this meant they'd have to go pick him up after work, on their own time, during their free time.

And, to be honest, not everyone wants to fuck with your stupid little wheelchair all the time, folding it in and out, and putting it in the trunk, only to have to take it back out and reassemble it just so you can go into some goddamn doctor's office.

Everyone starts new habits when they get back.

Devon, who looked so promising in the Ghan with his in-country online application to college and his plan to move to Denver and attend Metro State and study journalism, decided to party for six months in Vegas first.

Cox, our resident platoon musical prodigy, who cuts up a mean saxophone when he's sober and likes to tell us all about the various subtle but important differences between Mozart's earlier and later works, is getting ready to go to England.

Diego, after his successful in-country drive to cost the Army a million dollars in his campaign to deter people from reenlisting, reenlists. He won't say why.

Of course, deployment promises don't matter anymore. It's not as if you can die here in the States. That wasn't a "for real" promise, that was a momentary "I think I'm gonna die" promise.

There's a difference.

You don't die in Hawaii.

Unless you're Sergeant Mitchell.

If you're Sergeant Mitchell you die a few weeks after returning to Hawaii. One of those horrible cliché stories you hear where a drunk driver hits a perfectly innocent person who's sitting at a quiet intersection at one o'clock in the morning, patiently waiting out the red light even though there are no cars in any direction. Those are the peaceful moments of reflection when the radio is on. Maybe Tom Petty is playing. Maybe the Steve Miller Band. It's just you and the quiet 1 a.m. nighttime and a red-lit empty intersection.

That next weekend your friends all go out to have drinks as they think about you. Your friends all slowly get shit-faced as they morosely talk about good old fucking Mitchell. The fucking King. They talk about that piece of shit who drove drunk and hit him and killed him.

Then, the night over, they separate, make final plans and adjustments and negotiations for the bar they'll visit next weekend, and they all drive home with his memory filling their thoughts.

Of course, they all drive home drunk.

The auditorium is filled with soldiers who are screaming and yelling. It's like a rock concert. The retention sergeant who holds the stage frowns and tries to stare down as many as she can into silence. She's made the mistake of saying, "And for those of you who are going to leave the Army . . ."

This crowd goes nuts when you say that. Clapping. Cheering. Thunderous applause all around. This is after she has tried to entice us to stay in by explaining that within the next week she'll be getting in some nice polo shirts and new coffee mugs.

You should definitely sign back up for a coffee mug.

You have to be keen; you have to be clever; you have to know when to jump on a good deal when you see one.

You can't let life pass you by.

Sometimes you have to jump on the coffee mug deal.

The new lieutenant colonel grabs the microphone from the retention sergeant, and the crowd instantly quiets. You might interrupt a retention sergeant with some cheers, but not a lieutenant colonel.

"Who here thinks that the grass is greener on the other side? Who here thinks that civilian life is better than the Army?" A sea-to-shining-sea swarm of hands shoots into the air and waves excitedly back and forth.

The lieutenant colonel laughs for a brief second to show that he has a sense of humor and then suddenly gets all dramatic, yelling, "Well, I'll tell you what. You're all smoking fucking crack! I've got friends who have graduated from college and can't find work! I've got friends who were in the Army and left, and they tell me, 'You know what? That was the worst mistake I've ever made in my life.' Who here has a plan? Huh? Let me see a show of hands? Who here thinks they have some plan that can make it in the outside world?"

A few brave hands shoot up in the air. My hand shoots up in the air, too. Everyone knows that the lieutenant colonel is going to belittle them in front of everyone. He calls on his first victim, and the soldier tells him that he wants to attend college and study interior design. After the lieutenant colonel makes appropriate and necessary fun of his desire to be an interior designer, he interrogates him. Does he have an acceptance letter to college yet? Does he know how much to charge for his faggoty skill that will allow him to match pillow throw covers with curtains?

I pray to God that he calls on me. I wiggle and wave my arm with as much enthusiasm as I can. I'm that annoying student. *Teacher call on me! I know the answer! Ohh! Ohh! I know the answer!*

But he doesn't call on me.

He calls on some kid who wants to go into welding but hasn't yet contemplated the proper route to go.

They threaten us and scare us not to leave. A quick look around the auditorium shows that all exits are blocked by retention personnel. We're not leaving here until we sign up of our own free will, and they'll wait us out as long as it takes. They'll break us. If we leave, it'll be the biggest mistake of our lives. And they ask us, what exactly is it that we don't like about the Army? Will somebody please stand and tell them what is wrong with the Army?

It's like the relationship breakup where the other party refuses to break up. How can you break up with someone who insists that you're still a couple?

I know that recruiting numbers are down, that they're fighting two wars. But the threats, the pleading, the begging, the obvious manipulation and ploys are pathetic.

Have some fucking respect for yourself, U.S. Army. Act like a fucking man!

Nobody raises a hand, but I can hear everyone's thoughts. They're tired of being deployed. A quarter of the people in the audience have been deployed twice already. They've been outside the United States fighting for more years than they've been at home. You can't raise a family on that. You can't have a girlfriend with that.

But nobody says anything.

We can't think of anything we don't like about the Army.

I swallow hard and approach the women sitting on the lawn chairs facing the beach while Ryan carefully monitors my success from the bar as he nurses his drink. There are three of them. I lock eyes with the beautiful one and ask if she minds if I sit down and chat. She returns my smile and says that, no, as a matter of fact, she wouldn't mind at all.

I sit on the edge of her lawn chair, and introductions are made, while in my head I congratulate myself on my courage in approaching three women by myself. I'm usually a coward. It's the usual trite conversation. Where are you from? What do you do?

They work at a Navy shipyard in San Diego. Just like all the other pretty girls in Hawaii, they are here on vacation. They do paperwork or answer phones or something. I feign interest as best I can.

The inevitable softball is lobbed back at me, and I state that, unfortunately, for only a couple more months, I am indeed one more soldier of the type that seems to infest this island everywhere you go. We're like termites, I say, half laughing.

What do I do in the Army? I'm in the infantry.

Where have I been? Oh well, as a matter of fact, I just got back from Afghanistan.

Yes, yes, it is a good thing I went there and not Iraq, but you know what? It's really not as quiet as people seem to think it is.

What did I do over there? Did I fill out paperwork?

No, Goddamnit, I just told you I'm in the infantry. If you must know, I was at a Special Forces base deep in Taliban-controlled territory. Our area was so dangerous that the only way in or out for miles in all directions was by helicopter. Anybody who tried to drive to our base, Afghan or American, often ended up getting blown up and killed.

And as I explain what we did, doing patrols and raids on top Taliban targets with the Special Forces, I notice her nodding head scan the crowd for a new boy. She briefly rolls her eyes at her friend. Her friend briefly rolls her eyes back.

And then there's the polite extraction.

Sorry, it's been nice meeting you, but we have to go meet our friends. A few sympathetic eyebrow good-bye shrugs, and then it's over. I sit on their empty lawn chair as Ryan comes back to berate me for my poor performance.

Why do I feel embarrassed for having been in Afghanistan?

Why do I always want to lie about being a soldier?

The fireworks explode like colorful spiders over the Hawaii beach. And I jump. I lean forward from my chair and tap Ryan on the shoulder, "Holy shit! Did you see that?"

"What?" Ryan asks.

"Check it out," I say. I wait for the next explosion, and my body jumps lightly.

"Holy shit," Ryan says, studying my uncontrolled response. "Dude, you've got battle fatigue!"

I quickly get depressed, thinking it sad that my body is responding to so little battle with signs of battle fatigue. Yet, I am simultaneously elated to be experiencing some post-traumatic stress disorder, however slight.

Ryan pauses, waiting for the next fireworks explosion to see if his body responds, but it doesn't. "Fuck," he says. "That's not fucking fair, man. I want post-traumatic stress, too."

I sit in front of the computer staring numbly as I contemplate whether I like working more with my hands or more with computers. Like a slightly mentally dense child, I ponder this decision before lightly raising my hand, pressing a single key, and then returning my hand to the rest position on my lap as I see the response the computer gives me.

The Army's allowing me to start the process of leaving. This is good. We have only one month left after all. But I've heard stories of guys who finished the Army and were out using up their final vacation days when they were still called back. But our battalion is still active and alive. Thus far there have been no papers sending me to some new duty station. Hope starts to build. I cautiously wonder if I can start making plans.

The next question is whether I enjoy math or language. I'm taking a vocation aptitude test. A few years earlier I ran such tests as a probation officer, and now I am diligently awaiting the results of my aptitude test that will tell me which direction I should take in life.

After my questions are done, I enter the adjoining room, entirely empty save for myself and an angry young black woman. I hand her my test. She stares angrily at me. I realize I'm doing something wrong and look around the empty room. Then I realize I'm supposed to take a number. I take a number and sit down, staring at my numbered ticket.

The angry young black woman clears her throat and calls out, "Number fifty-seven! Number fifty-seven!"

I look at my ticket.

I'm number fifty-seven.

I stand and hand it to her, and she hands me my results.

Eager to find out what I should do with the rest of my life, I scan past the recorded compilation of my answers to the results, which inform me that I should consider a career in corrections or police work.

Have I ever considered a career in probation or parole?

I circle the base, obtaining signatures from offices I have never heard of, and turn in my Army gear to find out that I owe money for gear the Army hasn't yet shipped back from Afghanistan. I take classes and submit paperwork.

And then comes my D-Day.

This is my final "out" session.

For hours I work studiously with a counselor to get good solid decent hardworking signatures on reams of paper.

I keep scanning my watch.

I'm almost out.

I keep watching the doorway, waiting for some Army official to come in the room calling my name, alerting me that the stop-loss has just dropped into place and that on this, my last day in the Army, he has to deliver the unfortunate news that I'm not getting out.

I keep imagining that surely the next form would be the last. Then my counselor pauses and says, "You know, I don't know if you get both the National Defense Ribbon *and* the Afghan Service Ribbon." He leans back in his chair and calls over to the next cubicle. "George? Can this guy get both ribbons?"

George contemplates this in long-drawn-out thoughts that seem to last into eternity as he leans back in his own chair. They have no sense of efficiency. A signature is an hour's block of time. The printing of a single form? Another hour. The two decide that this matter requires further investigation, and soon a third party is brought in to consult on the matter.

I lean forward, saying, "Listen, I don't give a shit if I get any ribbons. Seriously, just don't even put me down for any ribbons. I really don't care."

My exit counselor stares at me with something approximating horror. "You'll need your ribbons! You'll need your ribbons! Someday you'll want to get a real job, and employers will look at this and see how many ribbons you earned!"

I'm eating a Triscuit from a plastic bag and I break out laughing so hard that I choke on it, causing both my counselor and George to rush to my aid and pound on my back as I lean forward. Little bits of Triscuit slowly fall from my mouth onto the floor.

"Fine!" I say, still clearing my throat and wiping Triscuit bits away from my lips. "Fine, give me ribbons. Whatever."

After adjustment of the dates for every training and school I have ever been to, all of which were entered incorrectly in some National Defense database, we're all finished.

"And here you go," my counselor says. His finger hovers over the print button on my final signature page. He pauses, and his eyes narrow, and the finger relaxes. "Oh, this is a problem. Hmm. Hmm. Inter-esting. Very interesting." My counselor says this in a way that seems to suggest even he has never seen a snag of this magnitude.

"What?! What?!" I ask desperately.

"Well, your life insurance policy. You took out twenty-five thousand while in Afghanistan, and the computer only has a prompt for fifty thousand. I'm going to get some clarification on this."

My counselor moves away from his cubicle to consult George. Soon they bring in a third party and then the floor supervisor. A whole slew of Army exit counselors is staring at the computer screen, each one hitting the F2 prompt in a slightly different manner, hoping for a new or radically different response than the previous person received. Finally, after much negotiation and discussion, it is decided that I will not be able to get out of the Army.

"What?" I don't know what else to say.

Suddenly it's harder to breathe. I feel the onset of a panic attack. My pulse quickens. My words slur and become incomprehensible. "What do you mean, not get out of the Army?"

"You'll have to take out additional life insurance. The minimum amount this prompt accepts is fifty thousand dollars of life insurance."

"I don't want fifty thousand dollars of life insurance."

My exit counselor shrugs and plasters a pearly wide-cheeked smile on his face.

Ten minutes later, and I'm at the appropriate office to purchase an additional twenty-five thousand dollars of life insurance that will cover me for the next forty-five minutes that I'm in the Army.

Thirty-five minutes into my new fifty-thousand-dollar life insurance policy, I'm out of the Army.

I end up missing the stop-loss by more than half a year.

Later that day, I brought my car to a screeching halt in an alley, jumped out, and threw all my Army uniforms into a Dumpster.

My plane ticket for Denver secure in my gym bag, I checked into a downtown Honolulu hotel room and looked out on the traffic below as I lit up a cigarette.

It was okay to smoke, since I'd already quit.

I realized that at twenty-nine years of age, I still had the same questions as when I was a more criminally minded teenager. What obligation did I have to my country? What exactly did citizenship require? What did it mean to be an American?

But now there were new questions. What was my moral responsibility to any conflict I engaged in? Did I have to own it, or could I just serve my country and let my country worry about it? Was any war or act of violence ever really justified? Or did it just create an exponential series of cause and effect that could ultimately end only in tragedy?

And what next for me? Well, Antarctica next. Two days earlier I had been hired by the National Science Foundation. It was time to leave the tropic waters of paradise and head south to the penguins. Still, I was bothered that I felt the same restlessness as when I first joined the Army. What did it mean that I had gone a year in Afghanistan and yet felt like the same person who enlisted three years earlier? What did that say about my life?

My cigarette out, I tossed it to the street below and thought, *Ahh, fuck it, who fucking cares.*

To what purpose?

To what better end?

In masturbation we trusted . . .

I ordered some porn and jerked off.

ABOUT THE AUTHOR

JOHNNY RICO graduated from the University of Colorado at Denver in the spring of 2001 with his Master's degree in criminal justice, at which point he worked as a probation officer in the Denver area. A month after September 11, 2001, Rico joined the Army under the delayed entry program. With C. Company, 2nd Battalion, 5th Infantry, of the 25th Infantry (Light) Division in Hawaii, he was sent to Afghanistan where he served as an infantryman in three different areas of operation. He was released from active duty in September 2005, and now permanently resides in the United Kingdom with his girlfriend.